CW00819159

"The twenty-first century global Christian fellowship is _____
logical loci: epistemology and ecclesiology. This boo _____
church. Authors Duerksen and Dyrness argue that th _____
form) and in the end, like the Buddha's raft, will be eli _____
its fullness. They suggest that the answer to our quai _____
more to do with eschatology than we have heretofore imagined. This book is a must-read for
anyone interested in our religious future."

Terry C. Muck, scholar of religion, comparative missiologist, and theological educator at Austin Presbyterian
Theological Seminary and Asbury Theological Seminary

"How should we understand the many diverse, emergent expressions of church across the globe
today? What is the relationship between these emergent expressions of church and the vision of
God's kingdom? Writing from their own deep missional engagements in Asia and the conviction of
their lifelong-missiological reflections, Darren T. Duerksen and William A. Dyrness make the case
for a renewed vision, critical theology, and constructive practice of being church as an emergent
phenomenon, empowered by the Spirit to witness the good news of Jesus in a world marked by
pluralism and diversity. Duerksen and Dyrness also break new ground by offering a comprehensive,
critical, and constructive theology of emergent church that truly embraces the diversity and plurality
of ways a church can be a faithful witness to the coming of God's kingdom. Seeking Church is essential reading for anyone interested in understanding the future of a decolonized Christianity,
where indigenous and subaltern emergent communities of faith, as well as new voices concerned
with transforming church structures, are challenging us to rethink church and seek to find it in new,
emergent, and hybridized forms that are able to witness faithfully to the coming of God's kingdom."

Jonathan Y. Tan, The Archbishop Paul J. Hallinan Professor of Catholic Studies, Case Western Reserve
University, Cleveland

"If we Christians seek a better fulfillment of church mission in the future, we do well to better understand the church's past. Seeking Church documents how the church changed its self-understanding in response to historically changing circumstances. As a sociologist, I found this socio-
logically informed theological reflection of great insight and value. I recommend this engagingly
written book for both individual and group study."

Douglas Porpora, professor of sociology at Drexel University, author of Landscapes of the Soul

"In decentering the 'church' from the mission of God and in inviting cultural, even religious, norms
to inform our appropriation of the biblical texts—what the authors call 'reverse hermeneutics'—
Drs. Duerksen and Dyrness, former missionaries both, follow the venerable tradition of missionaries bringing radical ideas to challenge the institutions back home. So much of 'received
authorities,' especially our own, are products of cultural accretions and historical contingencies.
We would recognize them for what they are if only we have the humility to hold up the thriving
Christian communities around the world as mirror to see ourselves."

Sze-kar Wan, professor of New Testament at Perkins School of Theology, Southern Methodist University

"The diversity of world Christianity forces us to reevaluate our more common hermeneutic of the
church. These two authors have combined theological, missiological, and social science perspectives
in a fresh analysis of both the church's history and those settings where the church is presently emerging
within unreached populations. It will prove to be an invaluable resource for comprehending ecclesial
dynamics where social, religious, and geopolitical barriers are prevalent. Seeking Church provides a
timely hermeneutic that opens us to new and innovative ways of extending the kingdom of God."

Brad Gill, senior editor, International Journal of Frontier Missiology

SEEKING CHURCH

*Emerging Witnesses
to the Kingdom*

DARREN T. DUERKSEN
and WILLIAM A. DYRNESS

Academic

An imprint of InterVarsity Press
Downers Grove, Illinois

InterVarsity Press
P.O. Box 1400, Downers Grove, IL 60515-1426
ivpress.com
email@ivpress.com

InterVarsity Press° is the book-publishing division of InterVarsity Christian Fellowship/USA°, a movement of students and faculty active on campus at hundreds of universities, colleges, and schools of nursing in the United States of America, and a member movement of the International Fellowship of Evangelical Students. For information about local and regional activities, visit intervarsity.org.

Scripture quotations, unless otherwise noted, are from the New Revised Standard Version of the Bible, copyright 1989 by the Division of Christian Education of the National Council of the Churches of Christ in the USA. Used by permission. All rights reserved.

Cover design and image composite: David Fassett
Interior design: Beth McGill
Images: ©Photography by Aubrey Stoll/Moment Collection/Getty Images

ISBN 978-0-8308-5105-8 (print)
ISBN 978-0-8308-7242-8 (digital)

Printed in the United States of America ∞

Library of Congress Cataloging-in-Publication Data

Names: Duerksen, Darren Todd, author. | Dyrness, William A., author.

Title: Seeking church : emerging witnesses to the kingdom / Darren T. Duerksen and William A. Dyrness.

Description: Downers Grove, Illinois : IVP Academic, an imprint of InterVarsity Press, [2019] | Includes bibliographical references and index. | Summary: "New expressions of church, including so-called "insider" movements, are proliferating among non-Christian religious communities worldwide. Drawing on the growing social-scientific work on emergent theory, Darren Duerksen and William Dyrness explore how all Christian movements have been and are engaged in a "reverse hermeneutic," where the gospel is read and interpreted through existing cultural and religious norms"—Provided by publisher.

Identifiers: LCCN 2019027278 (print) | LCCN 2019027279 (ebook) | ISBN 9780830851058 (paperback) | ISBN 9780830872428 (ebook)

Subjects: LCSH: Emerging church movement. | Church renewal. | Theology, Doctrinal. | Christianity and other religions.

Classification: LCC BV600.3 .D84 2019 (print) | LCC BV600.3 (ebook) | DDC 262.001/7--dc23

LC record available at https://lccn.loc.gov/2019027278

LC ebook record available at https://lccn.loc.gov/2019027279

| P | 24 | 23 | 22 | 21 | 20 | 19 | 18 | 17 | 16 | 15 | 14 | 13 | 12 | 11 | 10 | 9 | 8 | 7 | 6 | 5 | 4 | 3 | 2 | 1 |
| Y | 39 | 38 | 37 | 36 | 35 | 34 | 33 | 32 | 31 | 30 | 29 | 28 | 27 | 26 | 25 | 24 | 23 | 22 | 21 | 20 | 19 |

Contents

Preface

One night during the 2010 Third Lausanne Congress on World Evangelization in Cape Town, respected evangelical leader Chris Wright gave a rousing address titled "Integrity—Confronting Idols." In it he claimed that the greatest barrier to God's mission is God's people. In particular, he said, the church has too often embraced the idols of power and pride, popularity and success, wealth and greed. He called on leaders and churches to repent and seek to live out their witness in humility, integrity, and simplicity. In August 2017 the leadership of the Lausanne Movement reposted the lecture online, sparking renewed consternation and response.[1] Whatever else Wright's lecture and the responses might signal, they clearly reflect a growing awareness that all is not well in the Christian movement, and especially in the churches this movement has spawned around the world. While the church faces an increasing array of geopolitical challenges, the deepest challenge, on Wright's reading, is the failure of God's people to live out the good news in their lives and communities. The churches have failed to be the church!

While there is no doubt truth in Wright's claim, we want to argue that this failure is itself reflective of larger historical and cultural issues that call for reflection and critique. Thus, rather than focusing on these failures or even on the current geopolitical issues—growing economic inequality, newly militant religions, mass migration of desperate peoples, and political polarization—this book attempts a broader historical and developmental inquiry into the longer-term dynamics that lie behind these problems. This approach was prompted by general quandaries that motivated our research: the fundamental gulf that exists between cultures that reflect the influences of

---

[1]Christopher Wright, "Confronting Our Idols," Conference on Integrity (Cape Town: Lausanne Movement, 2010), video, www.lausanne.org/content/confronting-idols.

modernity and those that actively resist these influences; the divide between
societies influenced by the Enlightenment and those that are not; and the
general, and increasingly rancorous, religious inflection of these differences.
The tensions and divisions between traditional and modernizing cultures,
we believe, are implicated in many of the presenting problems the church
faces today but are too often overlooked by Western scholars. This has led
to the habit of measuring cultures and the resultant Christian institutions
against those familiar to Western Christians.

For example, an African scholar's recent study, *Megachurch Christianity
Reconsidered*, which arrived too late to be discussed in our book, has bril-
liantly argued that popular forms of megachurch in many places around the
world are responding to the malaise of educated youth and young families
trying to navigate the challenges and disruptions of modern life.[2] Rather than
simply importing a Western model of church into a different context, these
churches, in their teachings and social organization, are creating "roadmaps"
that provide their members stable pathways in the midst of economically,
politically, and culturally volatile times. Though we did not give attention to
these particular churches or processes, like the more religiously and culturally contextual churches we discuss, they represent an effort to navigate
the multiple and conflicting ways that traditional cultures confront, accom-
modate, or even resist modernizing systems. We have tried to thoughtfully
convey some of the unsettling diversity faced by the church in this globalizing
world and to argue that an emergent framework helpfully accounts for the
multiple forms and expressions of church to which this diversity gives rise.

Both authors have witnessed the struggles of the church firsthand as
missionaries—Duerksen in India and Dyrness in the Philippines—and subsequently as theological educators in the United States. More to the point, in
recently published works both have argued, with Wright, that misunderstandings surrounding the nature and character of God's people constitute one
of the most pressing issues facing Christians today.[3] In particular our research

[2]Wanjiru M. Gitau, *Megachurch Christianity Reconsidered: Millennials and Social Change in African Perspective* (Downers Grove, IL: InterVarsity Press, 2018).
[3]See Darren Todd Duerksen, *Ecclesial Identities in a Multi-Faith Context: Jesus Truth-Gatherings (Yeshu Satsangs) Among Hindus and Sikhs in Northwest India.* American Society of Missiology Monograph 22 (Eugene, OR: Pickwick, 2015); and William A. Dyrness, *Insider Jesus: Theological Reflections on New Christian Movements* (Downers Grove, IL: InterVarsity Press, 2016).

of so-called emerging or insider movements insistently pressed the question, What form or forms should the church be taking today? More specifically—given that the mission of God's people is finally God's work and that God seems to be moving in surprising and unexpected ways—how do those busy with the church and its structures respond to this divine work and the increasing diversity it represents? As Chris Wright's message implies, the main challenge all Christians face is this: How do we faithfully follow the Spirit's leading in deploying all our diverse gifts to foster our shared maturity in Christ (Eph 4:11-16)? This book is a modest attempt to address these questions.

Two convictions drive the argument of *Seeking Church*. First, we believe that the church of Christ has always reflected its social and cultural setting; it has read Scripture in terms of its cultural assumptions about community and human goods. This has led to a wide variety of possible social forms that, we believe, should be seen not as a cause for painful division as has too often been the case but as a potential basis for mutual learning. Second, we argue that the church in all its expressions is necessarily an emergent phenomenon. That is, the entities we call "churches" emerge from the interaction of their cultural assumptions, their special historical inheritances, and their understanding of God's revelation through Scripture. We illustrate these two convictions with case studies and amplify them with reflections on biblical metaphors for the church and on various practices that have emerged over time. Finally, we attempt our own description of normative ecclesial elements that should emerge and be evident in groups who follow Christ and consider the eschatological character of the church, which is journeying like a pilgrim toward the full revelation of God's reign in the renewed creation. Our hope and prayer are that a more deeply theological focus will encourage the humility and simplicity that Wright calls for, and at the same time stimulate our imaginations about the new creation God is fashioning around us.

We are both deeply grateful for the support and encouragement offered to us by many friends and colleagues who know more than we do about many of these things. Our citations offer the best glimpse of how much we owe others, but there are others who have lent a hand in more particular ways. Darren wants to thank H. L. Richard, Melanie Howard, Ryan Schellenberg, Douglas Porpora, David Elder-Vass, Christian Smith, Darin Lenz, C. Arnold Snyder, John Rempel, Randy Woodley, John Jay Travis, Robert

Enns, and Scott MacDougall. Bill could not have pursued this project without the generous support of Cory Willson, James Bradley, Makoto Fujimura, Emo Yango, Pascal Bazzell, Roger Hedlund, Melba Padilla Maggay, Paul Bendor Samuel, Dan Shaw, and John Goldingay. Both of us are grateful for the consistent encouragement of our editors at InterVarsity Press, Dan Reid and now Jon Boyd, and their competent staff.

1
. . . .

Is the Church in Crisis?

It is hard to know how to think about the Christian church today. Is the church as it exists today a cause for celebration or a reason to lament? One could make arguments either way. In some places it is clearly under attack—political, cultural, social, or even demonic. In North America, declining church membership is complicated by—and perhaps in part fueled by—the continuing polarization in the church over social and doctrinal issues. In Europe, despite the growing presence of African and Latin American immigrant Christians, the decline of the institutional churches appears unstoppable. In the majority world, despite a few bright spots in Africa and Latin America, Christians and their churches are often under severe pressure from newly militant Islam, Buddhism, or Hinduism. In parts of Iraq and Syria, struggling with years of violence, there is even talk of the disappearance of Christian churches altogether, many with centuries-long histories in the region.

But this is not the whole story. Reports from many places in the world give evidence of an explosive growth of Christian churches, some powered by the global Pentecostal movement and others forming spontaneously under influences that are mostly invisible to outside observers.[1] Even in places where Christianity faces serious challenges—like secularism in the West or newly awakened non-Christian religions in Asia—there are signs that God may be doing a new thing, something that calls for new wine skins for the new wine of the gospel.

These trends are interesting, and they are the staple of media reports. But the reality may be even more complex. Consider the different situations we have briefly described. When these various trends are examined closely, it

---

[1]For a current example of such news see *The Global Church Project: Exploring the Wisdom and Theologies of World Christianity with Graham Hill*, www.theglobalchurchproject.com.

becomes evident that the challenges faced by the church in North America are primarily about the institutional form (or forms) Christianity should take while the difficulties faced elsewhere are more often specific threats to the actual community of believers. The institutional form and the community of believers are both involved when we speak of church, of course, but they are looking at different aspects of "church," and they call for very different reflection and response.

It is this complexity, and the multiple factors behind this, that is the stimulus for these two authors to write this book. Both of us have had long experience with the forms of church and with communities of believers: Bill as a missionary in the Philippines and subsequently as a professor of theology and culture and an ordained Presbyterian (PCUSA) minister; Darren as a Mennonite Brethren missionary in India, as a researcher in new forms of the church, and recently as a professor of intercultural and religious studies. Both of us have come to feel that many of the anxieties faced in missions today, to say nothing of the bewildering array of institutional challenges Christians face in the West, relate centrally to the current identity of the church—to both its theological nature and its social character. Further, it is our conviction that too many treatments of *church* use the term uncritically as though it were something everyone understood when in actual practice *church* is used in a variety of ways that reflect widely different contexts. This diversity reflects not simply the fundamental divide we have already noted but the multiple cultural and historical situations where followers of Christ seek to faithfully live out the gospel. In this chapter we want to linger on some of the factors that contribute to this confusion about the church and then briefly lay out the argument of the succeeding chapters.

CHURCH AND KINGDOM

One important reason for many false assumptions about the church rests on the simplistic assumption that Christ's primary goal in his teaching and work was to inaugurate what we understand today as the Christian church. It is in the light of such priorities that mission in many people's minds is equated with church planting. While church planting is an important mandate of missions, there are two problems with this assumption regarding Christ's work. First, there is no doubt among scholars of the New Testament that Christ's primary message was the arrival of the kingdom or reign of God, not of the institutional church. At the very beginning of his ministry, Mark's Gospel tells us that Jesus came to Galilee announcing the "good news of God, and saying, 'The time is fulfilled, and the kingdom of God has come near; repent and believe in the good news'" (Mk 1:14-15). Further, from a careful examination of Jesus' teaching, especially his parables, it becomes clear that Jesus understood this reign to be present in his person and work. It was the arrival of this reign that was both a fulfillment of First Testament[2] prophecies about the coming of the Messiah and a realization of the reconciling and renewing work of God. This cosmic intervention of God in human form is what Paul would later call the new creation and what the New Testament claims will culminate in Christ's second coming. So, what Christ inaugurated, while it would later include the church, involved a renewing and reconciling work that had implications for the whole of creation and for all people.

"Church" (Gk. *ekklēsia*) meanwhile barely makes an appearance in Christ's teachings. The word appears on only two occasions in the Gospels, both in the Gospel of Matthew. The first is the famous account of Peter's confession that Jesus is the Messiah, whereupon Jesus promises that "on this rock I will build my church, and the gates of Hades will not prevail against it" (Mt 16:18). Catholics and Protestants differ on the interpretation of this passage, but scholars from both confessions would agree that it is a stretch to read back into it all that we understand now by "the Christian church." Rather, it is best seen as one way of thinking about the kingdom that Jesus preached and the concrete form that this would take. Whatever *church* meant, it would centrally involve the confession that Peter had made about Jesus' messianic mission, and nothing would be allowed to frustrate that mission. In the only other reference to church, also in Matthew, Jesus tells his disciples that divisions that disrupt the community of those gathered in his name are to be handled first privately before bringing in other witnesses: "If another member of the church sins against you, go and point out the fault when the

---

[2]We join other scholars in using the title First Testament instead of Old Testament to stress the nature of the Bible as a storyline and to avoid the connotation that the old is outdated. See James Sanders, "First Testament and Second," *Biblical Theology Bulletin* 17, no. 2 (1987): 47-49; and John Goldingay, *Old Testament Theology: Israel's Gospel* (Downers Grove, IL: InterVarsity Press, 2003), 859-63.

two of you are alone" (Mt 18:15). Clearly this indicates that the kingdom would take shape in the form of particular communities, but neither Jesus (nor Matthew) gives other details about what this means to him and his audience. It most probably would not have included many of the things we mean by *church* today, and it does not follow that this is simply to be equated with the Christian church as it developed in its long history.

This is not to say that the teaching of these verses is unimportant. In fact, one might argue that the two central theological components of the church that emerge in the book of Acts and in Paul's teaching are already present in these two appearances in Matthew. First, however one understands Peter's confession, it cannot be doubted that the church involves people's response to Christ, resulting in an intimate connection with God that Christ makes possible. As this develops later in the New Testament, the church centrally involves people whom God joins to Christ by the Holy Spirit, what Paul calls the body of Christ (e.g., Rom 7:4; 1 Cor 10:16). This is a central theological meaning of *church*, as we will argue in a later chapter. But, as the second appearance of the word indicates, this new reality involves people, joined to Christ, who are joined to each other by the Spirit to live together in a new community of mutual forgiveness. This latter aspect of "church" (Gk. *ekklēsia*, lit., "assembly") is seen consistently in the way God's work came to focus on communities, starting first with Jewish people and extending eventually to all ethnic and people groups.

Despite these important hints, Jesus gives no indication that he intended to found a separate religion with a distinct institution called "the church." It is clear from the Gospels that response to Jesus took many different forms that reflected the multiple situations of the hearer—from the Samaritan woman at the well who became a missionary to her community (John 4) to Nicodemus, the Jewish leader who came secretly to interview Jesus (John 3), to the Syrophoenician women whose faith resulted in the deliverance of her child from an unclean spirit (Mark 7). The kingdom work taking shape in Christ's life and ministry would elicit multiple responses and take many different forms, even if initially its focus was on the Jewish people and more particularly Jesus' disciples. But one must recognize that Jesus' primary work was to establish this divine kingdom, not only by his teaching and miracles but also and especially by his death and resurrection as manifested by the pouring out of the Holy Spirit in Acts 2. Notions of the church as a distinct and voluntary community came into existence gradually, as we will note in more detail in chapter two, but the church was always called to witness to the kingdom and become an embodiment of that new reality.[3]

The second problem with the assumption that Jesus came to found the church is that it ties Jesus' work—indeed God's purposes for creation—too closely to what eventually took shape as the Christian church. As missiologist David Bosch reminded us a generation ago, and as we mentioned above, the Gospels give no indication that Jesus intended to begin a new religion called Christianity. As Bosch put it:

> Jesus had no intention of founding a new religion. Those who followed him were given no name to distinguish them from other groups, no creed of their own, no rite which revealed their distinctive group character, no geographical center from which they would operate.[4]

Jesus came rather to bring about a radical renewal of the First Testament covenant people that was to bless the world. Bosch writes: "The community around Jesus was to function as a *pars pro toto*, a community for the sake of others. Never, however, was this community to separate itself from the others."[5] Jesus lived his life as a faithful Jewish believer, as did most of his earliest disciples. They saw no conflict between their Jewish faith and their call to follow Christ. It is true that already in the book of Acts the framework for what was to become "Christianity" was taking shape, and, despite Bosch's claim, there is reason to believe that much of what became known as "Christianity" was a part of God's purposes. However, what later became the institutional church does not constitute the center of Jesus' life and ministry. The kingdom, with its multiple forms, filled that spot. Moreover, it was the kingdom that would create the church, not the other way around. As Alfred Loisy famously commented in his 1902 book, whether with irony or regret,

---

[3]For a fuller account of the relationship between church and kingdom see George Eldon Ladd, *Jesus and the Kingdom: The Eschatology of Biblical Realism* (New York: Harper & Row, 1964), which has been one of the most influential sources for evangelical thinking on the kingdom and its relation to the church.

[4]David J. Bosch, *Transforming Mission: Paradigm Shifts in Theology of Mission* (Maryknoll, NY: Orbis, 1991), 50.

[5]Bosch, *Transforming Mission*, 50.

"Jesus foretold the kingdom, and it was the Church that came."[6] Though the church plays a crucial role as witness and embodiment of that kingdom, and might even be thought to be central in some ways, its reality does not constitute either the limit nor the extent and reach of the kingdom.

Throughout history the ambiguity associated with teaching on the church has been widely recognized by theologians. As the famous German theologian Wolfhart Pannenberg argues, "It is not self-evident that the concept of the church should be a separate dogmatic theme."[7] And in fact, Anthony Thiselton points out, the church was not really a separate area of doctrine before the Reformers. He concludes his survey by saying: "Whereas the kingdom of God is determinative, the church is characterized by provisionality."[8] This is a theme we will return to in the concluding chapter.

The implication of this for our argument will become clearer as we move forward. But here we signal that since God's work initiated in Christ extends beyond the church, there surely will be implications for the multiple forms of assembly that God intended to promote as kingdom work. And though the Christian church has a critical role to play in promoting this larger kingdom work, it will not be surprising if, as the history of the kingdom unfolds, the evidence of God's work will introduce social forms and structures that expand existing notions of "church" as they reflect what we might call God's larger kingdom—and even ecclesial—purposes. In preparation for exploring these possibilities, in the remainder of this chapter we want to reflect briefly on the contemporary situation of missions today in the light of recent history, and highlight the significance of this for thinking about the church.

Church and Missions

A further complication in reflection on the church results from the fraught history of relations between mission and church that we have inherited. On the one hand, missions, carried out frequently by activist Christians sent out

[6]Alfred Firmin Loisy, *The Gospel and the Church*, trans. Christopher Home (1902; New York: Charles Scribner's Sons, 1904), 166. Loisy did not doubt that Jesus intended some community but regretted that it came to take the shape of a civil association. Not everyone has agreed with him. His views were so controversial that he lost his position in a French Catholic university.
[7]Wolfhart Pannenberg, *Systematic Theology*, 3:21, quoted in Anthony C. Thiselton, *The Hermeneutics of Doctrine* (Grand Rapids: Eerdmans, 2007), 488.
[8]Thiselton, *Hermeneutics of Doctrine*, 488.

by supporting societies, from the start had an ambiguous—and frequently contentious—relationship with sending churches in the West. As Anne-Marie Kool points out, missions in the West were mostly born outside the church, and as a result, missions have often been considered an appendage.[9] Churches thought of mission—if they thought of it at all—as one of their many functions rather than as something essential to the nature of church. Missionaries, meanwhile, when they finally realized their goal was church planting rather than simply evangelization, had difficulty understanding what these "younger churches" should look like.

Stephen Neill in his classic history of missions recounts these difficulties in a lengthy chapter entitled interestingly enough "From Mission to Church."[10] He notes that the problems often stemmed from the fact that missionaries saw themselves as primarily activists seeking individual converts; thus, the church appeared mostly as an afterthought. Or else the founding of churches was carried out independently of the work of missions, with little mutual support and understanding between these efforts. Neill concludes that healthy national churches were rare because developments were driven by personal or nationalistic motives rather than by "any clear theological understanding of the nature of the church."[11]

These long-standing problems were on full display in the famous Edinburgh Missionary Conference of 1910, which is worth considering here as a case study of the struggle to understand and build healthy mission churches.[12] After more than one hundred years of missionary activity, planners of the conference felt there was much to celebrate. Two factors stand out as background to the conversations about the church. First, as Brian Stanley notes, the vast mobilization of resources reflected in the participation of multiple mission agencies from Europe and America lent a feeling of eschatological

---

[9]Anne-Marie Kool, "Changing Images in the Formation for Mission: Commission Five in Light of Current Challenges; A Western Perspective," in *Edinburgh 2010: Mission Then and Now*, ed. David A. Kerr and Kenneth R. Ross (Oxford: Regnum, 2009), 165. She argues that this has resulted mostly in a functional ecclesiology.

[10]Stephen Neill, *A History of Christian Missions*, ed. Owen Chadwick, 2nd ed. (New York: Penguin, 1986), chap. 12.

[11]Neill, *History of Christian Missions*, 383.

[12]This important conference has received significant recent attention on the occasion of its centennial. Two studies that we have found particularly helpful are Brian Stanley, *The World Missionary Conference, Edinburgh 1910* (Grand Rapids: Eerdmans, 2009); and Kerr and Ross, *Edinburgh 2010*.

expectation to the gathering. Never since the Reformation, or indeed since Pentecost itself, planners believed, had it been possible to anticipate that many in this generation might live to see the realization of the kingdom. Whether it was seeing the twelve hundred missionaries gathered together in one place, or because of the postmillennial eschatology popular at the time, they did their planning and assembled with a great sense of expectancy. This eschatological expectancy was surely fueled by the timing of the conference during the high point of British imperialism. On the first night as they all joined in singing "God Save the Queen," a visitor reported, the rafters shook and their spines tingled, suggesting yet another cause for optimism.[13] As Brian Stanley comments wryly: "The infectious power of British imperial motifs thus ironically played its part in making unity from the outset a dominant theme of the Edinburgh conference."[14] It was hard not to believe that the apparent triumph of Western civilization anticipated and facilitated the impending triumph of Christian missions.

Second, in the background of discussions of the church, and further fueling optimism, were assumptions about the triumph of Christianity and the imminent decay of other religions. Though some sought points of contact for the presentation of an alien gospel, many delegates believed that Christianity represented the fulfillment of these faiths. All agreed with J. N. Farquhar, who predicted that, since Christianity represented true wisdom, other religions were doomed to extinction. In fact, Sherwood Eddy announced, Buddhism and Hinduism were already "decaying."[15] As we will note later in this chapter, it is hard to imagine a more serious misreading of the situation with respect to the global progress of religion and its significance for mission and the church.

The triumph of Christianity is one thing, but what about the role of the church in all this? Here the feelings were decidedly less euphoric. In fairness, the state of "younger churches" took up a great deal of attention at the conference and was seriously considered: Commission II (of the eight major study commissions) examined "The Native Church and Its Workers." Brian

---

[13]Stanley, *World Missionary Conference*, 3-4, 81
[14]Stanley, *World Missionary Conference*, 81.
[15]Stanley, *World Missionary Conference*, 215-19.

Stanley in fact characterizes the conference as a church-centric gathering; delegates characterized the church as "the most efficient element in Christian propaganda."[16]

The conference and the report of the commission, however, give evidence that a focus on the church, to say nothing of a vision of a global church, was more a goal than a reality. For one thing, a mere 19 out of 1215 approved delegates were from the majority world. More surprising, one hundred years later, none represented Africa and only one came from Korea. (Latin America was not represented either since it was considered already evangelized.) Even so, a serious attempt was made to hear from these representatives. As the chair of the meetings, John R. Mott went out of his way to assure that these voices (along with the few women present) were heard out of proportion to their small numbers. But there is room to doubt that delegates were seriously listening. The final report of Commission II admitted that more needed to be done "to contribute to a definition of what the Church is, the definition of its essentials or real Catholic features."[17] It is not hard to see why this was so. The discussions of that commission were largely taken up with problems of missionary imperialism on the one hand and with the gap between the stipends of missionaries and those of national workers on the other. Though they employed the three-self understanding of church—self-governing, self-supporting, and self-propagating—they recognized this too was still an unrealized goal. Since churches were frequently not self-supported, they were manifestly not self-governing.[18]

But despite these weaknesses there were reasons for hope. Stanley finds the theological positions remarkably progressive for the time.[19] Vinoth Ramachandra, in his recent assessment of the conference, finds attitudes toward other faiths softening, reflecting both a high Christology and a dialogical approach to mission.[20] Conference delegates justly complained that, because of the long periods of probation and catechesis required of potential members, too much missionary time is spent keeping people out of church rather than

---

[16]Stanley, *World Missionary Conference*, 133.

[17]Stanley, *World Missionary Conference*, 109.

[18]Stanley, *World Missionary Conference*, 140.

[19]Stanley, *World Missionary Conference*, 149.

[20]Vinoth Ramachandra, "A World of Religions and a Gospel of Transformation," in Kerr and Ross, *Edinburgh 2010*, 148-49.

gathering them in. And they thoughtfully puzzled over what to do about mass movements to Christ, which were becoming increasingly common.[21]

Perhaps the comments of Gulnar Francis-Dehqani in the volume *Edinburgh 2010* best sum up the Edinburgh conference and its potential. He notes that "whilst the nature of missionary work was shifting to incorporate a more complex understanding of mission, a new theological language was not yet in place to express the changing experience."[22] The language still reflected a narrow evangelical experience, with its implicit Christian superiority linking the proclamation of the gospel with the spread of Western civilization. Now, he says, we have come to see mission in terms of dialogue and witness. But in 1910 perhaps nowhere was the lack of vocabulary more evident than in the conversations surrounding the emerging church outside the West.

And there were other critical lacunae in the 1910 conference. Not only was the voice of the majority world mostly unheard, but the absence of Roman Catholic missions assured that conversations on the church were limited to Protestant perspectives. The related absence of discussion on Latin America missed the opportunity to see new missional possibilities in that continent—whether Catholic or Protestant. The subsequent Congress on Christian Work in Latin America in Panama in 1916 was an important attempt to make up for this lack, though Catholic presence in those meetings was also limited.[23]

For evangelicals, significant opportunity to address the relation between mission and church would be delayed until the famous Lausanne Congress on World Evangelization of 1974 led by Billy Graham and John Stott.[24] There significant voices from the majority world were featured, and serious attention was paid to the place and role of the church. Howard Snyder addressed "The Church as God's Agent in Evangelism," Andrew Kirk offered

[21]Stanley, *World Missionary Conference*, 151, 156.
[22]Gulnar Francis-Dehqani, "Adventures in Christian-Muslim Encounters since 1910," in Kerr and Ross, *Edinburgh 2010*, 128; see 125-38.
[23]See Committee on Cooperation in Latin America, *Christian Work in Latin America* (New York: Missionary Education Movement, 1917); and Miguel Alvarez, ed., *The Reshaping of Mission in Latin America* (Oxford: Regnum, 2015).
[24]See the record of this conference edited by J. D. Douglas, *Let the Earth Hear His Voice: International Congress on World Evangelization Lausanne, Switzerland* (Minneapolis: World Wide Publications, 1975).

a serious review of "The Kingdom of God and the Church in Contemporary Protestantism and Catholicism," and Jonathan Chao considered "The Local and Universal Church in Evangelization." In the covenant that resulted from the meetings, paragraph six dealt with "The Church and Evangelism," maintaining that "the church is at the very center of God's cosmic purpose and is his appointed means of spreading the Gospel."[25] This church, however, must not only preach the cross but must itself be marked by the cross, by a living faith in God, and by love and honesty. The conclusion indicated the work still to be done: "The church is the community of God's people rather than an institution, and must not be identified with any particular culture, social or political system, or human ideology."[26] Seeing the church as the community of God's people was an important advance and an echo of the famous definition of the church as the pilgrim people of God from the Second Vatican Council a decade earlier. But to contrast the church with all particular cultures, or political systems or human ideologies, posed the question of what positive relationship to these inescapable realities the church would sustain. Or would the church continue to be an abstraction floating above the realities that constitute human life? Clearly the church exists in particular cultural forms and invariably takes on some political and social form. Moreover, despite Kirk's survey, no advance is made in understanding the relationship of the church to the kingdom of God, which is mentioned neither in Snyder's otherwise helpful article nor in the covenant itself.

As this brief survey illustrates, Protestants have made some headway in their understandings of church and of God's mission over the past one hundred years. The lack of definition regarding the church's relation to the mission of God in the world, evident in Edinburgh 1910, was partially addressed in Lausanne in 1974. Nevertheless, as we noted, important work on cultural realities had yet to be done before core issues could be addressed. One set of issues related to confronting and addressing newly militant religions on the one hand and dealing with the complexity of a global (and postmodern) culture on the other.

---

[25]"The Lausanne Covenant," Lausanne Movement, accessed April 3, 2019, www.lausanne.org/content/covenant/lausanne-covenant.
[26]Douglas, *Let the Earth Hear His Voice*, 5.

CHURCH AND RELIGIONS

The relationship of the church to other religions has been a point of much discussion and debate, particularly in recent years with the rise—and certainly not the decline—of the so-called world religions. Does the church stand out from its surrounding religious communities as a Christian "city on a hill," distinct and unrelated to all that surround it? Or is it the new "bread" that emerges when the leaven of the gospel enters into and infuses the very religions and cultures it encounters? Or is it some combination of these?

For our purposes it is helpful to again return to the World Missionary Conference of 1910 in Edinburgh. As we have seen, this was a moment of high missionary optimism, when church leaders from around the world predicted the impending triumph of Christianity over other religions. Ironically, however, this optimism was accompanied by another assessment—that, though other religions would eventually give way to Christianity, those religions nonetheless contained important truths that needed to be understood missiologically. J. N. Farquhar, whom we met above, was influential in this regard. Following the conference, his 1913 *The Crown of Hinduism* became one of the classic treatments of what was known as fulfillment theology, arguing that missionaries should seek out the truth and "gleams of light" within the Hindu faith and demonstrate that Christianity fulfills these.[27] It was a view that was in many ways remarkably open to and positive about other religions, if only because of what other religions could eventually become rather than what they were in their present state.[28]

The point of debate during this and subsequent decades was whether there is continuity or discontinuity between Christianity and other religions. Farquhar and those at Edinburgh cautiously affirmed continuity: other religions have some continuity with Christianity insofar as they are fulfilled and completed by Christianity. During the 1930s and post–World War II, however, the debate erupted and divided into two firm camps. Some in the growing theological liberalism argued the need for what Harvard University philosopher William Ernest Hocking called a new "world faith" that would

---

[27]J. N. Farquhar, *The Crown of Hinduism* (1913; repr., New York: Oxford University Press, 1919), 54.
[28]Farquhar, *The Crown of Hinduism*, 51; see also Ramachandra, "World of Religions," 148-49.

emphasize continuity among all religions and the supremacy of no single one, especially Christianity.[29]

Others, influenced by the dialectical theology of Karl Barth, emphasized a radical discontinuity between "man-made" religions and God's completely separate and unique revelation. This was probably most clearly articulated in the 1938 conference of the International Missionary Council (IMC) in Tambaram, India. Guided by a book prepared for the conference by Hendrick Kraemer, the conference explored and affirmed the ultimate discontinuity of the true Christian faith from all other religions.[30] Though Kraemer encouraged Christians to be humble and respectful of other religions, he maintained that no "point of contact" was possible between these and Christ's revelation. This created a tension between the church and other religions, but for Kraemer this tension was something to be embraced, not softened. As he later wrote, "The deeper the consciousness of the tension and the urge to take this yoke upon itself are felt, the healthier the Church is. The more oblivious of this tension the Church is, the more well established and at home in this world it feels, the more it is in deadly danger of being the salt that has lost its savor."[31]

Interestingly, at the 1938 International Missionary Council a group of Indian theologians presented a contrasting viewpoint. Calling themselves the "Rethinking Christianity" group, these writers sought to argue that it was entirely possible, indeed crucial for the future of Christianity in India, for the Christian faith to be expressed in Indian (meaning Hindu) concepts.[32] Though their views helped to temper the overall skepticism toward other religions, Kraemer's discontinuity viewpoint proved to be highly influential for the conference and for Western Christians for years to come. Evangelicals in particular would not substantially revisit the question of other religions until the 1990s.

---

[29]William Ernest Hocking, *Living Religions and a World Faith* (New York: Macmillan, 1940). See discussion in Harold Netland, *Encountering Religious Pluralism: The Challenge to Christian Faith & Mission* (Downers Grove, IL: InterVarsity Press, 2001), 40.

[30]Hendrick Kraemer, *The Christian Message in a Non-Christian World* (New York: Harper, 1938).

[31]Hendrick Kraemer, *The Communication of the Christian Faith* (Philadelphia: Westminster, 1956), 36.

[32]See their response to Kraemer following the conference: A. J. Appasamy, V. Chakkarai, and P. Chenchiah, *A Christian Approach to Hinduism: Being Studies in the Theology of A. J. Appasamy, V. Chakkarai, and P. Chenchiah,* (Madras, India: Christian Literature Society, 1956).

Other Christian traditions, however, more quickly began to reevaluate the continuity between Christianity and other religions. Of particular note is the major shift that the Roman Catholic Church made with Vatican II. Traditionally, the Catholic declaration of "outside the church there is no salvation" was often interpreted as a statement of discontinuity—God's work occurred only in the (Catholic) church, and this work could not occur in or through other religions. With Vatican II, however, a door was opened to the "unseen" work of God in the hearts of "all men of good will."[33] Karl Rahner, an important contributor to Vatican II, later proposed that in some cases certain persons in other religions may receive enough of God's grace to make that person an "anonymous Christian."[34]

As mentioned, it has only been since the 1990s that some evangelicals have begun to reassess the ways in which the church may understand and relate to other religions.[35] In 1992 a commission of the World Evangelical Fellowship met in Manila and discussed, among other topics, the issue of other religions. At that time writers such as Clark Pinnock and John Sanders had begun to propose ways in which the Holy Spirit may be at work in other religions.[36] This influence was seen in the Manila conference where, while affirming a strong commitment to the authority of Scripture and the uniqueness of the person and work of Jesus Christ, participants were still unable to reach a consensus on the question of whether people may "find salvation through the blood of Jesus Christ although they do not consciously know the name of Jesus."[37] As a result, the declaration called for further

[33]Pope Paul VI. *Gaudium et Spes*. December 7, 1965, Papal Archive. The Holy See, www.vatican.va/archive/hist_councils/ii_vatican_council/documents/vat-ii_cons_19651207_gaudium-et-spes_en.html.

[34]Karl Rahner, *Ecclesiology: Questions in the Church, the Church in the World*, vol. 14 of *Theological Investigations*, trans. David Bourke (London: Darton, Longman & Todd, 1976), 283.

[35]Evangelicals were perhaps made even more reluctant because of their reactions to the developing ecumenical statements and theologies of the World Council of Churches (WCC), which during this time highlighted the need to set aside exclusivist theologies and engage in humble dialogue with other religions.

[36]Clark H. Pinnock, *A Wideness in God's Mercy: The Finality of Jesus Christ in a World of Religions* (Grand Rapids: Zondervan, 1992); and John Sanders, *No Other Name: An Investigation into the Destiny of the Unevangelized* (Grand Rapids: Eerdmans, 1992).

[37]"The WEF Manila Declaration," in *The Unique Christ in Our Pluralist World*, ed. Bruce J. Nicholls (Grand Rapids: Baker Books, 1994), 14. See also discussion in Veli-Matti Kärkkäinen, *An Introduction to the Theology of Religions: Biblical, Historical and Contemporary Perspectives* (Downers Grove, IL: InterVarsity Press, 2003), 147-48.

study on the question. That this group was willing to acknowledge a lack of consensus on this point and called for continued dialogue signaled an openness, however reluctant, to a development of thought in the way churches understood other religions.

In the decades since the Manila conference, the global public has been confronted with many realities and developments with regard to religions. The most prominent singular event was arguably the Muslim terror attacks on September 11, 2001, which catapulted into the global awareness the reality and challenges of Muslim terrorist groups. Religious radicalization, however, did not start or end with 9/11. Rather, as many have observed, globalization has caused various religious communities to reaffirm their beliefs and identities over against the threat of others.[38] This process of "sacralization" often causes religious communities to return to what they see as their fundamental and core values and to solidify differences between them and others. In extreme cases such communities use physical, political, and psychological violence to protect their communities and beliefs from others. Accompanying, and often sparked by, this resurgence are increasing levels of voluntary and forced migration, bringing people of different religious backgrounds into closer proximity with each other and increasing the sense of threat on all sides.

How does the church, and particularly evangelical churches, understand itself and its relationship to other religions in this context? The 2010 Lausanne Congress on World Evangelization at Cape Town, South Africa, provides an interesting barometer and contrast to the Manila conference nearly twenty years earlier. Whereas Manila opened up the possibility of discussion regarding how God may be at work in other religions, Cape Town makes no mention of this. Instead, the Cape Town Commitment strongly affirms the classic and important "truth" of Jesus Christ as the "Savior, Lord and God,"[39] and emphasizes how this truth combats "relativist pluralism,"[40] and that other religions "replace or distort the one true God."[41] However, the commitment also seeks to affirm these statements from a place of humility,

---

[38]See most prominently Peter Berger, ed., *The Desecularization of the World: Resurgent Religions and World Politics* (Grand Rapids: Eerdmans, 1999).

[39]"The Cape Town Commitment: A Confession of Faith and a Call to Action," *Kairos* 5, no. 1 (2011): 175.

[40]"Cape Town Commitment," 191.

[41]"Cape Town Commitment," 173.

declaring, "We repent of our failure to seek friendships with people of Muslim, Hindu, Buddhist and other religious backgrounds. In the Spirit of Jesus, we will take initiatives to show love, goodwill and hospitality to them."[42] It also rejects "lies and caricatures about other faiths" and affirms the "proper place for dialogue with people of other faiths."[43] Thus, the statements of Cape Town (in contrast to Manila) seek to affirm the theological and religious boundaries between Christianity and other religions while coupling this with a posture and attitude of love toward persons of other faiths.

The understanding of the relationship between the church and other religions articulated at Cape Town 2010, however, is not representative of all Protestants and evangelicals. Some European and North American mainline Protestant churches have given increased attention to interfaith dialogue and partnerships, particularly with Muslim communities in those nations. Among evangelicals, there have been several theologians that have begun to explore the continuity between Christianity and other religions and the ways in which God's church may have constructive relationships with other religions.[44] Missiologists have increasingly employed the concept of cultural contextualization, which, as we will note, analyzes the cultural forms of other religions that can be meaningfully contextualized to Christianity.

Overall, however, in recent years there has not been a wide and sustained conversation among mission and ministry practitioners, particularly among evangelicals, about the ways in which other non-Christian religions may have some continuity with the church. As mentioned above, much of this can be explained by increased globalization, the move among many to strengthen their own religious communities and commitments, and the fear of the religious "other" that this generates. In a climate generated by fear, there is little motivation to consider if and how there is continuity between Christianity and other religions and religious communities. Rather, discontinuity becomes a sociological and theological default, strengthening and hardening the boundaries between communities and religions in a world whose boundaries feel increasingly threatened.

---

[42]"Cape Town Commitment," 203.
[43]"Cape Town Commitment," 203.
[44]See for example Gerald R. McDermott and Harold A. Netland, *A Trinitarian Theology of Religions: An Evangelical Proposal* (New York: Oxford University Press, 2014).

The development of the fraught relationship between the church and religions raises a fundamental question that calls for treatment here: what do we mean by *religion*? This question surely constitutes a major factor confounding the conversation about church and religions. Part of the problem lies with the word itself. How does the church reflect a religion? What exactly does it reflect in doing so? Defining *religion* is similar to the proverbial problem of defining *time*—it seems self-evident until one actually tries to put words to it. But for all the various definitions of *religion*—and there are many—there are at least two things upon which contemporary scholars agree. The first, as scholars such as Wilfred Cantwell Smith, Clifford Geertz, and J. Z. Smith have suggested, is the idea that religion was, and to some degree continues to be, a concept that comes from outside of religions themselves and does not adequately describe various religious traditions.[45] As Richard King has noted, early Greco-Roman uses of the concept referred to ritual practices and paying homage to the gods. With the rise of Christianity, however, it was redefined as "a matter of adherence to particular doctrines or beliefs rather than allegiance to ancient ritual practices."[46] This model tends to emphasize a theistic belief and a "fundamental dualism between the human world and the transcendent world."[47] Such conceptions reflected particular ways of understanding the Christian religion in the West but did not and do not always adequately describe the religions of other contexts.[48]

The second area of agreement is that the idea of "world religions" is also largely a Western concept born out of the Enlightenment and responds to the need to make sense of a changing world. As Tomoko Masuzawa demonstrates in her influential book *The Invention of World Religions*, until the mid nineteenth century Europeans and North Americans typically described the

---

[45]Wilfred Cantwell Smith, *The Meaning and End of Religion* (New York: Macmillan, 1963); Clifford Geertz, "Religion as a Cultural System," in *Anthropological Approaches to the Study of Religion*, ed. Michael Banton, 1-46 (London: Routledge, 1966); and Jonathan Z. Smith, *Imagining Religion: From Babylon to Jonestown* (Chicago: University of Chicago Press, 1982).

[46]Richard King, *Orientalism and Religion: Postcolonial Theory, India and "The Mystic East"* (New York: Routledge, 1999), 35-37. See also discussion by H. L. Richard, "Religious Syncretism as a Syncretistic Concept: The Inadequacy of the 'World Religions' Paradigm in Cross-Cultural Encounter," *International Journal of Frontier Missiology* 31, no. 4 (2014): 209-15.

[47]King, *Orientalism and Religion*, 37.

[48]This question is discussed in more detail by one of us in William A. Dyrness, *Insider Jesus: Theological Reflections on New Christian Movements* (Downers Grove, IL: InterVarsity Press, 2016), chap. 3.

world as made up of Christians, Jews, Muhammadans (Muslims), and the rest.[49] Western affinities for taxonomy began to be more specific about "the rest" in subsequent decades, but it was only in the wake of World War I and the uneasy calm before World War II that American universities started to write texts that categorized and studied what became known as "world religions." The context is instructive: the West was increasingly aware of a globalizing world where an event in one part of the world could have great, even devastating, effects on another. In order to navigate this new era, it was imperative to become more educated and aware of the various religions that were at work in these countries as these were impinging on the West.[50]

What this required, however, was to somehow define and order in Western and Christian terms that which often defied categorization. An important example is the "religion" of Hinduism. As H. L. Richard and others have shown, historically the non-Muslims of the Indian continent did not understand themselves as sharing a common set of beliefs and practices known as Hinduism, much less call themselves Hindus. In the eighteenth century onward, however, and particularly through interaction with British Christian colonialists and missionaries, Britons and then Indians started to categorize the widely ranging traditions of the subcontinent as an identifiable religion.[51]

This signals an important point that we intend to explore in this book—that from a social science perspective the category of religion itself is an elastic concept and is not as self-evident as is often assumed. Missiologists and Christians who would try to distinguish the church from surrounding religions can thus run the risk of creating a category that, for members of that community at least, does not accurately describe them or what they value and the place this has in their lives. This can also run the risk of trying to arbitrarily separate the church and its members from something that God can and does use to shape the church in unique ways.

---

[49]Tomoko Masuzawa, *The Invention of World Religions: Or, How European Universalism Was Preserved in the Language of Pluralism* (Chicago: University of Chicago Press, 2005), 47.

[50]Masuzawa, *Invention of World Religions*, 41.

[51]H. L. Richard, "New Paradigms for Religion, Multiple Religious Belonging, and Insider Movements," *Missiology* 43, no. 3 (2015): 297-308. See also Geoffrey A. Oddie, *Imagined Hinduism: British Protestant Missionary Constructions of Hinduism, 1793–1900* (Thousand Oaks, CA: Sage, 2006).

Church and Culture

If one were asked to name what has changed in the practice of missions since the Edinburgh conference, the increased awareness and engagement with other faiths would immediately come to mind. But if one were to ask what has changed in our reflection on mission, one candidate would certainly be the influence and spread of the social sciences in understanding the context and appropriate methods of missions. Starting in the 1960s the Roman Catholic Church began to reflect on what was called inculturation; evangelicals entered the conversation in the 1970s and began to speak of contextualization.

This conversation was given impetus by the 1974 Lausanne Congress to which we have already referred, but, as we noted, even there one sensed work remained to be done in applying newer social science methods to missions and its relation to the church. Arguably, the major achievement of that decade in this respect was the Consultation on Gospel and Culture sponsored by Lausanne and held at Willowbank in Bermuda in January 1978.[52] In the report resulting from that colloquium, paragraph eight, addressing "Church and Culture," began with the recognition that if the gospel must be contextualized, so must the church.[53] To older models of imposing Western forms of church, the statement proposes the dynamic-equivalence model (proposed at the conference by Fuller Seminary professor Charles Kraft), which better allows the church to freely and creatively develop in ways that can stand up to colonial imposition and have a positive impact on the indigenous situation. The influence of Kraft—whose *Christianity in Culture* would appear the following year—is clear in this statement.[54] In his address to the consultation Kraft described the process that would foster authentic indigeneity and, in turn, natural growth within churches. This process gets beneath the surface of the forms of a given culture to the meanings these hold so that emerging elements of church life—preaching, worship, sacraments—have equivalent meaning to biblical forms. The goal, Kraft writes, is that a church "produces an impact on its society equivalent to the impact

---

[52]Presentations published in John R. W. Stott and Robert Coote, eds., *Down to Earth: Studies in Christianity and Culture* (Grand Rapids: Eerdmans, 1980).

[53]Stott and Coote, *Down to Earth*, 329. This paragraph constituted pp. 329-36, the longest paragraph in the statement.

[54]Charles H. Kraft, *Christianity in Culture: A Study of Dynamic Biblical Theologizing in Cross-Culture Perspective* (Maryknoll, NY: Orbis, 1979).

that the original church produced in its cultural environment."[55] This process, he believes, allows the Holy Spirit to work in novel ways—producing results, he observes, that missionaries frequently oppose! This represents an advance over previous attempts to impose foreign structures, but there is a clear assumption at work that we want to challenge. Kraft implies that there is such a thing as a biblical notion of the church, and this simply needs to be "translated" into its native equivalent forms. But what is that biblical form? Is it the temple worship of Jesus and his disciples? Is it the house church of Paul, or the developing structure of the Pastoral Epistles? Some participants at Willowbank must have had similar questions because the final statement, after introducing the dynamic-equivalence model, wonders whether "by itself it is large enough and dynamic enough to provide all the guidance that is needed."[56]

This understanding of church and early attempts at contextualization were both developed within the general framework of communication theory, which seeks to understand how best to communicate the Christian message within indigenous thought patterns, or how best to translate the Scripture from Hebrew or Greek into native languages. But, important as this advance was, it carried limitations; the church does not exist like a text waiting to be communicated. It is rather a dynamic, culturally situated emergent reality that is formed under multiple influences. As a result, and at this early stage in the growing awareness of cultural diversity, cultural analysis was not used to consider the nature of the church in particular cultures. Given the central role cultural forms play in the formation of church subcultures, to say nothing of ritual practice and symbolic forms, this was a strange omission. There is an irony here: the study of various cultures had its origin in the study of community values and family (kinship) patterns, just the sort of data, one would think, that would contribute to a deeper insight into communities of faith and worship. But the application of this wisdom to the church did not occur. The church was considered an abstract theological reality rather than an actual community of people necessarily existing as a subculture within a larger social group.

---

[55]Charles H. Kraft, "The Church in Culture: A Dynamic Equivalence Model" in Stott and Coote, *Down to Earth*, 224.

[56]Stott and Coote, *Down to Earth*, 330. It goes on to point out that the analogy with Bible translation is not exact since the translator in this case is the whole community.

In fairness to Kraft, much has happened in social science since he wrote his article and his influential book. Three developments are relevant to our discussion of church. First, during the 1980s and following there has been what has been called the "turn to the subject" in anthropology. This attitude encourages increasing attention be paid not only to indigenous values and practices but to what the people themselves make of their situation. Sherry Ortner, in a now classic article, argued that culture consists of "serious games" in which persons and groups adopt and rewrite cultural norms.[57] The obvious implication of this for missionary practice was to focus less on the message (and the messenger) and more on the listeners and their world. Some of the implications of this for the development of missionary practice were explored by Robert Schreiter in his 1985 book, *Constructing Local Theologies*, which argued that response to Scripture will emerge in ways consistent with local knowledge and values.[58] Though the implications of this for the growth and development of church communities are considerable, they have been mostly ignored in the missionary literature.

A second development has been the growing awareness of the dynamic and changing nature of cultures. Older ideas of culture understand cultures as fixed structures of values and practices that anthropologists enter and seek to explore. With the growing interaction of global, pluralist realities, it is clear that such essentialist notions are no longer plausible. Kathryn Tanner has described the possibilities this opens for thinking about theology. Cultures are not self-contained units, she argues; when understood within a global and historical context, they are "seen instead as dynamic, interactive phenomena" with porous boundaries and mixed identities.[59] The emphasis on the agency of people and the hybrid character of culture does not mean that the various cultural entities are incommensurate; if this were so, communication and transfer of cultural goods, so vital to globalization, would be impossible.[60] This is especially true if we believe that the Spirit of God is at work within the structures of creation, drawing people to acknowledge God.

---

[57]Sherry B. Ortner, "Theory in Anthropology since the Sixties," *Comparative Studies in Society and History* 26, no. 1 (1984): 126-66. This article is considered a classic description of anthropologists' "turn to the subject."

[58]Robert J. Schreiter, *Constructing Local Theologies* (Maryknoll, NY: Orbis, 1985).

[59]Kathryn Tanner, *Theories of Culture: A New Agenda for Theology* (Minneapolis: Fortress, 1997), 54.

[60]Tanner's discussion at times seems to imply a radical cultural relativism.

A third, more recent development, and one that will inform our approach to church, is the rise and influence of emergence theory on the understanding of communities and cultures. Already in 1986, and signaling the new, dynamic view of culture described above, James Clifford posited, "'culture' is not an object to be described, neither is it a unified corpus of symbols and meanings that can be definitively interpreted. Culture is contested, temporal, and emergent."[61] Theories of emergence have grown in use and importance in recent years as scholars have sought to make sense of the growing complexity that is developing and being discovered in social and natural sciences. Such theories are being applied in areas such as philosophy, physics, sociology, biology, organizational studies, and religious studies.[62]

We will develop the contours and importance of emergence theory further in chapter three. In brief, emergence theory seeks to account for new entities. It does so by suggesting that, in many cases, new entities are more than simply the sum of their parts. That is, though social entities such as a political movement, a neighborhood, a soccer club, or a church are composed of many people and various shared practices and beliefs, these combine to create a whole that is greater than the parts.

How does emergence differ from other ways of accounting for social entities? Some social science theories are descriptive, listing and analyzing the various cultural symbols, practices, values, and so on that the group collectively shares. Take the example of the "team spirit" that a soccer team

---

[61]James Clifford, "Introduction: Partial Truths," in James Clifford and George E. Marcus, eds., *Writing Culture: The Poetics and Politics of Ethnography* (Berkeley: University of California Press, 1986), 19.

[62]For example, in philosophy see Paul Humphreys, *Emergence: A Philosophical Account* (New York: Oxford University Press, 2016); Jaegwon Kim, "Making Sense of Emergence," *Philosophical Studies* 95 (1999): 3-36; and John R. Searle, *The Rediscovery of the Mind* (Cambridge, MA: MIT Press, 1992). In physics see Murray Gell-Mann, *The Quark and the Jaguar: Adventures in the Simple and the Complex* (London: Abacus, 1995). In sociology see Margaret S. Archer, *Realist Social Theory: The Morphogenetic Approach* (New York: Cambridge University Press, 1995); and R. Keith Sawyer, *Social Emergence: Societies as Complex Systems* (New York: Cambridge University Press, 2005). In biology see Stuart A. Kauffman, *At Home in the Universe: The Search for Laws of Self-Organization and Complexity* (London: Oxford University Press, 1995). In organizational theory see Benyamin B. Lichtenstein, *Generative Emergence: A New Discipline of Organizational, Entrepreneurial, and Social Innovation* (New York: Oxford University Press, 2014). In religious studies see Christian Smith, *Religion: What It Is, How It Works, and Why It Matters* (Princeton, NJ: Princeton University Press, 2017).

may develop during the course of a season. A descriptive approach may focus on the language, skills, and values the team begins to share around winning. Another approach focuses on the rules that shape belief and behaviors. A team adopts a cognitive model or map that provides the rules of the game needed to communicate and succeed in a given social context. With this approach we may look at the social rules that the wider society provides the team regarding what it means to win. Each of these is helpful. An emergent approach, however, analyzes the relationships between different people and groups and what that interaction in turn creates. In the case of the soccer team an emergent approach would suggest that the team's identity and "spirit" emerges from their interactions with each other, the rules, equipment, and wider social norms. As they interact with these and each other, a new entity called a "team" with "spirit" begins to emerge.

The implications of these three developments for thinking about church will be the common theme in the chapters that follow, but here we note that growing emphasis on local agency and on cultural complexity as illuminated by emergence theory bears important significance for reflection on the church. As one example, consider again Stephen Neill's discussion of church and mission. He notes that there have traditionally been two problems in forming indigenous churches. First, converts have often spent long periods of time watching and even participating in the church the missionaries introduced before thinking about forms that might be appropriate for them. When they do begin this process, the patterns they have learned are hard for them to ignore. Second, Neill points to the difficulty new converts have in answering for themselves the myriad questions that naturally get asked in the complex process of community formation. What might preaching look like in my context? How do we practice Communion or baptism? How do we discipline members? Neill notes that it is no more possible for them to work out by themselves the Pythagorean theorem than it is to invent the church from scratch.[63] The situation is further complicated, Neill notes, by the fact that it is common for new converts, for various reasons, to be resistant to new and indigenous forms of church. They may see their culture as restrictive or lacking resources for developing new forms of church, or

---

[63]Neill, *History of Christian Missions*, 396-97.

this may even be seen as an evil from which they have been delivered. Neill concludes with this wisdom:

> The old non-Christian past must sink below the horizon. That which has come from the West must be so absorbed and assimilated that it can be transformed and re-expressed in categories different from those of the world of its origins. But this is the work of generations, not of years.[64]

Neill is making a critical point that we intend to consider in this book. Cultural influences are subtle, change and mutual influence are often slow and imperceptible, and the church practices and beliefs that eventually emerge in any given context are not entirely predictable. But this also means that the resistance new converts have to new forms may not be the end of the story, and at the same time assimilation of foreign forms may not be entirely evil. In fact, we will see in what follows examples of converts who have accepted new forms and then decided over time that the new, emergent entity is not reflective of who they are or wish to be. Others may from the beginning initially resist the gospel because of its foreignness but then over time move toward those forms. Still others may live in a world of dual belonging, or become migrants who take their homes with them as they are planted in a new setting. The point is that all these options express unique cultural dynamics, and none of these processes is normative or incompatible with God's kingdom work. In every case, we will argue, both the newer understandings of cultural flows and influences and the subtle urgings of the Holy Spirit should encourage us to be open to new forms of church. Or better, we might discern new possibilities for communities as charged spaces where persons can hear new accents of the gospel and grow in their own way toward maturity in Christ.

At the Lausanne-sponsored Congress on World Evangelization of 2010 in Cape Town, celebrating the one-hundred-year anniversary of Edinburgh, the final statement reflected much more this newer—complex but exciting—understanding of mission, even as its delegates reflected a truer vision of the global church:

> Jesus calls all his disciples together to be one family among the nations, a reconciled fellowship in which all sinful barriers are broken down through

---

[64]Neill, *History of Christian Missions*, 398.

his reconciling grace. This Church is a community of grace, obedience and love in the communion of the Holy Spirit, in which the glorious attributes of God and gracious characteristics of Christ are reflected and God's multi-coloured wisdom is displayed.[65]

WHAT THIS BOOK ATTEMPTS

The focus of this book is theological reflection on the sociocultural formation and growth of communities who follow Christ, or in some particular ways are drawn to Christ. As we have already implied, we want to approach this in terms of emergence theory, which stipulates that social communities arise over time in ways that reflect their interaction with specific historical and cultural dynamics. These trajectories are often fragile and contested but also deeply expressive of the social identities of the actors. At the same time, the fact that such communities reflect and embody particular cultural situations, we will argue, should not keep us from discerning ways in which the Spirit of God is at work in these diverse situations forming people into the likeness of Jesus Christ. Another way of saying this is to claim that people's deeply ingrained cultural values offer potential vehicles even if, at times, they also can raise obstacles to the work of God drawing people to appropriate worship. Developing the process of discerning where church exists will be a subtheme of the book and a particular focus of chapter seven.

The following chapters will seek to provide elements to unwrap our theme. Chapters two and four argue that all actual instances of church in history (chap. 2) and in the contemporary world (chap. 4) are emergent entities that reflect their particular social situation. Further, the processes involved in developing churches provide what we will describe as a "reverse hermeneutic" in which the cultural situations interpret the gospel in their own terms, providing both illumination and obfuscation for the emerging shape of the church. Chapter two will explore this in the early period of the church through the fall of the Roman Empire, then in the period of the Reformation, both in the magisterial Reformers' and the developing believers' churches. Chapter three will develop further emergence theory in the light of current examples of church development. Making use of emergence theory and

---

[65]"The Cape Town Commitment," 188.

Margaret Archer's "constraining" and "competitive" conditions to illumine recent history of thinking about "church" in India, we will seek to argue that the church is today, as it has always been, an emergent phenomenon.

Chapter four will explore in detail further contemporary examples of the cultural production of church or, in some cases, frustrated attempts to produce particular communities of believers who follow Christ. We will explore examples largely drawn from Asia, where the most significant cases known to us exist today. Chapters five and six will seek to raise more specifically theological issues. In chapter five we explore biblical models of understanding church: the body of Christ, the pilgrim people of God, and the community of the spirit. Chapter six asks in particular how the practices of worship, particularly the sacraments, might be understood in terms of emergence theory and as reflective of God's purposes within culture. We will note ways in which theological arguments stipulating that these practices are divinely inscribed often ignore the actual history and background of sacramental practice, and are blind to the way their "divinely inscribed" practices invariably carry traditional values. Here we continue to insist that cultural production and emergent biblical values are not in inherent conflict but rather can be mutually productive of multiple communities of faith.

In chapter seven we will argue that the central thrust of biblical teaching on church is best described in terms of the transformative presence of the Spirit of God, drawing the creation and people toward a community of every tongue, people, and nation who will worship God. We will explore in detail what ecclesial markers might allow emerging churches to be identified. The final chapter will note the way in which the biblical church is an eschatological reality whose final home and goal is the worship of the Lamb in heaven. This perspective of church as an eschatological community provides both the substance of the preaching of followers of Jesus and leverage for our critique of all cultural and political forms.

2

The Church as an Emergent
Phenomenon in History

INTRODUCTION

We have argued in the first chapter that contemporary discussions of the Christian church face multiple challenges that make a straightforward definition of the church as a universal phenomenon difficult or impossible. This chapter and the next will seek to establish reasons why this difficulty exists and how we can think about and respond to this situation constructively. In this chapter, making use of historical and theological categories, we will argue that the church has always taken shape within particular historical and cultural situations and that these circumstances invariably facilitate a unique hermeneutical process that is determinative for the shape of the church in a given period. In the following chapter we will seek to describe the same process, using contemporary examples, from the perspective of the social sciences in general and emergence theory in particular.

Since the Reformation, the developing study of interpreting Scripture has been called the science (or method) of hermeneutics. During the last two hundred years scholars of Scripture and theology have begun to apply the methods of explaining and applying Scripture (and other texts) more generally to our human inclination to interpret our life in the world. Since Schleiermacher, these methods, often described as a general hermeneutic, have been used to interpret products of culture or institutions "thickly"— that is, in terms of a specific set of values and commitments. This (mostly unconscious) interpretive process describes how people "make sense of," that is, interpret, their lives in terms of larger narratives and religious commitments. In the last generation this process has led some scholars to wonder if this process could be taken full circle: What if our understanding

of life in the world could then be used as a "reverse hermeneutic"? Hermeneutics has traditionally described the process of drawing out meaning from
Scripture. What if we were to reverse this hermeneutical direction and use
the values and insights of culture to illuminate aspects of Scripture? Alter-
natively, how might these serve to obscure or distort those readings?[1]

There is no longer any question that our cultural perspective critically
influences what we will find valuable and convincing in Scripture. Most
people accept and understand this. For example, few Western readers of
Scripture find much use for the complex biblical genealogies in the First
Testament or Matthew 1. However, students in Africa find these a wonderful
authorization of the truth of Scripture; it assures them that it has been
handed down from the ancestors and ultimately from God. Of course, it is
not hard to see that viewing Scripture through our own cultural lens carries
risks; our culture can also blind us to things that Scripture teaches. However,
recently scholars have begun to argue that being embedded in particular
cultural forms is an advantage to be exploited, and not simply an obstacle
to overcome. This process has sometimes been referred to as "reversing the
hermeneutical flow," that is, discovering ways in which cultural forms actually illuminate parts of Scripture that might otherwise be invisible to us.[2]
Of course for this to become a positive process, and to properly understand
biblical instruction, Christians of all times and places need the illumination
of the Holy Spirit.

In this chapter, then, we make use of the idea of reversing the hermeneutical flow in order to illustrate the way historical forms of church have necessarily reflected, for better or worse, prevailing cultural forms and practices.
Further, we argue that the reading of Scripture at any given time has constituted what we will call a reverse hermeneutic. That is, Christians in the early
church, or during the Reformation, found ways to construe accepted cultural

---

[1]There are many sources that have contributed to this conversation, but the most important is
surely Hans-Georg Gadamer, *Truth and Method*, trans. Richard Heinemann and Bruce Krajewski
(New York: Seabury Press, 1975).

[2]One of the most prominent proponents of this practice is Larry Kreitzer, who has shown ways
contemporary film and fiction shed light on parts of Scripture. See Larry Joseph Kreitzer, *Gospel
Images in Fiction and Film: On Reversing the Hermeneutical Flow* (Sheffield: Sheffield Academic
Press, 2002). For a critique of this attempt see William Romanowski and Jennifer L. Vander
Heide, "Easier Said Than Done: On Reversing the Hermeneutical Flow in Theology and Film
Dialogue," *Journal of Communication and Religion*, 30, no. 1 (2007): 40-64.

forms of community as possible ways of embodying the community of those who follow Christ as this is prescribed in Scripture. While we will point out the dangers each form represented, we mean for this to be a straightforward and descriptive exploration of what was an inevitable process of interpreting scriptural teaching in terms of notions of community they already understood.[3] These various periods represent the standard chapters of what we call church history, and our brief review of this is highly selective and overly brief—especially in omitting any treatment of the medieval church. But these case studies, we trust, will show that diversity in forms of church has been a constant throughout history and that this diversity, though frequently a source of tension and conflict, also pays tribute to the translatability of the Christian gospel into multiple shapes and forms. This may prepare us to see ways the newer forms of church today may be more properly appreciated and understood.

THE EARLY CHURCH

The earliest churches grappled with and adapted to cultural contexts in various ways. When Gentiles began to express interest in and devotion to Christ, for example, Jewish Christ-followers had vigorous debates among themselves regarding their practices and the nature of the gospel (see, for example, Acts 15 and Gal 2). As a result of these debates, the church's ecclesiology and self-understanding found a basis in the work of the Holy Spirit and people's response to this work rather than in a chosen cultural lineage.

In these instances the narrative indicates that God's miraculous intervention, such as with Paul in Acts 9 or with Cornelius in Acts 10, created new understandings of the gospel, which in turn reshaped the church's self-understanding. While it is true that the church's ecclesiology often changes in response to new God-given revelation, we also want to pose the question, In what ways might God have used or been at work in the midst of cultural contexts and practices to uniquely shape the early church? This, as we have indicated, is a reversal of the way in which the question is often posed. It is normally assumed that the church's self-understanding and practices arose from its ideas, which then shaped or modified its practices. While ideas

---

[3]For a defense of the necessity of received culture for the practice of hermeneutics, see James K. A. Smith, *The Fall of Interpretation: Philosophical Foundations for a Creational Hermeneutic* (Downers Grove, IL: InterVarsity Press, 2000).

certainly informed the church's theology and practice, we pose the reverse question of how these ideas may have been shaped in part by the cultural context in which the churches existed.

When participants in the early churches began to meet together, they utilized and adapted to the most convenient spaces and forms available to them. Though churches organized themselves differently by location, it is apparent that many met in domestic homes and shaped themselves similar to the *collegia,* or voluntary organizations, that were common in Greco-Roman towns and cities.[4] Associations varied widely in focus and organization but were commonly organized for occupational, religious, or social purposes and provided members with an opportunity for relationships that were unavailable through other civic structures.[5] Prospective members were sometimes required to pay a fee to join and then were allowed to participate in regular gatherings, including banquet meals, and to make decisions about activities and functions. The associations appealed to and were open to people from diverse backgrounds and thus often provided those of lower status with a place for participation.[6] Associations thus helped to connect people and form bonds across social barriers, especially in an age when people were feeling less connected to the wider cities and societies.

The Christian associations fulfilled for its members many of the same functions as other Greco-Roman associations. They too provided members

---

[4]Richard S. Ascough, *Paul's Macedonian Associations* (Tübingen: Mohr Siebeck, 2003), 17. On the discussion regarding the importance of volunteer associations, also see Richard Last, *The Pauline Church and the Corinthian Ekklēsia: Greco-Roman Associations in Comparative Context* (New York: Cambridge University Press, 2016); Edward Adams, *The Earliest Christian Meeting Places: Almost Exclusively Houses?* (New York: Bloomsbury; T&T Clark, 2016); and John S. Kloppenborg, "Associations, Christ Groups, and Their Place in the Polis," *Zeitschrift für die neutestamentliche Wissenschaft* 108, no. 1 (2017): 1-56. Many of these authors challenge the earlier scholarly consensus that claimed most early churches met as guests of a household patron. On house churches see Roger W. Gehring, *House Church and Mission: The Importance of Household Structures in Early Christianity* (Peabody MA: Hendrickson, 2004); and Bradley Blue, "Acts and the House Church," in *The Book of Acts in Its Graeco-Roman Setting*, ed. David W. J. Gill and Conrad Gempf, 119-221 (Grand Rapids: Eerdmans, 1994).

[5]Alan Kreider, *The Patient Ferment of the Early Church: The Improbable Rise of Christianity in the Roman Empire* (Grand Rapids: Baker Academic, 2016), 52.

[6]As John Kloppenborg has discussed, associations rose in popularity in an age when democratic structures were changing, if not declining in some areas. With the lessening of democratic practices in many cities came an increased concentration of power in the elite. Associations helped to provide a space for *isonomia* (equality among all citizens) that was not always available in other spheres of society. Kloppenborg, "Associations," 15.

with a space in which they could create a small community that crossed social boundaries. In particular, those of lower statuses were welcome and given a place where they could participate in community life. As Kloppenborg remarks, the Christian associations created the opportunity for a sense of "fictive citizenship," not based on the city or state but one reflective of the new community of God.[7]

How did they create such a sense of inclusion and bonding? One important feature of the Christian associations was the meal gathering. By the first century CE banquet meals were common among family households and associations, providing such groups with entertainment or philosophical discussion and helping them bond, establish social boundaries, and display and modify social statuses.[8] The structure of a typical banquet gathering normally consisted of two parts, the meal and the symposium or drinking/entertainment party.[9] Christian associations, like other associations, though probably more often, gathered on a regular basis for worship around a meal, eventually known by Christians as the agape meal. This, as we will discuss in later chapters, distinctly shaped practices such as the Eucharist and formed the context out of which metaphors such as the "body of Christ" emerged.

As a social form, however, the small association gatherings around meals would have looked to many outsiders like one of the many other associations of their region. This is not to say that the church leaders mimicked other associations in their entirety. Rather, early church leaders went to great lengths in their written descriptions to show that, though the Christian gatherings were associations in the broad sense, they were also distinct from others. Thus, Tertullian, a church leader and prolific North African author in the early second century CE, argued that, unlike other associations, his association did not charge a fee for membership. The members also sought to help

---

[7]Kloppenborg, "Associations," 21.

[8]Dennis E. Smith, *From Symposium to Eucharist: The Banquet in the Early Christian World* (Minneapolis: Fortress, 2003), 9-12, 35.

[9]"Symposium" was used interchangeably to refer to the entire banquet event, or to the latter part of the event involving entertainment (D. E. Smith, *From Symposium to Eucharist*, 49). See also Gerard Rouwhorst, "The Roots of the Early Christian Eucharist: Jewish Blessings or Hellenistic Symposia?," in *Jewish and Christian Liturgy and Worship: New Insights into Its History and Interaction*, ed. Albert Gerhards and Clemens Leonhard (Boston: Brill, 2007), 303-5; and Paul F. Bradshaw and Maxwell E. Johnson, *The Eucharistic Liturgies: Their Evolution and Interpretation* (Collegeville, MN: Liturgical Press, 2012), 1-8, 17.

those inside and outside of the association and created a unique sense of equality among themselves.[10]

Though imperial authorities usually allowed associations to function unhindered, they often kept a close eye on them since they provided a place where subversive movements could develop.[11] This was no less the case for Christian associations, which encountered varying levels of scrutiny and persecution throughout the first three centuries. Church leaders responded by encouraging their members to persevere and to be strong witnesses for Christ. But what would help them in this endeavor? As Alan Kreider has shown, these church leaders developed perseverance by cultivating habits that allowed them to inculcate the virtue of patience. Of course, correct beliefs were important, and early catechisms certainly emphasized learning and memorizing particular teachings. But of equal, if not greater, importance was the need to develop habits of conduct that shaped believers' relationships with each other and the wider society. For example, Cyprian, bishop of Carthage in the third century, developed a list of 120 precepts for catechumens, a document known now as *To Quirinius* 3. Notably, 48 of these, or a little over a third of the total, regard correct beliefs while the rest cover a range of behaviors that should characterize the catechumen.[12]

Cyprian's emphasis on the formation of behaviors and character was not only intended to help his people withstand persecution but was also a response to changing cultural norms. Cyprian's churches, like so many other churches of his time and after, began to receive prospective members from a greater diversity of background and with differing moral practices and expectations. In response, early church leaders formalized and in many cases lengthened their formal initiation process for membership. This was a practice common among volunteer associations, and particularly religious associations.[13] In the case of the Christian associations, however, such a process was focused on helping people to reshape their behavior, transforming old morals and habits into new.[14]

---

[10]As discussed by Kreider in *Patient Ferment*, 56-60.

[11]Kreider, *Patient Ferment*, 52.

[12]As discussed in Kreider, *Patient Ferment*, 161-65.

[13]Richard S. Ascough, "Greco-Roman Philosophic, Religious, and Voluntary Associations," in *Community Formation in the Early Church and the Church Today*, ed. Richard N. Longenecker (Peabody, MA: Hendrickson, 2002), 3-19.

[14]As Kreider has shown, the four-part catechesis model of the third-century apostolic tradition may have been a common practice for many churches. Kreider, *Patient Ferment*, 147-84.

Though church forms based on the associations continued to be utilized throughout the second and third centuries, churches began to innovate and modify more and more in light of new circumstances. For instance, starting in the early second century many churches began to introduce a second worship service, this time meeting on Sunday mornings before members had to go to work.[15] Though practices varied by location, churches gradually began to separate and distinguish between the morning Eucharist service and the evening agape meal. Alongside changes in services came changes in the church buildings. Church communities grew in size and needed to meet in larger spaces, including larger remodeled rooms (*domus ecclesiae*) and eventually in large modified halls (*aula ecclesiae*) that were fully dedicated to church gatherings.[16] As the church communities and buildings grew in size, the agape meal became more and more difficult to sustain. As Cyprian remarked in the mid third century, the main church had grown such that "when we dine we cannot call all the people together to share in our meal."[17] Eventually the agape meal was discontinued altogether in favor of the morning Eucharist service.

But just as the Greco-Roman associations and related practices shaped churches in their initial stages, so too did the accommodation to larger gatherings. With the shift to Sunday mornings, for example, rather than worshiping by facing each other in the midst of a meal, participants now sat in rows to face the leaders—the clergy. The Eucharist, originally a full meal during which church members would enjoy fellowship and pray and remember Christ, was now symbolized by small amounts of bread, wine, and water.[18] All these developments served important purposes and shaped the church in ways that arguably allowed it to grow and adjust to new contexts. But each development was a reverse hermeneutic—a "reading" of the gospel and the purpose of the church via the changing cultural contexts and needs of the time. Many of these changes were gradual. In the fourth century,

---

[15]Persecution also played a part in this shift. By mid second century the church in some locations, such as Bithynia and Rome, abandoned the evening service in favor of a morning service that met before daylight. Kreider, *Patient Ferment*, 189.

[16]L. Michael White, *The Social Origins of Christian Architecture*, vol. 1, *Building God's House in the Roman World* (Valley Forge, PA: Trinity Press International, 1996), 120.

[17]Cyprian, *The Letters of St. Cyprian of Carthage*, trans. G. W. Clarke (New York: Newman Press, 1986), 3:107.

[18]Kreider, *Patient Ferment*, 190-93.

however, changes would come much more quickly; by this time the influence of the associations and meal traditions on the life of the church would be a distant glimmer.

THE IMPERIAL CHURCH IN THE TIME OF NICAEA

A common starting point for reflections on the church in Western theology is the creed that grew from the famous Council of Nicaea in 325 CE (as it was amended in 381 in the First Council of Constantinople). There the church is defined in the classic statement: "We believe in the one, holy, catholic, and apostolic church." These four qualities were considered, and are still believed by many church communions in the West, to constitute the essential nature of the Christian church. But in fact this formulation, even as it provides a valuable reading of the teaching of Scripture, embodies a reverse hermeneutic that reflects the concerns and pressures of that period.

How is this so? When Emperor Constantine saw the famous cross in the sky at the battle of Milvian Bridge in 312 and declared himself a follower of Christ, things began to change dramatically for the rapidly growing Christian church.[19] The most obvious change was that, after periods of intense persecution, the Christian church became one of the approved religions of the Roman Empire and, indeed, the religious group favored by the emperor. Early in 313 Constantine and Licinius, who ruled in the east, issued a letter called the Edict of Milan, extending to Christians the "free and unrestricted opportunity of religious worship." In addition, Christians were to receive back all of their properties and churches "without any hesitation or controversy at all." And while Constantine and Licinius state that they have the general, and the Christian's public welfare in mind, it is also clear that they are principally concerned that "any Divinity whatsoever," but particularly the *summa divinitas* [supreme Deity] of the Christians, may "preserve and prosper our successes together with the good of the state."[20] Christians are

---

[19]Though it is often said that this represented Constantine's conversion, this is untrue. He did not formally join the church or receive baptism until shortly before his death in 337 CE. See Kreider, *Patient Ferment*, 251-52.

[20]Constantine Augustus and Licinius Augustus, "The Edict of Milan," trans. University of Pennsylvania, *Translations and Reprints from the Original Sources of European History* (Philadelphia: University of Pennsylvania Press, 1897-1907), 4:28-30, https://sourcebooks.fordham.edu/source/edict-milan.asp. See also Robert M. Grant, *Augustus to Constantine: The Rise and Triumph of Christianity in the Roman World* (New York: Harper & Row, 1990), 236.

pictured here as those who practice their religion, much as pagans continued to worship their gods. Now, however, the Christian God has been called on to offer support for the empire!

That people were free to worship publicly led to a building boom of Christian churches, a project led by the emperor himself. As mentioned above, instead of meeting in small groups in homes, Christians began to gather together in larger meeting halls—both basilicas (large public buildings in the Roman world) made into worship spaces and before long purpose-built structures. This very process implied that Christianity was a religion for all people and not simply for the few, and it inevitably affected how *church* would come to be understood.[21]

While initially Christians celebrated the emperor's support of the church and of Christians—gratitude for which was made clear in Eusebius's famous early history of the church[22]—there were troubling implications that would emerge only gradually. For one thing, the freedom and support the faith now enjoyed led to an influx of new members into the newly opened churches, and the high standards of catechism that had been regularly practiced were gradually compromised. Teaching about the church began to change to reflect this new situation. In 250 CE, Cyprian wrote his 120 requirements for church membership described above, so that the church member's beliefs and behaviors could withstand tension and persecution. A century later Cyril of Alexandria taught that the church was constituted by a mystical unity in Christ.[23] Notice that while the former defined this group by particular standards of behavior, the latter began to define *church* in philosophical and spiritual categories.

Cyprian, we recall, was responding to a particular situation of intense persecution, a peril that would eventually cost him his life. Cyril was facing a different threat, one he felt equally dangerous to the nature of the church, the challenge posed by the Alexandrian priest Arius, who denied the deity

---

[21]Margaret Miles has argued that the practice of building large spaces for worship communicated the universality of the Christian faith. See Margaret R. Miles, *Image as Insight: Visual Understanding in Western Christianity and Secular Culture* (Boston: Beacon Press, 1985), chap. 2. Grant notes that the building program was part of Constantine's project of unifying the church (*Augustus to Constantine*, 246).

[22]See *Eusebius' Ecclesiastical History*, early fourth century. Many modern editions.

[23]On these differences see J. N. D. Kelly, *Early Christian Doctrines*, rev. ed. (New York: Harper, 1978), 400-406.

of Christ and thus threatened the unity of the church. A similar threat emerged in North Africa, Cyprian's home territory, at the same time that Cyril was teaching the mystical character of Christ's body. In 311 one of the bishops of Carthage was accused of being a *traditor* (one who had betrayed other Christians by offering sacrifices during the persecution), and many churches calling themselves Donatists (followers of a Berber bishop Donatus Magnus) separated from the Roman Catholic Church. These believers, mostly indigenous Berber, were the true heirs of Cyprian.[24] Like that bishop, they were rigorists who sought to preserve the purity of the church by insisting that only those who had resisted persecution should be allowed into the church. Though condemned by Catholic authorities, large numbers of Donatist churches continued to exist, especially in North Africa, and threatened the unity of the Christian church—at least in the eyes of the Catholic (and imperial) authorities.

Interestingly, these movements often had antecedents in the earlier period of the church and had previously been tolerated. Indeed, Cyprian was deeply respected. But now, especially in the eyes of the emperor, such divisions in the church were felt to be dangerous, not only religiously but, more importantly, politically. As a response to these perceived challenges to the unity of the church Emperor Constantine called a council in Nicaea in 325. The council, convened and funded by the emperor, became the first major, worldwide council of the Christian church. The major achievement of this ecumenical council of Christian bishops was to settle the issue of Christ's full deity and thus respond to Arius's teaching in Alexandria. This was affirmed by the critical phrase of the creed, that Christ was "of the same substance of the Father" (Gk. *homoousios*), a phrase not incidentally added at the express intervention of the emperor himself.[25] Histories of the church tend to overlook the extent and implications of this political support. Not only did the emperor convene and subsidize the council, but afterward he

---

[24]Mercy Odoyuye, the Nigerian theologian, argues that this was a clear example of the church's inability to respond appropriately to the indigenous (African) values and an imposition of Latin and Roman understandings of institution on the church. Mercy Amba Odoyuye, *Hearing and Doing* (Nairobi: Acton, 2000), 15-28.

[25]Kelly, *Early Christian Doctrines*, 233. Kelly notes that the emperor was pushing for agreement in the service of promoting unity (*Early Christian Doctrines*, 237).

did not hesitate to use political pressure to enforce the decisions of the council.[26] Robert Grant notes that despite the support of the emperor himself nothing was really settled: "The question of heresy was not settled even when the Emperor worked as a Christian with Christian bishops and gave guidance in their council."[27]

So the unity and catholicity of the church were promoted, not simply on biblical grounds but also in part because of the political pressures posed by Arian believers in Alexandria and the Donatist churches in North Africa.[28] Regarding the latter case, the council's statement on the inherent holiness of the church counters the Donatists' assertion that the church must be visibly and actually holy to truly reflect the holiness of God. How, the Donatists wondered, could the Catholics countenance the fact that certain members of the Catholic Church were manifestly *not* holy in their practice? Here the teaching of Cyril became relevant, providing a way to interpret scriptural teaching on holiness in ways that allowed the church to be conceived as a mixed body. The holiness of the church, according to Cyril, resides not in the actual members of the church but in the reality of Christ, to whom believers are mystically joined by the Holy Spirit. This teaching would be confirmed a hundred years later by Augustine, who was still facing the challenges of Donatism in his North African home. The church, Augustine taught, is a mixed body that by the life principle of the Holy Spirit becomes the mystical body of Jesus Christ, all joined together in a single body of believers.[29] Its holiness resides not in its human members but in the mystical body of Christ, to which believers are joined in baptism.

But Augustine took this teaching on unity a step further. Early in his career he was troubled by the application of political power (even violence) to force schismatics into the church. In an early writing he confessed: "I am displeased that schismatics are violently coerced to communion by the force

---

[26]See Joseph H. Lynch, *The Medieval Church: A Brief History* (London: Longman, 1992), 15-16. Lynch notes that not only did the emperor summon and subsidize the council but he then "used the Imperial power to gain adherence to the decisions."

[27]Grant, *Augustus to Constantine*, 242. He notes that subsequent councils fared no better in this respect.

[28]Kelly's account is particularly strong in emphasizing how seriously these church fathers took the text of Scripture in their deliberations.

[29]Kelly, *Early Christina Doctrines*, 414.

of secular power."[30] Later, after he had seen the damage the Donatists had done to the unity of the church, he came to evaluate such pressures in a more positive light. As he wrote in his *Retractions*, he had come to believe his earlier views were mistaken: "I had not yet learned either how much evil their impunity would dare or to what extent the application of discipline could bring about their improvement."[31]

Notice the differences in evolving understandings of the church. Earlier the community of believers was defined by the character of the community that composed it whereas later the church came to be defined by its spiritual and theological nature. Neither can be said to be better than the other because both pick up on critical aspects of scriptural teaching. Moreover, we note that threats to the unity in the church emerged from below in the disturbances caused by Donatist churches and Arian influences in Africa while efforts promoting unity came from above, enforced by the reigning political arrangements—and the power of the empire. While we cannot judge one image of church as right and another wrong, we should also not fail to recognize that the differences also reflect the social and political arrangements in which Christians found themselves in these two periods. The church took shape in these places, in part, as a situated interpretation of Scripture.

One further episode in this history is worth recalling. Even with the support of the emperor, theological issues like those raised by Arius in North Africa continued to trouble the church. In the fourth century these questions led another Egyptian monk, Eutyches, to argue that Christ had one nature in which divine and human natures are combined without division, which seemed to observers in the west to deny Christ's human nature. In 451 the Council of Chalcedon, convened by Emperor Marcian, met to define Christ's two natures in one person, "unconfusedly, unchangeably, indivisibly, inseparably."[32] Once again, even with the support of the emperor, large segments of the church in the east refused to accept this definition. The decision in fact exacerbated and formalized the divisions in the church for succeeding centuries. As one scholar noted, these controversies divided Christians throughout the eastern half of the empire,

---

[30] Augustine, *Retractions*, 31, quoted in Kreider, *Patient Ferment*, 289. This was written about 397 CE.
[31] Augustine, *Retractions*, quoted in Kreider, *Patient Ferment*, 289n40.
[32] This is the main article of what came to be called the Chalcedonian definition.

leading to the formation of institutionalized communities—West Syrian or Syrian Orthodox and Coptic churches—that had their own bishops and monasteries, but were united in their rejection of Chalcedon and the Roman emperors who sought to enforce the Dyophysite [two nature] language as the touchstone of orthodoxy.[33]

This fractured situation reflected not only doctrinal but also linguistic, political, and cultural differences, and it surely made the seventh-century victory of Muhammad and his armies much less difficult.

THE REFORMATION CHURCH

Church history texts frequently speak of the transformative changes in notions of the church that resulted from the Reformation, but in critical ways very little changed, especially with respect to the political situation of the churches. Some might even be surprised to learn that the emperor of what survived of the Holy Roman Empire, Charles V, still played a critical role in the eventual shape the Reformation churches would take. In 1521 when Martin Luther appeared before Charles in the famous Diet of Worms and refused to recant, the unity of the church, which was under serious attack, had already became a serious concern of the emperor.[34] Europe during this time was undergoing historic changes in its political order, changes that would cause two centuries of turmoil and violence. Because the various territorial reforms contributing to these divisions were incomplete in the early sixteenth century, it was inevitable that emerging churches would be embroiled in political conflicts. So it is not surprising that Charles responded to Luther's resistance by imposing a ban on the evangelicals, essentially criminalizing them in the interest of "internal peace."[35]

So even though Luther wanted to institute a "pure" form of Christianity in the church at Wittenberg, he was constrained by the contested political powers around him. While he was allowed to leave Worms in 1521 under imperial

---

[33]Richard E. Payne, *A State of Mixture: Christian, Zoroastrians, and Iranian Political Culture in Late Antiquity* (Berkeley: University of California Press, 2016), 184.

[34]For this point see Peter H. Wilson, *The Heart of Europe: A History of the Holy Roman Empire* (Cambridge, MA: Harvard University Press, 2016). "Papal concordats with individual monarchs since the early 12th century fostered the growth of more distinct national churches across much of Europe" (109).

[35]Wilson, *Heart of Europe*, 110.

protection, for his own safety he soon had to be hidden away in Wartburg
Castle by the sympathetic Elector of Saxony. Because of the quarreling political
powers and their shifting territorial claims, it was not clear who was entitled
to decide which version of Christianity was correct. Was it the emperor, a
prince, a magistrate, or the people? What was clear, and had been clear since
the time of Constantine, was that though theological issues were in the purview
of the pope and bishops, political issues were in the hands of political powers.[36]

Luther basically took over this division of labor in his famous teaching of
the "two swords." God, he argued, ruled the world through these two designated authorities, the political sphere by the power of the magistrates and
the spiritual by the power of the spiritual sword—which for Luther of course
was the word of God and not the pope. Often overlooked is the way this
formulation of powers enforced, and justified theologically, not only relations between the medieval church and emperor but the understanding of
Constantine himself. Robert Grant cites a letter of Constantine to the
bishops that stipulates, if they are bishops "to those inside the Church, I am
a Bishop to those outside"—that is, throughout the empire.[37] There is the
(incipient) two-swords doctrine in its purest form!

In the 1520s and 1530s, Luther and his colleagues inevitably formulated
their new conception of the church in light of the fragmented jurisdictions
of power and authority. When in 1529, at the Second Imperial Diet of Speyer,
the emperor's brother Ferdinand denied the right of subjects to form
churches within their own territories, the evangelicals filed a formal protest
and thus earned the designation *Protestants*. In 1530 councils of various
cities along with a group of princes presented the emperor with their
statement of core beliefs in what later became the Augsburg Confession,
and thus was born the "confessional state."[38] Contained in this statement
was indeed a new conception of church, separated from the authority of the
pope, consisting of three components: the community of saints, the gospel,
and the sacraments. With a stroke, the hierarchy was eliminated while the
jurisdiction of the temporal sword was extended to institute and protect the

---

[36]Wilson, *Heart of Europe*, 109.

[37]Grant, *Augustus to Constantine*, 245.

[38]Lee Palmer Wandel, *The Reformation: Towards a New History* (New York: Cambridge University
Press, 2011), 100-101. And see Wilson, *Heart of Europe*, 109-10. This confession was presented
to and thus implicitly authorized by the emperor.

church within its physical boundaries. Luther designated authority for the spiritual sword not to priests but to "ministers," trained now to teach and preach the Word of God, as the only proper authority in the church. Most importantly, this freedom to preach the Word of God implied a further freedom, what later became known as the right of private judgment. Both Luther and Calvin denounced the notion of implicit faith—that one believed implicitly the teachings of the religious community to which one belonged. Rather, Luther stressed the need for personal faith and the priesthood of all believers.[39]

There is something new, perhaps even radical, in this decoupling of spiritual authority from the structure of the church.[40] But as newer histories of the Reformation recognize, it was the uniquely fragmented character of imperial politics that provided the soil in which this notion of church could take root.[41] Moreover, the development of these confessional churches—Lutheranism in Germany, Presbyterianism in Scotland and Ireland, Anglicanism in England—continued for two centuries to promote a unitary and national form of the church in which dissent was not allowed. It would be the radical Reformers who would take Luther's ideas further.

The same complexities accompanied John Calvin's efforts to rebuild the church some decades after Luther's initiatives. He too sought to found the church afresh on the Word of God—as preached and taught in the assembly. For Calvin, the Word of God is the unique instrument of the Spirit to mediate the truth of salvation that is accomplished in Christ's incarnation, reestablishing the broken relationship of a fallen humanity.[42] As Roger Haight notes, Calvin's church was formed over against the view that the church is "always open and observable," a visibility exhibited in the hierarchy.[43] Calvin,

---

[39]Nicholas Miller traces the notions of the separation of church and state as enshrined in the US Constitution to these early ideas of Luther. See Nicholas P. Miller, *The Religious Roots of the First Amendment: Dissenting Protestantism and the Separation of Church and State* (New York: Oxford University Press, 2012), 19-27. We thank James E. Bradley for this reference.

[40]But this freedom was not complete. Cf. Miller: "The line the church drew around the conscience with the spiritual sword the state could enforce with the civil sword." N. Miller, *Religious Roots*, 19.

[41]See on this Wandel, *Reformation*, 102.

[42]For this and what follows see François Wendel, *Calvin: The Origins and Development of His Religious Thought*, trans. Philip Mairet (London: Collins, 1963), 292-96. He points out how Calvin here has recourse to definitions prominent in Cyprian and Augustine.

[43]Roger Haight, *Christian Community in History*, vol. 2, *Comparative Ecclesiology* (New York: Continuum, 2005), 87.

by contrast, insisted the true church appears in the pure preaching of the word and the lawful administration of the sacraments.

On the one hand, the church in its visible form is given to believers as a necessary instrument and the earthly means to believers' sanctification. While initially Calvin, like Luther, stressed the hidden and invisible nature of this body, over time (and under the influence of Martin Bucer), he came to stress the physical presence of the gathered body of Christ. In this sense, as Lee Palmer Wandel has noted, Calvin is moving closer to the Anabaptist believers' notion of church, which we consider next. But there is this critical difference: these groups of believers scattered abroad, without any physical center, all under the authority and obedience of Christ, seek to remake the political order after the image of this new community. And so, on the other hand, these moves of Calvin and the ruling Council of Geneva also resulted from a desire for political autonomy from the Duke of Savoy—who had the power to appoint bishops. Gradually the ruling council, under William Farel's influence and later under Calvin's leadership, assumed more and more authority.[44]

Partly as a result of Calvin's situation in the city of Geneva, and the clergy's ability to order worship freely within this jurisdiction, Calvin was able to institute a new order of church. In 1537 he presented to the council a series of articles that laid out his conception of church.[45] It was to be a body of those who confessed this new faith (now obligatory for all who wished to remain in this city), but also a living community of the kingdom of Christ.[46]

It was in this last tenet that Calvin's notion of church differed from Luther's (and from that of the believers' church). Like Luther, Calvin insisted the church was a community formed by the gospel and properly administering the sacraments. Unlike Luther, Calvin resisted the separation of the spiritual and the temporal worlds.[47] He believed all of life should reflect this kingdom of Christ, and the whole world was to be a theater in which God's glory should be manifest. How one dressed, what one's work produced, and

---

[44]Haight, *Christian Community*, 2:89-90. Though the council chafed under this clerical influence and, in 1538, expelled Calvin, they recalled him in 1542.

[45]Wendel, *Calvin*, 50-51. On Calvin's movement toward the believers' church see Wandel, *Reformation*, 103-4.

[46]Attendance at services was legally required in Geneva. Haight, *Christian Community*, 2:121.

[47]Wandel notes that Luther here was still shaped by his experience as a monk; Calvin had never been a monk. Wandel, *Reformation*, 107.

how government was structured were all to be an outward expression of the Christian's faith in Christ.

Both Luther and Calvin sought to base their understanding of church on the teaching of Scripture; both were consummate exegetes who knew their Hebrew and Greek. And so critical elements of the biblical teaching—justification by faith for Luther and the need to bring members to fullness of Christ (Eph 4:11-13) for Calvin—were recovered. But their notions of the nature of the church were different, and the differences rested in part on the different political situations in which they worked. Calvin lived his life in a city that was ruled by the council of magistrates and sought always to see political and religious power as complementary. But he never sought to put the political powers under the tutelage of the church authorities. Ministers of the church were to educate and catechize the citizens—including the children—and to explain to magistrates what the Word of God requires. But this meant for him that church was the visible community limited to a particular territory—to Geneva or Basel or Strasbourg.[48] This meant too that Calvin had a greater tolerance than Luther for multiple forms of church that reflected these different places. Since place mattered, he resisted investing any particular form with ultimacy.[49]

Luther's church formed itself along a north-south axis of lands ruled by German princes, all traditionally aligned in contested ways with the emperor. After Luther's death, these groups splintered; even the Augsburg Confession could not hold them together.[50] But the princes lamented this division and in 1580 came together to publish the Book of Concord, which would henceforth serve as the core of Lutheran belief. But still this confession could not bind these groups together. As Peter Wilson comments, written creeds did not provide sufficient grounds for unity: "Fixing arguments in writing simply made the disagreements more obvious."[51]

Calvin, too, late in his life came to lament the divisions that had overtaken the churches, pleading in the *Institutes* not to reject any assembly

---

[48]Wendel, *Calvin*, 309-10.

[49]Haight, *Christian Community*, 2:125-27. Haight notes that Calvin's recognition that Christians may be in the minority, and that forms of church might emerge from below, looked forward to the end of Christendom.

[50]Wandel, *Reformation*, 102.

[51]Wilson, *Heart of Europe*, 109.

where the Word of God is preached and sacraments are administered, "even if it otherwise swarms with many faults."[52] But no movements toward the visible unity he sought gained any traction in his time, and a major hindrance to such aspirations were the conflicting political structures that kept neighboring groups from expressing visibly their unity in Christ.

Meanwhile, the Catholics had their own reasons to lament the chasm that the Reformation opened up, and in 1545 Pope Paul III convened the Council of Trent, in part to restore the unity in the church. While representatives of the pope invoked the memory (and authority) of the Council of Nicaea and even issued invitations to evangelicals to attend, the council served rather to exacerbate than to heal those divisions. Part of the reason became evident in the first matter of business of the council in April 1546. This session stipulated that the Latin Vulgate, "tested in the church by long use over so many centuries," should be kept as the authentic text for public readings and further that no private interpretation (or new translation) should be allowed to abrogate and pass judgment on its true meaning apart from the teaching of the mother church.[53] So the new conception of authority in the church—the vernacular Bible translated from the original languages—celebrated by the Protestants was specifically forbidden to Catholic believers. Meanwhile, traditional authority residing in the hierarchy would continue to define *church* in ways specifically distinct from the Protestants. Though there was no imperial power adequate to assure the submission to its decisions, Trent continued to represent itself as the heir of 1500 years of Christian tradition. The Roman Catholic Church was the church of Nicaea, of the Lateran councils, the church Christ himself founded on Peter's confession and which Paul spread throughout the empire. The evangelicals, despite their claims to recover the true faith, were now labeled as schismatic, subjective, and individualist.[54] But what these bishops had forgotten was the political turmoil that their own concordats had set off in previous centuries. They could not imagine a church whose spiritual polity would enable it to exist amidst all these different lands. If they had paid

---

[52]*Institutes*, 4.1.12 (see John Calvin, *Institutes of the Christian Religion*, ed. John T. McNeill, trans. Ford Lewis Battles [Philadelphia: Westminster, 1960]).

[53]Cited in Wandel, *Reformation*, 110.

[54]Wandel, *Reformation*, 114-16.

attention, they would have seen groups forming all around that offered the potential for a new form of church.

THE BELIEVER'S CHURCH

As we turn to the early "radical Reformation" or Anabaptist movements, we come to what many regard as the beginnings of the modern, voluntary, congregational form of church, now widely seen in various Baptist, Pentecostal, community, and independent churches. In tracing the origins of this form and theology of church, many have often started with the Anabaptists' emphasis on Bible study, derived from Luther's principle of *sola scriptura* and the priesthood of all believers.[55] This was certainly evident in the practices of early Anabaptists, who would gather to read and memorize translations of the Scriptures.[56] Also from Luther they adopted what they felt was a straightforward biblicism, directly applying the teachings or "pure gospel" of the Bible to their own lives. This biblicism in turn influenced their ecclesiology, where the teachings of Jesus and the example of the early churches, particularly in the book of Acts, provided for them a picture of God's true intention for his church. Based on "self-evident" readings of Scripture, for example, the Anabaptists argued that churches should be voluntary, locally based, and characterized by teaching, study, prayer, and sharing.[57]

Though the Anabaptists certainly felt they were creating churches from a straightforward application of Scripture, the development of their understanding of church was much more complex. In particular it is evident that their interpretation was shaped by a reverse hermeneutic involving their

---

[55]This was emphasized particularly by prominent Anabaptist scholars in the mid twentieth century who sought to revise previous historical accounts portraying Anabaptists as fringe extremists. For example, Anabaptist historian Harold Bender wrote, "The Anabaptists, being Biblicists and usually unsophisticated readers of the Bible, not trained theologians or scholars, and having made a more complete break with tradition than the reformers, were more radical and consistent in their application of the principle of sole Scriptural authority. They sought to obey the Bible in simple faith, without calculation of consequences for the socio-political or ecclesiastical order." Harold S. Bender, "Bible," in *Global Anabaptist Mennonite Encyclopedia Online* (Herald Press, 1953), revised January 16, 2017, http://gameo.org/index.php?title=Bible&oldid=144829. See also David L. Weaver-Zercher, *Martyrs Mirror: A Social History* (Baltimore: Johns Hopkins University Press, 2016), 6.

[56]Thomas N. Finger, *A Contemporary Anabaptist Theology: Biblical, Historical, Constructive* (Downers Grove, IL: InterVarsity Press, 2004), 27.

[57]Anabaptists did, and some still do, add to this the importance of sharing common goods among believers and administering some form of church discipline.

social and political contexts. Reformers such as Luther and Calvin, as we have seen, responded to and adapted their understanding of church to various political developments, including the increasingly fragmented loci of power and authority. This in turn influenced the possibility of creating national churches. There were, however, further social changes occurring in late medieval Europe that helped shape additional ways in which church would be understood, particularly by Anabaptists.

One such development was the shift in late medieval Europe from hierarchical feudalism to *Gemeinden*, or communes.[58] Communes were associations, usually at the village level, consisting of the principal male householders. Though communes varied from region to region, they often elected officers by majority vote and convened regular communal assemblies to review various issues important to the community. Their principal function was to help the common people of the village gain and safeguard access to local resources, like hunting, forest lumber, land, and markets, and to assist them in coordinating and managing crops and crop rotation.[59] The communes also provided communal courts to judge minor crimes and legal disputes and gave the village a collective voice for negotiations with the local nobles.[60]

Communes had gradually grown in number over the previous two hundred years as feudal estates diminished in size and power and, by the early sixteenth century, had become quite prominent in various parts of central Europe.[61] This growing communalism created a "horizontal principle"[62] that operated along and in varying levels of tension with the

---

[58]Werner O. Packull, *Hutterite Beginnings: Communitarian Experiments During the Reformation* (Baltimore: John Hopkins University Press, 1995), 16. Though scholars have highlighted the significance of this overall shift, they also note that late medieval understandings of community, and the exact structure and political authority of communes, differed from region to region. See R. Po-Chia Hsia, "The Myth of the Commune: Recent Historiography on City and Reformation in Germany," *Central European History* 20, no. 3 (1987): 212-13; and Bob Scribner, "Communities and the Nature of Power," in *Germany: A New Social and Economic History*, ed. Bob Scribner (New York: Arnold, 1996), 1:291-326.

[59]Peter Blickle, *From the Communal Reformation to the Revolution of the Common Man*, trans. Beat Kumin (Boston: Brill, 1998), 12. See also James M. Stayer, *The German Peasants' War and Anabaptist Community of Goods* (Montreal: McGill-Queen's University Press, 1991), 29.

[60]Scribner, "Communities and the Nature of Power," 1:300-301.

[61]Blickle, *From the Communal Reformation*, 194.

[62]However, as Scribner shows, communes were certainly not utopian settings of egalitarianism, instead displaying their own systems of hierarchy, status, and disputes. Scribner, "Communities

vertical feudal-oriented hierarchy and power of nobles and princes.[63] Because of this there was often tension between the communes and the local nobles. This began to be felt more acutely in the decades of the late fifteenth and early sixteenth centuries when nobles and princes became increasingly concerned over their own declining financial wealth and wary of the growing power of some of the communal associations. As a result, some nobles exerted control and coercion over the village communes, increasing taxes and servitude.[64]

Another social development that would have a profound impact on understandings of church was a growing anti-clericalism in the church, led by those who sought to address, reform, or counter the hierarchical control and abuses of the church clergy structure. Prior to Luther, various reformers had challenged these, usually seeking to reform the structures themselves. By Luther's time, however, frustrations had grown such that Luther sought to "do away with the clerical estate altogether since it was no longer needed as a mediator between God and human beings."[65]

The growth of communalism and the critique of church hierarchies formed what Hans-Jürgen Goertz has described as the *Sitz im Leben*, the vital context, for a reimagining of the church.[66] As Luther and other Reformers (and proto-Anabaptists) started to articulate their new understandings of church in this context, two characteristics were soon widely agreed upon and shared—the communal determination of doctrine (based on the ability of the laity to read and interpret Scripture for themselves) and the right of communities to choose their own pastors. The new vision amounted to what Blickle has called the "communalization of the Church."[67]

Less clear in all of this was what constituted a Christian community or church. Was it the gathering of godly believers, the local parish, or a parish combined with its political structures? It is on this question, and the ways

---

and the Nature of Power," 301-303.

[63]Blickle, *From the Communal Reformation*, 12.

[64]Finger, *Contemporary Anabaptist Theology*, 21.

[65]Hans-Jürgen Goertz, "Karlstadt, Müntzer and the Reformation of the Commoners, 1521–1525," in *A Companion to Anabaptism and Spiritualism, 1521–1700*, ed. John D. Roth and James M. Stayer (Boston: Brill, 2007), 3.

[66]Goertz, "Karlstadt, Müntzer," 3.

[67]Blickle, *From the Communal Reformation*, 193.

in which Scriptures were interpreted to answer it, that the Anabaptist movement began to separate itself from the wider reform movements and articulate a distinctive voluntary, separatist ecclesiology.

Initially most Reformers and Anabaptists generally shared the assumption that Christian community should be geographically defined and in some way include the political structures of the area. For example, some of the earliest Anabaptist leaders in Zurich were at first followers of Ulrich Zwingli, a Catholic priest-turned-pastor who established small-group Bible studies and gave sermons following Luther's teachings. Zwingli tended to identify Christian community with the parish, including the civic structures, and successfully gained the Zurich city council's support of his reforming ideas.

Some of Zwingli's followers, including Conrad Grebel and Felix Mantz, seemed to have initially agreed with Zwingli's concept of a parish church. As they met in Bible studies in Zurich and participated in church services in neighboring towns, these followers began to teach that the local communes had the ability to collectively interpret Scripture and determine their own leadership and finances. But as these groups came into conflict with local nobles and church leaders, these teachings were interpreted in ways that reflected the desire of these villages to have greater autonomy from civic and church hierarchies. Soon Zwingli's disciples were teaching against images in the church, unworthy priests, and the tithe that was collected and managed by the Zurich city council.[68] The latter was important because local communities could then stop supporting "good for nothing monks, who have stolen their living from the people long enough" and instead redirect it to pastors whom they would appoint themselves.[69]

These teachings began to spread to rural villages throughout the area. In response, Zwingli wrote a pamphlet and proposal, ultimately adopted by the Zurich council, arguing that God has mandated the government to maintain

---

[68]C. Arnold Snyder, *Anabaptist History and Theology: An Introduction* (Kitchener, Ont.: Pandora, 1995), 53.

[69]C. Arnold Snyder, *The Life and Thought of Michael Sattler* (Scottdale, PA: Herald Press, 1984), 67-68. Brady says that by 1500 perhaps only 100 out of around 3,000 villages in the region had gained the right to appoint their own parish priests, though pressure was mounting from villages to obtain the same right. Thomas A. Brady, Jr., *Communities, Politics, and Reformation in Early Modern Europe* (Boston: Brill, 1998), 425.

peace in society. Consequently, if the government ordered a tithe, it was everyone's responsibility to pay it.[70] The implications were substantial for the understanding of Christian community: the city government was mandated by God with certain authority, including that which would govern and help to order a church. There was an irony in this, for while Zwingli argued that a city council and its church should be free from outside clerical authority, he did not agree that these same freedoms should extend to local towns, communes, and their churches. In short, the identity and well-being of the church were closely tied to the civic authority of its area, and the two still needed to work together on issues of finances and pastoral leadership.

Grebel, Mantz, and others of Zwingli's followers did not agree and continued to push for greater reforms. In 1524 several families in rural villages outside of Zurich refused to baptize their infants, and not long after that several of Zwingli's disciples began to rebaptize adults in light of their interpretation of Scripture. However, even at this stage, the ecclesial implications of this were not immediately apparent or made explicit. Rather, as J. Denny Weaver has argued, the Anabaptists still shared with the Reformers the parish understanding of church, assuming that the church encompassed the whole of a given social and civic system.[71] That is, Christian communes desired to have the autonomy to reinterpret baptism, control the tithe, or appoint their own pastors, but they would also seek the endorsement of their local city or town councils to support this.[72]

The growing desire for local autonomy, and particularly the practice of adult baptism, raised the concern of Zwingli, Luther, and other Reformers about the potential for such practices to create social disorder. This fear was well founded. In the 1510s and 1520s the communes and peasant groups around Zurich and the surrounding regions became progressively more upset at restricted freedoms and economic hardships. Increasingly, the local communes articulated demands to nobles, including the right to choose their own pastors, and defended these with slogans from religious reformers.

---

[70]C. Arnold Snyder, "Swiss Anabaptism: The Beginnings," in Roth and Stayer, *Companion to Anabaptism and Spiritualism*, 54.

[71]J. Denny Weaver, *Becoming Anabaptist: The Origin and Significance of Sixteenth-Century Anabaptism* (Scottdale, PA: Herald Press, 2005), 54. See also Snyder, *Anabaptist History and Theology*, 12.

[72]Weaver, *Becoming Anabaptist*, 58.

By 1525 the unrest galvanized into organized uprisings that were soon
suppressed by armies of local princes. The uprising and its suppression,
known as the Peasants' War of 1525, marked a decisive shift in both the Reformers' and Anabaptists' understanding of church.[73] While some Anabaptist
leaders were sympathetic to aspects of the communal reform movement,
Luther and Zwingli famously opposed the popular uprising by again appealing to the God-given role of the state to maintain order.[74] Such populist
movements also prompted Luther to affirm that, though Scripture could and
should be read by the masses, there were those who, via their education and
superior understanding, should retain the ultimate interpretive authority.

As we have noted, the Anabaptists did not arrive at a fully developed free
church or believers' church ecclesiology. Rather, two principal features of
later Anabaptist ecclesiology emerged gradually, through a reverse hermeneutical process. The first feature was a local church community that collectively determined its own doctrine and leadership. The anti-clericalism of
the wider Reformation remained strong and was further strengthened by the
persecution the Reformers experienced from the political authorities. Many
of the principles, including a true "priesthood of all believers," continued to
survive and were carried forward in Anabaptist religious communities.[75]
Whereas the Peasants' War caused Luther and other Reformers to pull back
from their initial belief that the congregation "has the right and power to
judge all doctrines and to appoint and remove all teachers," the Anabaptist
movement continued to emphasize a leveling of authority. This was expressed
as early as 1527 in the Schleitheim Confession and was evidenced by the increased numbers of peasants and craftsmen in the movement following 1525.[76]

A second emergent feature of Anabaptist ecclesiology was identification
of the church as a separate and voluntary group. Here again persecution and

---

[73]Stayer, *German Peasants' War*, 50.

[74]Michael Driedger makes the point that Luther and other Reformers grew concerned about the
need to maintain public order and "worked to contain the radical implications of his early activism and ideas." Michael Driedger, "Anabaptists and the Early Modern State: A Long-Term View,"
in Roth and Stayer, *Companion to Anabaptism and Spiritualism*, 512.

[75]Snyder, *Anabaptist History and Theology*, 15.

[76]Though many of the initial Anabaptist leaders were educated clergy, after five years most leaders,
and a strong majority of church members, were coming from communities of poor and near-
poor classes. Claus-Peter Clasen, *Anabaptism: A Social History, 1525–1618* (Ithaca, NY: Cornell
University Press, 1972), 318-23.

the suppression of the Peasants' War caused Anabaptists to reinterpret Scripture and articulate a separatist ecclesiology that made clear distinctions between the church and the world. As we have seen, initially Anabaptist leaders did not distinguish clearly between a church of "believers" and the "official religion" of a region. As Snyder summarizes, "The strong 'separation of the world' ethic that pervaded later Anabaptism was not a *necessary* original component of believers' church ecclesiology, but was a further theological interpretation that was encouraged, in part, by the encounter with a decidedly hostile world."[77]

As the early Anabaptists increasingly failed to gain the support of civic leaders, they began to call into question the link between the church and society or "the world." As we have seen, under Luther and Zwingli the state or world was ordained by God to keep order, and because of this close relationship the actions of the government could in a sense be sacralized. However, after persecution and the Peasants' War, the Anabaptists rejected the idea that God's kingdom or the church encompasses the entire social order.[78] If governments continued to frustrate attempts by the local commune to shape its own teachings and practices, then the government was ultimately not operating in accordance with God's will. What this meant for churches was critical. Christian communities could no longer be understood to include, much less be governed or protected by, state governments. Rather, churches were now understood to be Christian communities with responsibility to a single spiritual kingdom and Prince. As a result, rather than addressing the wider political and economic issues of an area, as the peasants' revolt had done, the Anabaptist communities pulled away from that world, resisting it nonviolently when necessary but giving up any hope of its support or protection.

This voluntary, separatist notion of church would continue in small ways among fringe Anabaptist and Baptist groups for decades to come. However, it was not until this form of church interacted with still other social and cultural developments that it would grow to a much more prominent model.

---

[77]Snyder, *Anabaptist History and Theology*, 181 (emphasis original). See also Adolf Laube, "Radicalism as a Research Problem in the History of Early Reformation," in *Radical Tendencies in the Reformation: Divergent Perspectives*, ed. Hans J. Hillerbrand (Kirksville, MO: Sixteenth Century Journal Publishers, 1988), 22.

[78]Weaver, *Becoming Anabaptist*, 54.

The Modern (Western) Church

Though Martin Luther had celebrated the right of private judgment, it was the believers' church that took the next step in defining the nature of the church in ways expressive of this personal decision. Indeed, Luther's political commitments and assumptions, which we have described, led him eventually to oppose the Anabaptists, whom he understood to constitute a threat to the social order. It was the contribution of believers' churches, in their various forms, that insisted people must be given freedom to join the community of Christ's followers by their own mature decision and should decide for themselves as adults to receive baptism. These two ideas, the right of private judgment and the notion of the gathered church, were to have incalculable influence on emerging ideas of the church and, as they were taken abroad by the missionary movement, on the majority church around the world.

Luther's early thought was to have definitive influence on these ideas. As he wrote in his 1520 tract, "An appeal to the ruling class of German Nationality": "Each and all of us are priests. . . . Why then should we not be entitled to taste or test, and to judge what is right and wrong in faith?"[79] Luther, when he became alarmed at the potential for social disruption the enthusiasts caused, later moved away from the implications of this position. But these early writings were to have decisive influence on the developing ideas of toleration, especially in Holland.

The influence of the believers' church on the developing ideas of toleration and freedom of assembly was important but indirect.[80] Ironically, though Luther came to be suspicious of the Anabaptists in his setting, his own early writings had a profound influence on that movement. Menno Simons (1496–1561), founder of the Mennonites who lived and worked in Holland, claimed Luther's influence as decisive in forming his ideas of the church. Later, John Smyth (d. 1612), founder of the Baptist churches, was influenced by the Mennonites in Holland and became a defender of religious liberty in England. Most famously, John Locke, while in exile in Holland in the 1680s and as a

---

[79]Cited in Nicholas Miller, *Religious Roots*, 22.

[80]Miller argues the impact of their lives (and suffering!) probably had more influence than their writings. N. Miller, *Religious Roots*, 29. The discussion that follows draws from Miller, *Religious Roots*, 33-39.

result of interaction with Quaker William Penn and the example of the Mennonites, wrote his "Letter Concerning Toleration."[81]

The religious roots and the focus on church are clear from Locke's pamphlet. He did not support relativism in matters of ethics or religion; nor was he basing his ideas solely on reason, as many later interpreters have assumed. For Locke, toleration was based firmly on the teachings of Christianity and on the New Testament in particular, which he cites frequently. And it is the freedom of the religious conscience in matters of worship that he emphasized. Accordingly, he assumes the church to be "a voluntary society of men, joining themselves together of their own accord in order to [conduct] the public worshipping of God in such manner as they judge acceptable to Him." Interestingly, only later does Locke go on to define the authority of the magistrate, which is separate from that of the spiritual authority of the church, as also having its source in the "consent of the people."[82] What is primary then is the right of private judgment and free assembly in spiritual matters; the free compact that forms the state is parasitic and reflective of this spiritual freedom embodied in the voluntary church.

John Locke is often cited as the principal exponent of Enlightenment views of religious liberty, and one of the principal sources of this idea. But recent scholarship has demonstrated that these Enlightenment ideas followed rather than preceded the successful practice of religious toleration by groups like the believers' churches and, somewhat later, non-conformist Baptist and free churches in England and Scotland. These ideas came early to the American colonies, many of whose leaders had spent time as exiles in Holland. In particular William Penn, the founder of Pennsylvania, insisted that religious liberty should be the birthright of settlers in that state. As a result, Philadelphia was an early center of tolerance. As the place where Penn's influence and Locke's ideas dominated, it was the natural center for the development and eventual inscription of these ideas in America's founding documents.[83]

For our purposes it is important to stress that the case for toleration was never a secular idea; it was from the beginning a biblical and theological

---

[81]John Locke, "Letter Concerning Toleration." Written in Latin in 1685, published in English in 1689; text available at https://socialsciences.mcmaster.ca/econ/ugcm/3ll3/locke/toleration.pdf.
[82]Locke, "Letter Concerning Toleration."
[83]See Benjamin J. Kaplan, *Divided by Faith: Religious Conflict and the Practice of Toleration in Early Modern Europe* (Cambridge, MA: Belknap Press, 2007); and N. Miller, *Religious Roots*.

notion.[84] And the significance of this was understood not simply to allow individuals to believe for themselves but to encourage them to join without coercion in communities of worship. Though these ideas flourished sooner in the middle colonies, eventually (in 1828) disestablishment came to New England, and the congregational form of church government became common. By the early nineteenth century it was assumed that the church consisted of individuals who had decided to join themselves together in a worshiping community. In America during the early republic, fueled by the Second Great Awakening, the Methodists and Baptists, and a multitude of other independent groups influenced by this voluntarism, spread across the frontier and gave American religion its distinctive character.[85]

One of the fruits of the notion of church as a gathered community was the freedom to join with other like-minded people to accomplish a variety of common purposes in voluntary societies. This came to be a defining characteristic of America during the early republic. Upon his arrival in America, Alexis de Tocqueville noticed "in most operations of the mind, each American appeals only to the individual effort of his own understanding." This gives the citizens, he noticed, a bias toward free institutions, societies bound together by "interests" rather than "ideas."[86] And in America's early history, associations of common interests led to the proliferation of voluntary societies, such as the American Bible Society and the American Abolition Society among many others, aimed at promoting virtue and suppressing vice.[87]

But here is where our story takes a dramatic turn, for it was precisely this voluntary impulse that fueled the missionary movement that originated during this period. Mark Noll, in fact, has argued that the success of the American missionary impulse, which was to prove so influential in founding churches in the majority world, "was accomplished through voluntary

---

[84]N. Miller, *Religious Roots*, 39. He points out that even scholars arguing for the influence of humanism on Luther's ideas admit that in the end New Testament passages weighed more heavily.

[85]The populist and democratic character of this period is described in Nathan O. Hatch, *The Democratization of American Christianity* (New Haven, CT: Yale University Press, 1989). In chap. 6 he describes the character of churches formed under the influence of the universal conviction that one can think for oneself in matters of religion.

[86]Alexis de Tocqueville, *Democracy in America* (1863; Cambridge: Sever & Francis, 1963), 2:2, 6, 354.

[87]These are described in some detail in George Marsden, *The Evangelical Mind and the New School Presbyterian Experience: A Case Study of Thought and Theology in Nineteenth-Century America* (New Haven, CT: Yale University Press, 1970).

means" and was the result of a "voluntary Christianity."[88] Not only were missionaries themselves sent and supported by newly formed voluntary mission societies, Noll points out, but they exported the notion that believers should take the initiative to do the work of forming churches for and by themselves. Consistent with the history we have been tracing, this impulse was inspired by their emphasis on the individual conscience rather than tradition and history. It featured an elective affinity involving free market initiatives, and it resulted, Noll argues, in multidimensional efforts "stunning in their breadth, complexity and depth."[89] Noll acknowledges that this often led to efforts that ignored the lessons (and baggage!) of history and were more activist than thoughtful in market relationships.[90] But these are only the unfortunate deviations, he thinks, of an impulse that has had mostly positive effects on the majority-world church. He summarizes his claim in this way: "The [successful] American missionary programs . . . are the most conversionistic in their message and also the most voluntaristic in their methods."[91]

Noll recognizes that these have had enormous influence in majority-world Christianity, but he argues that this has less to do with heavy-handed American manipulation (and funding), though these were sometimes present, than with conditions that in many places were ripe for this message. These voluntaristic impulses, he thinks, were able to make the gospel relevant to the emerging Enlightenment self and were more likely to encourage believers to chart their own way forward.[92] Moreover, these characteristics were modeled by missionaries in a way that have, he argues, "become standard in the rest of the world."[93] So the voluntaristic impulse is not a colonial imposition but a template that has come to be widely accepted and embraced by local actors and for local reasons because, he concludes, the "world is coming more and more to look like America."[94]

---

[88]Mark Noll, *The New Shape of World Christianity: How American Experience Reflects Global Faith* (Downers Grove, IL: InterVarsity Press, 2009), 12.

[89]Noll, *New Shape of World Christianity*, 40.

[90]Noll, *New Shape of World Christianity*, 45.

[91]Noll, *New Shape of World Christianity*, 85. Noll's thesis that the voluntary society is the key vehicle for Protestant missionary activity is not new, as he admits, but can be traced to the work of Andrew Walls.

[92]Noll, *New Shape of World Christianity*, 43, 85.

[93]Noll, *New Shape of World Christianity*, 110.

[94]Noll, *New Shape of World Christianity*, 116, 189.

But is this true? Looking at the world taking shape in the twenty-first century, can we really say the world is becoming more like America? Isn't it the case that, in many ways that matter to Christian mission, the world is looking more and more unlike America, and the presence of the freedoms necessary for voluntaristic activity are increasingly under threat. And isn't it the case that these differences have special relevance for reflection on the social shape of church in the majority world?

Let us acknowledge for the sake of argument that notions of voluntaristic Christianity are the clear fruit of the gospel message, and that they have found traction in many places in the world. One thinks, for example, of the wild proliferation of churches in places like Nigeria or Kenya, where free-market initiatives are common. Or one can point to growth of Pentecostal groups, funded by a voluntaristic ethos, becoming visible in Latin America. One can even argue that these ideas have found footing in China in the growth and expansion of the house-church movement. One might even go further and admit that the impulse resulting from the rights to private judgment and to free association, rooted as they are in the liberating work of Christ in the gospel, have had an immense and largely positive impact on the development of free and economically prosperous societies in many places in the world. In fact, the highly significant research of Robert Woodberry has shown that there is a strong correlation, and perhaps even a causal connection, between places where conversionistic Protestant missionaries worked in the nineteenth century and societies that have the highest levels of education, health care, and economic and political stability.[95]

In response to Noll's thesis we would make two points. First, one wonders whether this emerging Enlightenment self, as it has been carried around the world through the processes of globalization, is always congenial to biblical notions. Does it not frequently reflect secularized versions of this self, what might be called the modern liberal self? These secularized ideas were widely disseminated after World War II and have been enshrined in documents like the famous United Nations' Universal Declaration of Human Rights.[96] These

---

[95]Robert Woodberry, "The Missionary Roots of Liberal Democracy," *American Political Science Review*, 106, no. 2 (2012): 244-74. And see Andrea Palpant Dilley, "The Surprising Discovery about those Colonist, Proselytizing Missionaries," *Christianity Today*, January 8, 2014, 40, www.christianitytoday.com/ct/2014/january-february/world-missionaries-made.html.

[96]We will leave aside for the moment whether and to what extent these documents themselves owe

traditions often assume the primacy of an individual self that is ultimately autonomous and self-motivated. Roberto Goizueta has argued that these notions, basic to both conservative and liberal political traditions in the West, are often hostile not only to many indigenous traditions but to biblical values.[97] Such notions of self assume that religious beliefs reside in the individual rather than being embodied in religious communities. Church membership, on this view, is freely chosen or rejected by the individual, inspiring the frequent refrain of many millennials who claim to be spiritual but not religious while resisting membership in any church community.

Roberto Goizueta argues that within Hispanic culture (and one could argue in many cultures in the world) such notions are simply incoherent. For many such groups, community is preexistent and constitutive of the self. For the Hispanic, Goizueta writes, it is not an abstract relationship to Christ mediated by texts that matters, important as these texts are. Rather, it is through the concrete and embodied relationships with Jesus himself—for example, by touching his image or kissing his feet—that we come to know him, just as surely it is in our embodied and historical relationships with our family that we come to know them.[98] The point is, we are constituted by these actual (and physical) relationships. Communities form individual selves, not the other way around. The latter is subsequent and dependent on the former. As Africans like to say, "I am because we are." These notions do not make individual agency impossible, but they condition this in ways not recognized by modern secular notions of the self.

The second point is equally important: How do we understand communities where communal solidarity, not individual initiative, is basic to identity? We have acknowledged the many places where the church as a voluntary society has found acceptance. But what about those places where this has been resisted? The many places in the world where this idea is viewed with suspicion are frequently places where the Reformation and

---

a debt to religious notions we have been tracing. The matter is thoroughly discussed in Nicholas Wolterstorff, *Justice: Rights and Wrongs* (Princeton, NJ: Princeton University Press, 2008). Our discussion here will focus on the way these ideas are often promulgated and understood.

[97]See Roberto S. Goizueta "Liberalism," in *Global Dictionary of Theology*, ed. William A. Dyrness and Veli-Matti Kärkkäinen (Downers Grove, IL: InterVarsity Press, 2008).

[98]Roberto S. Goizueta, *Caminemos con Jesús: Toward a Hispanic/Latino Theology of Accompaniment* (Maryknoll, NY: Orbis, 1995), 54n12, 168.

Enlightenment play no role in the effective history of people. This calls into question a central claim in Noll's argument: the assumption that elective affinities proposed by missionaries appeal to the emerging Enlightenment self. What of those places where such notions of the self are absent?

These places, interestingly, are often thought to be those most resistant to the gospel. But perhaps we should ask, Might the resistance be, in part, to Western notions of the voluntary church rather than simply to the gospel? The question this raises, and which the rest of this book will seek to address, is the following: What forms and practices might constitute the church in places like this? Granted that the church as voluntary society has made inroads in many places, what about those places where these ideas are foreign, or where political and cultural restrictions make such freedoms impossible?[99] What shape might the church take in those places?

---

[99]The literature on the influence of the missionary movement clearly implies that things like representative government are an often unrecognized fruit of the gospel message . Even if this would be an eventual (and hoped for) result, it cannot be expected as a criterion for forming churches in the first place.

3

Emergent Ecclesial Identity and Mission

W e have thus far argued that the church is one integral part of the wider work of God in this world. And we have asserted that its expression of God's work is always and everywhere interpreted through a reverse hermeneutic— a reading of the gospel through the lens of one's own culture. In this way the church from its inception, and throughout its history, has always made sense of its mission and God's work in the world via its cultural context.

Such a stance perhaps makes some Christians nervous. They may wonder: If this is the case, is the church then simply a product of its context? In recent decades, some have made sense of this question by posing a difference between the gospel and culture and considering how the two relate to each other. Andrew Walls, for instance, discusses what he calls the "indigenizing" principle and the "pilgrim" principle of the gospel.[1] The former, he says, accentuates the believer's cultural rootedness and leads one to "live as a Christian and yet as a member of one's own society."[2] Countering this is the "pilgrim" nature of the gospel, which challenges the context and reminds the believer "that he has no abiding city and warns him that to be faithful to Christ will put him out of step with his society."[3]

While these two "principles" point to important dynamics in the relationship between culture and the gospel (and, by extension, the church), there are at least two problems with this way of framing the issue. First, we would suggest that this framework has a fundamental flaw, and thus poses

---

[1] Andrew F. Walls, "The Gospel as Prisoner and Liberator of Culture," in *The Missionary Movement in Christian History: Studies in the Transmission of Faith* (Maryknoll, NY: Orbis, 1996).
[2] Walls, in "Gospel as Prisoner and Liberator," 7.
[3] Walls, in "Gospel as Prisoner and Liberator," 8.

the wrong question. The flaw, similar to what we noted in chapter one regarding Charles Kraft's *Christianity in Culture*, is the assumption that the church somehow exists above and apart from culture. Instead, we contend that the church can never transcend its culture. As our previous chapter has shown, even those churches that have sought to counter culture do so using existing cultural categories!

Second, the interaction between culture and the gospel (and church) is complex and cannot be adequately framed as a dichotomous tension between two poles. Others have recognized this complexity and have offered alternative ways of framing the relationship. For example, the Lutheran World Federation's Study Team on Worship and Culture in Nairobi, Kenya, surmised that Christian worship and culture relate dynamically with each other in at least four ways.[4] Christian worship, they propose, is transcultural, contextual, countercultural, and cross-cultural. It is transcultural in that there are those elements that transcend time, space, culture, and confession.[5] It is contextual as it enables "the meanings and actions of worship to be 'encoded' and re-expressed in the language of local culture."[6] Since some aspects of culture are "sinful, dehumanizing, and contradictory to the values of the Gospel," worship at times needs to be countercultural.[7] And, finally, worship should cross cultures in order to enrich the whole church.[8]

The Nairobi statement provides helpful nuances in the discussion of the relationship between Christian worship and culture. However, the document reflects a flaw similar to that which we discussed above—an assumption that the church and its practices somehow exist above or outside of culture and that the task of the church is to adopt or counter (depending on the situation) cultural values in order to most accurately reflect that transcendent reality. The church, in a sense, mediates the interaction of gospel and culture by rationally and objectively analyzing a culture and then adjusting its understanding and practices of the gospel, including its worship, accordingly.

---

[4] Study Team on Worship and Culture, "Nairobi Statement on Worship and Culture: Contemporary Challenges and Opportunities," *Lutheran World Federation*, Calvin Institute of Christian Worship, January 1996, https://worship.calvin.edu/resources/resource-library/nairobi-statement-on-worship-and-culture-full-text.

[5] Study Team on Worship and Culture, "Nairobi Statement on Worship and Culture," par. 2.3.

[6] Study Team on Worship and Culture, "Nairobi Statement on Worship and Culture," par. 3.2.

[7] Study Team on Worship and Culture, "Nairobi Statement on Worship and Culture," par. 4.1.

[8] Study Team on Worship and Culture, "Nairobi Statement on Worship and Culture," par. 5.1.

This, as we will discuss in a moment, reflects a particularly modern (and often Western) understanding of culture.

While it can be helpful to discuss the different postures that Christian worship, the gospel, and church can have in relation to culture, we suggest reframing the question. Rather than posing a dichotomy between the gospel and culture and then discussing the ways a church should or should not reflect its culture, we suggest shining a light on a process that is already and always at work. This process is a dialectic or, perhaps more accurately, a multi-lectic process. That is, church identities, practices, and theologies come into existence through the ongoing interaction among its people (with all of their various cultural perspectives and social locations) and between them and God. This is a process that deserves much more careful scrutiny.

But as we reframe the question, some may ask: What about the agency of God and, to a lesser extent, his people? Are not God and people the ultimate controllers of this process? Regarding God's agency, in chapter five we will discuss several of the biblical metaphors for the church, all of which make God central to the identity and purpose of the church. Here we can note that, whereas Scripture is clear on God's authority in relation to his work and people, it also suggests a wide range of ways in which God interacts with, guides, and shapes these in the midst of cultural contexts. As Peruvian scholar Ruben (Tito) Paredes has said, culture is "the vehicle used by God to interact with humans as well as the vehicle to carry out his mission in this world."[9] Though Christians may disagree on where and how God may be at work in cultures, all will agree that he certainly has the agency and ability to do so.

What about people's agency? The ability of people to bring the gospel and effect change has certainly been a hallmark of the Western modern missionary movement since at least the eighteenth century. The sense of people's missional agency and abilities gained even greater strength and sophistication in the mid to late twentieth century as Christian mission workers studied and integrated the social sciences, and particularly cultural anthropology, with mission practice. While the social sciences provided important correctives to colonialist and ethnocentric approaches to mission, they also

---

[9]Tito Paredes, "Integrity of Mission in the Light of the Gospel: Bearing the Witness of the Spirit; Perspectives from Latin America," *Mission Studies* 24, no. 2 (2007): 235.

reinforced the already prominent sense of people's ability to master other cultures, if not politically and militarily, at least in terms of cognitive understanding. The goal became to gain this cultural knowledge in order to shape the gospel and its mission enterprise according to the needs of the cultural context. This sense that cultures can be studied and mastered, and that the gospel and mission can be manipulated accordingly, led to what missiologists such as Samuel Escobar have criticized as "managerial missiology."[10]

Much more could be said about the perhaps inflated sense of personal agency that has permeated much mission work and scholarship. However, while we can and do affirm that God has given to people agency and the ability to actively participate in his mission, an overemphasis on this can obscure an interactive hermeneutical process that is always occurring. In recent years new theories in the social sciences have looked more carefully at the process by which people and groups interact with their context to create new structures and meaning. In this chapter we turn to one particular theory known as critical realism and its discussion of *emergence*, which offers a compelling explanation of how social groups like churches come into being. We put emergence in conversation with our theology of church and reframe our question: What is the process by which social groups emerge, and how does this help us develop a missiological understanding of how churches emerge out of and reflect their contexts?

SOCIOLOGICAL INTERPRETATIONS OF CHURCH

Churches are social groups and as such often make considered decisions regarding their practices, doctrines, music, buildings, and other concerns. Who or what guides social groups like churches in making these decisions? Social science has recognized and discussed two sources: people themselves and the social/cultural context. Theories that emphasize persons' power to form and shape groups give priority to people's agency. That is, people have the ability to create new cultural artifacts, create new groups, or resist—or change—certain things in their culture. They normally do this in order to

---

[10]Samuel Escobar, "Evangelical Missiology: Peering into the Future at the Turn of the Century," in *Global Missiology for the 21st Century: The Iguassu Dialogue*, ed. William D. Taylor (Grand Rapids: Baker Academic, 2000), 111.

increase their own interests, well-being, power, and social status and to satisfy other desires.[11] This was the viewpoint typical of Enlightenment thinkers such as David Hume and Adam Smith. In recent years this has been revised and reformulated in the social sciences in theories such as rational choice theory, which analyzes the overall "product" that a church or society produces and to what degree people are motivated to "invest" in it.[12] In short, theories of this persuasion emphasize the ability of individuals to evaluate their own context and to make rational choices to modify, change, or adapt it for their own purposes.

On the other side are theories that emphasize the power of the social and cultural contexts. These point out the degree to which people are shaped, often unconsciously and from the day they are born, by their context. Though it may seem like they are making choices regarding their culture, the choices they make are in many ways determined for them. If person-centered theories make people the controllers of the context, the social/cultural-centered theories make people and their groups subservient to their context. In the social sciences this latter approach was championed by theorists such as Émile Durkheim, Talcott Parsons, Mary Douglas, and others. For these, though individuals were central to social structures and perhaps played some role in shaping them, on the whole social laws or principles operated on human beings and were the primary shapers of social groups.[13] Durkheim famously equated society with a deity's ability to create, saying, "Just as society largely forms the individual, it forms him to the same extent in its own image. Society, therefore, cannot lack the material for its needs, for it has, so to speak, kneaded it with its own hands."[14]

---

[11]Christian Smith, *To Flourish or Destruct: A Personalist Theory of Human Goods, Motivations, Failure, and Evil* (Chicago: University of Chicago Press, 2015), 6.

[12]See for example Rodney Stark and Roger Finke, *Acts of Faith: Explaining the Human Side of Religion* (Berkeley: University of California Press, 2000); Laurence R. Iannaccone, "Rational Choice: Framework for the Scientific Study of Religion," in *Rational Choice Theory and Religion: Summary and Assessment*, ed. Lawrence A. Young (New York: Routledge, 1997), 25-44; and Laurie C. Stoll, "Church Growth and Decline: A Test of the Market-Based Approach," *Review of Religious Research* 49, no. 3 (2008): 251-68.

[13]As Paul Hiebert shows, McGavran was highly influenced by Durkheim's emphasis on social structures. Paul G. Hiebert, "French Structuralism and Modern Missiology" (paper presented at the Christian Perspectives on Anthropological Theory Conference, Biola University, La Mirada, CA, April 6-8, 2000).

[14]Émile Durkheim, *Suicide: A Study in Sociology*, ed. George Simpson, trans. John A. Spaulding (New York: The Free Press, 1951; first published in French in 1897), 323.

This view, strongly influenced by positivism, sees social structures as following universal laws. Drawing from this, many missiologists of the twentieth century were (and continue to be) on a quest to discover these social "laws," seeking the causal relationships that bring about certain phenomena, including "successful" churches. But, as Christian Smith observes, positivism fails to account for the diverse and complex realities of social life.[15] This partially accounts for church-growth missiologists' struggle to explain why certain approaches work in certain contexts but not others. Though there are many reasons for this, certainly one explanation is that many theorists within this approach have not, or cannot adequately, account for the agency of people in any given context.

A CRITICAL-REALIST ACCOUNT OF EMERGENCE

Most of us probably feel that there is some truth in both ways of accounting for the decisions that we make. We acknowledge that our context shapes us in profound ways, but we also feel we possess and use the ability to make our own decisions, some of which can even go against certain cultural norms. Indeed, some social theories have sought to hold both sources together. One such theory that social scholars and missiologists have turned to in recent years is emergence theory, particularly a form known as critical realism (CR).[16] One of CR's principal proponents, Margaret Archer, argues that it provides a way for us to see that "we are simultaneously free *and* constrained and we also have some awareness of it."[17] In other words, we as individuals (and groups) are not simply subject to the values, power, and practices of our cultures, but neither do we make choices free of any influence or constraint from these.

---

[15]C. Smith, *To Flourish or Destruct*, 20-21. Also see Porpora's more extended discussion. Douglas V. Porpora, *Reconstructing Sociology: The Critical Realist Approach* (Cambridge: Cambridge University Press, 2015), 32-45.

[16]Of sociologists see C. Smith, *To Flourish or Destruct*; Margaret S. Archer, *Realist Social Theory: The Morphogenetic Approach* (New York: Cambridge University Press, 1995); Dave Elder-Vass, *The Causal Power of Social Structures: Emergence, Structure and Agency* (New York: Cambridge University Press, 2010); Porpora, *Reconstructing Sociology*. Of missiologists see Sherwood Lingenfelter, *Agents of Transformation: A Guide for Effective Cross-Cultural Ministry* (Grand Rapids: Baker Academic, 1996); Darren Todd Duerksen, *Ecclesial Identities in a Multi-Faith Context: Jesus Truth-Gatherings* (Yeshu Satsangs) *Among Hindus and Sikhs in Northwest India*, American Society of Missiology Monograph 22 (Eugene, OR: Pickwick, 2015).

[17]Archer, *Realist Social Theory*, 2 (emphasis ours).

This is an important component for our understanding of church. For, as we illustrated in the last chapter, churches have always made sense of the gospel and been guided and constrained in their understanding via their own context. In this respect we would agree with those who would emphasize the power that context has over people's choices. But we do so with the caveat that CR highlights: people are still agents and have the ability to survey and decide from a whole set of possibilities, even if their cultural context has limited the number of choices they think are possible and viable. When, for example, we read Scripture, our cultural context allows us to see many possible themes that could be emphasized to shape and guide a church. But our cultural context also often limits the possible themes that we see at any given time. From a theological standpoint, we would affirm that God by his Holy Spirit is actively at work in this process as well, giving people the ability and agency to understand truths about God and his work and to make choices while also providing social constraints that limit what people grasp and do.

If churches are not formed by fully autonomous agents or by universal social "laws," what forms them? Critical realists answer this by introducing us to a concept called *emergence*. Though this word has been used among Christians in various ways in recent years (such as the "emergent church"), the focus here is not on a particular church movement. Rather, for social theorists, *emergence* describes the process of interaction between a context and persons and what results out of that interaction. As Christian Smith explains, social emergence is "the process of constituting a new entity with its own particular characteristics and capacities through the interactive combination of other, different entities."[18] In other words, if we can better understand how people, a context, and the gospel interact with each other, we can likewise better understand the unique expressions of church that emerge from that interaction. Emergence is attentive to ways in which expressions of church are unique to a context and could only survive and thrive in and because of that context.

But what does it actually mean to say that social groups such as churches are emergent, and what are we looking for? Smith summarizes the main

---

[18]C. Smith, *To Flourish or Destruct*, 36.

components needed for something to be recognized as emergent. We will look at each of these in turn to provide a framework with which to describe the ways churches, including the insider groups on which we are focusing, come into being.

EMERGENCE OF NEW ENTITIES

Christian Smith first states that emergence occurs when two or more entities combine or relate to each other, resulting in the formation of a new entity that did not exist before. On a social level this can happen within a group as well as between groups. Within a group, when individuals come together, there often emerges a collective identity that transcends the combination of individuals.[19] The individuals involved will sense this identity and may describe the "we-ness" they feel. That sense of we-ness—that the group as a whole has its own identity and energy and qualities—is a sign that a new social entity has emerged. For many societies, such senses of we-ness precede personal and individual awareness—"I am because we are," the African maxim that we cited earlier. Regardless of when a group becomes aware of it, however, they would recognize it in the old saying, the whole is more than the sum of its parts.

What causes this group identity to emerge? On a social level the process often begins with shared circumstances, interests, and concerns. But these in themselves are not enough to create the strength and characteristics of an emergent group identity. Rather, as people are brought together (such as being born into a family) or come together through common interests, there needs to be a special bond through interactions or relations between people that result in a shared commitment.[20] It is this commitment, formed through relations, that creates the emerging sense of we-ness within a social group.[21] In like manner a new entity called a church emerges, giving its

---

[19]Some may hear echoes of Durkheim's concept of "social facts," or facts about society that cannot emanate from or be reduced to a single individual. However, though similar, Durkheim ascribed to these facts a high level of coercive control, giving limited room for personal agency.

[20]Pierpaolo Donati and Margaret S. Archer, *The Relational Subject* (Cambridge: Cambridge University Press, 2015), 25, 107-8. Critical realists, and we, include in this as well our relations with our material world, which we leave to the side for the moment. See for example Archer's discussion of the relation of individual to the material: Margaret S. Archer, *Being Human: The Problem of Agency* (New York: Cambridge University Press, 2000), 121-90.

[21]Thus, for example, for children, families are initially involuntary structures with the potential

members a sense of we-ness when they relate with each other and have a sustained sense of commitment to the gospel, to one another, and to their values and practices.

DEPENDENCE ON THE PARTS

Smith's next criterion for something to be emergent is that the new entity is dependent on the interaction of the parts. We have already discussed the importance of relations and interactions for the emergence process. But what Smith stresses here is the *continual* dependence of the new entity on the components that compose it. Again, this can occur both within and between groups.

Above we talked about how within social groups there often emerges a sense of we-ness that transcends the individuals involved. However, though this new, emergent entity exists at a "higher" level than the individuals, it is nonetheless dependent on the individuals and their interaction, including each person's energy, gifts, ideas, and skills, whether they are aware of this or not. Indeed, in places such as Africa, individuals may become aware of the we-ness of the group into which they are born without reflecting on how they and others contribute to it. Regardless of when or if they become aware of it, the group gains its identity through the interaction of its people. In the New Testament some of the writers certainly had something like this in mind, though they were of course not expressing modern-day sociocultural theory. In chapter five we will discuss some of the prominent metaphors that biblical writers employed, such as Paul's description of the church as the "body of Christ" (e.g., Rom 7:4; 1 Cor 10:16). The biological body is formed by the relations of its parts to each other. However, while the body has a collective identity, each part is important for giving the body its unique characteristics and abilities. The body, like the church, is more than the sum of its parts, but without those parts it could not function in its own unique way.

NEW CHARACTERISTICS, NEW LOGICS

Smith's last point regarding emergence says that, though it is dependent on the lower entities, the new entity possesses its own characteristic qualities

---

for emergent properties and identity. However, it is only if and when the people in a family relate to each other through shared commitments that a sense of we-ness emerges.

or properties. Once again, such properties occur both within a group, such as a church, and between groups. Because social settings are complex and not highly predictable, it is often difficult to anticipate the exact forms of the new qualities and properties. Though this is the case, there are three general characteristics that apply to most emergent entities: relational goods, evils, and logics.

Relational goods. As people relate to one another around shared commitments, they often experience through the group what Margaret Archer and Pierpaolo Donati call "relational goods." Between people, these could include senses of trust, safety, cooperation, empowerment, or support. It could also be a valued outcome, such as the good harmonization and performance of a musical ensemble, a social or health service provided by a neighborhood nonprofit, or the trust and support developed within a church small group that prays together.[22]

It is true that persons and groups may enjoy goods that are not emergent. For example, a person may gain helpful knowledge from a sermon whether or not she relates to anyone in the church (for example, through a podcast). So what differentiates a relational good from other goods? One way to determine this is to consider whether a good can be distributed among people and enjoyed without any relations. If a couple divorces, they can divide their assets, children, and other things between them. However, the emergent, relational goods that were generated by the couple or family, such as trust, positive family identity, understanding, and encouragement, would cease to exist because the relations that generated them have ceased to exist.[23] Nonrelational goods, such as material goods, can be very important to individuals but are not dependent on a group for their existence. Only relational goods are characteristic of and can be enjoyed by an emergent group or church.

Relational evils. The opposite is also possible. That is, when people or groups relate to one another, it is possible that relational evils emerge. These, in a similar way to relational goods, only exist as long as the people are relating with one another (though the memory of it and some of its effects may outlast the relationship). For example, two co-workers might agree to

---

[22]Donati and Archer, *Relational Subject*, 199.
[23]Donati and Archer, *Relational Subject*, 66. Indeed, it may be that these goods began to decrease well before the divorce in response to deteriorating relations between the spouses.

work on a project together but, in the midst of it, have misunderstandings and differences of opinion that make them angry and resentful toward each other. These are relational evils that may cause them to abandon the project or vow never to work together in that way again. Unhealthy relations in a church may result in the relational evils of mistrust, hurt, or betrayal and outcomes such as church divisions. Likewise, unhealthy relations between groups result in similar experiences of mistrust, hurt, and even violence. For example, the long history of strained relations between the United States and Muslim nations and groups has resulted in many relational evils, including deep mistrust between Christians and Muslims, violence between groups, and war.

Relational logics. If people's relations can create goods and evils, they can also generate the emergence of change or of stasis. Within a group as well as between groups, this is most often noticed when new ideas and practices are introduced by one or more parties. In such cases, when individuals or groups choose to engage the ideas (and they may not), a new outcome may emerge; they may affirm and continue in their existing beliefs and practices (stasis) or change or modify these in some ways. Since in this book we are interested in the ways in which new ecclesial groups have emerged and continue to emerge, we might ask, What are some common ways in which such interactions may prompt a church to change, or for a new ecclesial group to emerge? What relational patterns or "logics" do they often follow? Margaret Archer proposes several such logics. We will highlight the two she calls the constraining contradiction and the competitive contradiction as prominent examples.[24]

The first of these, the *constraining contradiction*, occurs when people in a group embrace two or more ideas or frameworks that are distinguishable but in some way rely on each other. These frameworks have some clear differences, but one cannot be discarded outright without undercutting a significant aspect of the other(s). For example, persons in a church may disagree over the role of the Holy Spirit in people's lives. Those in subgroup A may become more "charismatic" in their views and seek to elicit the Holy Spirit's power and intervention in many places and ways. Those in subgroup

---

[24]Archer, *Realist Social Theory*, 230-34, 39-43.

B may disagree with this emphasis and some of the changes it brings to their prayer and worship practices. However, subgroup B cannot dismiss subgroup A's ideas completely since their own concept of the Trinity not only allows for but necessitates the existence of an active Holy Spirit.

Such contradictions remain "constrained" when there is a strong unity in the group in terms of material interests or commitments. Such unity, and the presence of some similarity of commitments, causes the group to stay somewhat unified while seeking ways to deal with the tension of contradicting ideas. Some persons may address the tension by becoming ideologically agnostic and remaining uncommitted to either idea. However, those that remain committed to their ideologies usually respond by trying to correct or contain the contradiction. In a church conflict, for example, the church leadership may try to correct the beliefs of one subgroup or socially constrain the groups from elevating the conflict. In either case, what emerges is a modified set of beliefs, rituals, or social practices that reflect the correction or containment necessary for the group's continued unity.

The *competitive contradiction* also involves two or more contrasting ideas. However, in this case there is little if any perceived similarity between them, and the social group is divided by other material or social interests. Thus, group A not only holds an idea that is perceived to directly contradict that held by group B, but they are separated by social, ethnic, or material differences. In this situation it is difficult for people to remain nonaligned, and they usually yield to pressure to side with one group or the other. As sides are defined, they then seek to resolve the tension, not by correcting or minimizing the differences but by eliminating and having victory over the other on the ideational (and sometimes literal) battlefield. However, though the goal is usually to achieve victory and eliminate the other, the actual consequence is often "ideational pluralism" or sustained differentiation between the groups and their ideologies.

Another way of thinking about emergent logics of various groups, and one that is relevant to the example we use at the end of this chapter, is to attend to cultural logics at work in producing the various contradictions we have discussed. In an influential study of modernization in Latin America, sociologist Cristián Parker has shown that rural (mostly premodern) groups moving to the city do not automatically become modern and secular; rather, they develop what Parker calls a different, semimodern cultural logic.[25] Confronted with somewhat contradictory values, these groups deal with and constrain the tension by modifying aspects of these values. The resulting cultural pluralism influences the way various religious groups adapt to their new setting, favoring some groups—traditional faiths, Pentecostalism— while challenging others. Similarly, in India and other places missionary logics that reflected a modernizing Western culture often conflicted with local (and mostly informal) cultural logics, producing unexpected contra- dictions. The forms the Christian churches assumed necessarily reflected, and sometimes even encouraged, these contradictions.

God, Reverse Hermeneutics, and Ecclesial Emergence

Our discussion of emergence has drawn much from the social sciences. But, as we've insisted, though they are social groups, churches are not only social groups. Rather, churches are an integral part of God's kingdom work. And though God is present throughout creation, and even in other religions, he is present and at work in his church in a special and unique way via his Holy Spirit, and especially through the teaching and preaching of Scripture. How does a theological understanding of the church connect with, and even en- hance, our account of the emergent church as a social group?

To understand this, recall the importance of relations in the emergent process. That is, when people relate together, particularly through shared commitments, new properties emerge, such as the sense of we-ness, which in turn can assist in strengthening an existing church or in the formation of a new church. In a like manner, our theological understanding of church involves the real presence of God and the potential for a relationship be- tween God and people. When people recognize the presence and work of God in their midst and relate to him through various practices, such as prayer, worship, and preaching, new properties and relational goods emerge. We will speak about these in a later chapter as theological practices, that is, activities in which both humans and God are freely involved. Thus God is actively at work as an agent in the emergent process of church. His power and revelation are always available for people to interact with according to

---

[25]Cristián Parker, *Popular Religion and Modernization in Latin America: A Different Logic* (Maryk- noll, NY: Orbis, 1996).

their own cultural understandings, and, when they do, the entity called church emerges.

We can say more about this interaction by returning to our discussion from chapter one on hermeneutics. If biblical and theological hermeneutics is conceived as a way of relating to the gospel, or a gospel tradition, might this not potentially be an emergent process? Recall that, rather than thinking of hermeneutics as a linear, one-way process of the gospel speaking to and shaping the person or church, we must also recognize the presence of what we have called a reverse hermeneutic. Not only do the gospel and the teachings of Scripture shape people, but people shape interpretations of the gospel. As Hans Georg Gadamer argues, the process is one in which the horizon of our culture—which represents what is possible for a people to grasp—fuses with the horizon of Scripture—which represents the renewing work of God as this centers in the life, death, and resurrection of Christ. In emergence terms, God relates to us through his gospel message, and we relate to him through our cultural, social, and religious contexts. Out of this interaction emerges a particular expression of the gospel—one that is not entirely new but stands as a fresh and unique articulation. When this expression gains longevity through ongoing interaction by more and more people, and the formation of ecclesial institutions around this expression, there emerges a theological tradition. A theological tradition, in emergence terms, is the result of an initial interaction—a dialectical hermeneutic—between culturally embedded people and God's gospel message.[26]

We have worked through some rich but complex sociological concepts to argue that churches are the result of emergent processes involving relations among people, their contexts, and God. In addition, as churches interact with other groups around them, these interactions too create new entities, goods, evils, and logics, which in turn influence the groups, further shaping the church and other groups. We have come a long way from the simplistic, predictable positivism that often underlies modern notions of church formation and church planting. Though the emergent account of the church is perhaps messier and more complex, it also helps us account for the church's richness and diversity. In addition, emergence helps us account for the way

---

[26]See Henning Wrogemann, *Intercultural Theology*, vol. 1, *Intercultural Hermeneutics* (Downers Grove, IL: InterVarsity Press, 2016), 57-59.

in which churches reflect multiple understandings and images of God, his work, and his gospel.

In the remainder of this chapter we will illustrate these concepts by analyzing the relatively recent emergence of one particular church—the Indian church—along with the group's common associative identity as non-Indian and Dalit. We hope that in doing so we can demonstrate how the concept of emergence can help us understand the context and formation of churches. In the following chapter we will then turn to specific case studies from various contexts, including one from North India that looks at how some Christ-followers are responding to their histories and, through various strategies, are hoping for a new type of ecclesial group to emerge.

The Indian Church and Its Emergent Identities

Religious discourse in India often questions the degree to which Christianity is truly Indian.[27] At both political and local levels Christians often face direct or implicit accusations that they are in some ways part of a religion that is foreign or other. The roots of this characterization and the process of its emergence in India can be traced back to the early missionary work in the region.

The history of Christianity in India is long, stretching back to the Saint Thomas or Syrian Christians in South India sometime in the first three centuries CE.[28] These early Christian communities came to have a relatively high level of status among the Hindu and Muslim communities in the area.[29] Christianity also remained largely confined to southern India up until the sixteenth century. However, with the coming of colonial Christianity via Portuguese, Dutch, and British powers, churches were established in other regions around India. But it is the missionary work of the nineteenth- and twentieth-century British colonial era that has perhaps most directly contributed to the contemporary emergent identity of Indian Christianity.

---

[27]The same question is posed of Indian Islam as well, but we will focus on the experience of the Indian Christian community.

[28]The designation Saint Thomas Christians relates to the claim by many of these groups that the apostle Thomas came to the region and founded churches there in 52 CE. Though this claim is debated and disputed by many scholars, most agree that a Christian community existed in the region by the third or fourth century CE.

[29]Chad M. Bauman, "Hindu-Christian Conflict in India: Globalization, Conversion, and the Co-terminal Castes and Tribes," *Journal of Asian Studies* 72, no. 3 (2013): 636.

In North India, where we will focus, the British East India Company was initially not favorable to missionaries and their work in its territories. However, in 1813 the company changed its policies to allow for greater freedom for missionary work in its territories with the result that more missionaries began to arrive from Britain and elsewhere. The initial outcome of this increase in missionary presence and activity, in terms of converts and churches, was generally quite minimal during the first half of the nineteenth century.[30] This began to change, however, following the 1857 uprising. In that year a substantial number of Indian soldiers in the British East India Company regiments rebelled, in part over rumors of planned forced conversions to Christianity, resulting in a bloody and lengthy revolt.[31] Though deaths and atrocities occurred across religious communities, the stories reaching British newspapers largely focused on the killing and martyrdom of British and Indian Christians at the hands of the "violent" Indians. When the British reestablished control in 1858, the evangelical community in Britain, which had itself been growing in numbers and strength, rallied and sent an increasing number of missionaries who were more assertive in evangelistic message and methods.[32] As a result of their work, over the following decades more Indians converted to Christianity and more churches were established, particularly in urban centers.[33] The emergent impact of this missionary activity, however, went well beyond the addition of converts and churches. As the missionaries' efforts proceeded, their presence and work accelerated the emergence of various relational goods, evils, and logics.

Relational goods. There can be no doubt that, from the perspective of missionaries and Indian Christians themselves, Christianity brought about many relational goods. The churches that were established, though not

---

[30]For example, Webster says that during the first half of the nineteenth century in northwest India missionaries reported fewer than two hundred converts. John C. B. Webster, *A Social History of Christianity: North-west India Since 1800* (New Delhi: Oxford, 2007), 73.

[31]For a helpful summary of the uprising and the various factors contributing to it, see William Dalrymple, *The Last Mughal: The Fall of a Dynasty, Delhi, 1857* (New York: Penguin, 2006).

[32]For example, the Society for the Propagation of the Gospel in Foreign Parts (SPG), the mission organization of the Church of England, committed itself to doubling the number of missionaries and to focusing in particular on converting the educated classes of prominent cities. Stephen Neill, *A History of Christianity in India: 1707–1858* (New York: Cambridge University Press, 1985), 346.

[33]Again by example from northwest India, Webster says that the number of converts rose from 200 to 3,912 by 1881. Webster, *Social History of Christianity*, 117.

without various struggles, facilitated the message of salvation through Christ, created emotional and material support, and helped bring about many other outcomes that Indian Christians celebrated and for which they were proud. This, as we will discuss shortly, was particularly the case for Christians from Dalit castes, for whom Christianity and the Christian community provided a source of dignity. As one Dalit convert expressed it, "I wanted to become a Christian so I could be a man. None of us was a man. We were dogs. Only Jesus could make men out of us."[34]

Tensions, contradictions, and strategies of constraint. The interaction of a colonial and Western form of Christianity with other religions also created relational logics that in turn created evils of distrust, competition, conflict, and even violence that have unfortunately characterized the church and its reputation throughout India.

As missionaries, and particularly those who arrived after 1857, began to evangelize among Hindus, Muslims, and Sikhs, they brought with them the close association of Christianity with British culture. In their experience, evangelical Christianity had brought about many positive changes and reforms in English society. However, the conflation of Christianity with British society and culture meant that Christianity had indeed become thoroughly British and Western.[35] But could it not also be Indian? Certainly the missionaries thought so, though they understood this in a wide variety of ways. However, the answer was not as obvious to Hindus, Muslims, and Sikhs, particularly those who had been educated in British institutions. To many of them the thorough intertwining of Christianity with British nationality and Western culture in general, together with the missionary antipathy to other religions, invoked the belief that Christianity was a threat to Indian culture and religious traditions and thus needed to be resisted. As the century went on, the sense of rising anxiety was palpable, particularly among the more educated Hindus, Muslims, and Sikhs. For example, in 1894 the editor of a Punjabi Sikh newspaper wrote:

[34]J. W. Pickett, *Christian Mass Movements in India: A Study with Recommendations* (New York: Abingdon, 1933), 36.

[35]Andrew F. Walls, "The Evangelical Revival, the Missionary Movement, and Africa," in *The Missionary Movement in Christian History: Studies in the Transmission of Faith* (Maryknoll, NY: Orbis, 1996), 79-84.

An English newspaper writes that the Christian faith is making rapid progress and makes the prophecy that within the next twenty-five years, one-third of the Majha area will be Christian. The Malwa will follow suit. Just as we do not see any Buddhists in the country except in images, in the same fashion the Sikhs, who are now, here and there, visible in turbans and their other religious forms like wrist bangles and swords, will be seen only in pictures in museums. Their own sons and grandsons turning Christians and clad in coats and trousers and sporting toadstool-like caps will go to see them in the museums and say in their pidgin Punjabi: "Look, that is the picture of a Sikh—the tribe that inhabited this country once upon a time." Efforts of those who wish to resist the onslaught of Christianity are feeble and will prove abortive like a leper without hands and feet trying to save a boy falling off a rooftop.[36]

In this light missionaries were seen as those who sought to replace or destroy invaluable cultural and religious practices and identities. To invoke one idea—that Christianity should be accepted by India because it was the true religion—invoked the other—that Christianity should be resisted because it sought to destroy and supplant Indian religion and culture, which was being portrayed as false.

In terms of relational logics, this contradiction could potentially manifest as a constrained or a competitive contradiction, depending on the interests and approach of those involved. Missionary responses throughout the nineteenth and early twentieth centuries and their interaction with various religious movements illustrated both.

Many missionaries sought to shape the emerging logic as a constraining contradiction. In this, we may recall, two groups share various commitments and interests but are confronted with two ideas that are neither completely similar nor completely compatible. In the interest of preserving a certain level of unity and relations the parties seek to correct the other, make mutual concessions to minimize the differences, or in other ways seek to contain the conflict. One way some missionaries sought to address the contradiction was through their focus on social and economic development,

[36]Giani Ditt Singh, *The Khalsa Akhbar*, May 25, 1894, quoted in Nikky-Guninder Kaur Singh, *The Feminine Principle in the Sikh Vision of the Transcendent* (New York: Cambridge University Press, 1993), 153. It is unknown which English newspaper Singh refers to, or if such an article was even written. Regardless of its historical veracity, however, this account demonstrates what many Sikhs (and Hindus and Muslims) believed to be a primary objective of British Christians.

often expressed by the establishment of hospitals and schools. These educational and medical institutions, many of which grew to great prominence and exerted significant influence on Indian society well into the twentieth century, were for missionaries a demonstration of their desire to help India and a reflection of the social consciousness of a growing number of evangelicals in England.[37] If their religion, they would want to say, sought to eliminate certain cultural and religious traditions, it was only because Christianity and its related spiritual, social, and economic institutions were more beneficial to the development of society. In the missionaries' minds their presence and efforts were expressions of care and not of threat. In this way they hoped that their actions would help to affirm the truth of Christianity and "correct" the perception that Christianity was a threatening and destructive religion.

The efforts of various missionary Indologists, those who studied the languages, religious texts, and beliefs of Hinduism and other religions, represented another strategy to contain the contradiction.[38] Though most missionaries acquired knowledge of local languages and, to varying degrees, the beliefs of various religious communities, some took particular interest in scriptural languages, such as Sanskrit, studied and translated ancient scriptural texts, and learned from and engaged in discussions with religious leaders on these topics. One such person was the lay missionary John Muir, an employee of the British government in Bengal from 1829 to 1853 who was intensely interested in presenting the Christian faith to Hindus. Muir was convinced that the most effective way to do so was to refrain from characterizing other religions negatively and avoid engaging their adherents with the harsh and combative language that was typical of many of his missionary colleagues. In its stead, he argued, missionaries should use a conciliatory approach, discussing with educated Hindus the merits of religion, and ultimately the Christian religion, using Sanskrit. To this end he devoted himself to the study

---

[37] A particularly influential group in this regard was the Clapham sect, an evangelical wing of the Church of England founded by John Newton, which included social reformers such as William Wilberforce. Richard Fox Young, *Resistant Hinduism: Sanskrit Sources on Anti-Christian Apologetics in Early Nineteenth-Century India*, Publications of the De Nobili Research Library 8 (Leiden: Brill, 1981), 51-52.

[38] We use the title Indologists to refer to those who were academically trained in Indian languages and texts and employed at universities, as well as those who studied these on the field and as a part of other vocations, often missionaries and British East India employees.

of Sanskrit and published a five-volume series on Sanskrit texts, as well as a work called *Matapariksha*, "The Investigation of Religions."[39] Muir's more conciliatory approach was viewed with skepticism by many of his evangelical colleagues while his clearly evangelical concern to demonstrate the truth of Christianity provoked hostile responses from various educated Hindus.[40]

A later example of someone who took such an approach was Dr. H. D. Griswold, a missionary in India from 1890 to 1926 who studied Sanskrit at Oxford and Vedic religion under Max Weber in Berlin. Though critical of the way in which certain Hindu groups, such as the Arya Samaj, interpreted Hindu texts, Griswold expressed great appreciation for these groups' attempts to develop and reform Indian society and promote Hindu teachings.[41] Webster summarizes the approach of Griswold and similar missionaries: "Instead of juxtaposing Christianity as true and Hindu religion as false, they offered a much more positive assessment of Hinduism's moral and spiritual power."[42] Thus, though missionaries such as Muir and Griswold affirmed some distinctions between Christianity and Hinduism, they sought to minimize the sense of threat that was emerging.

Strategies of competition. While some missionaries saw a contradiction that could be constrained (that Christianity was good for India and that Christianity sought to displace Indian religion and culture), most missionaries saw a contradiction that could only be competitive. True to the nature of a competitive contradiction, these missionaries saw two contradictory claims—that, according to their Enlightenment standards of reasoning, Christianity was the true religion and therefore the best religion for India and that Hinduism and other religions were detrimental for India. Typical of this approach were missionaries who found Hinduism, Islam, Sikhism, and other Indian religions to be illogical and barbaric, and representative of the depravity of Indian culture that needed to be displaced by Christianity in order to raise India to its full potential. It was only natural that in response many Indians who valued their religious traditions could not accept the missionaries' premise.

---

[39]Neill, *History of Christianity in India*, 373.
[40]Young, *Resistant Hinduism*, 59.
[41]Webster, *Social History of Christianity*, 141-43.
[42]Webster, *Social History of Christianity*, 143.

One of the prominent results and expressions of this contradiction was the emergence of religious reform movements. As missionaries promoted religious competition through their activities and conversions, Hindu, Sikh, and Muslim religious reform movements started to emerge throughout North India.[43] The history and origin of each of these groups is unique, but all shared a commitment to counter the Christian missionary rhetoric and "threat" and to defend and strengthen their respective religious community over against each other and Christians.[44] The leaders of these groups utilized the latest technological innovations, such as developments in print communication and commerce, to organize and mobilize more followers.[45] Ironically, groups that for centuries had had no clear religious profile, and that had often lived peacefully with other religious groups, began to assert their newly developed identity—sometimes even with violence.

The agents involved in competitive contradictions usually pursue some form of victory and the elimination of the other and its power. However, as Margaret Archer shows, the unintended consequence is usually "ideational pluralism" or sustained differentiation.[46] In the emerging religious identities of North India, the various religious groups sustained their differentiation by increasing structural and cultural boundaries between each other. On the one hand, this resulted in certain outcomes that many eventually regarded as positive. For example, the increase in religious pluralism, and people's awareness of that pluralism, in many ways aided in the eventual emergence of a secular state.[47]

On the other hand, Christianity was seen to be in competition with important aspects of Indian religion and identity, including an emerging Indian nationalism. The burgeoning nineteenth- and early-twentieth-century nationalist movement often appealed to India's religious traditions

---

[43]Webster, *Social History of Christianity*, 135. Five of these coalesced into associations and helped set the stage for further organizations. These included the Brahmo Samaj (1863), the Anjuman-i-Punjab (1865), the Anjuman-i-Islamia (1869), the Amritsar Singh Sabha (1873), and the Arya Samaj (1877).

[44]Bauman, "Hindu-Christian Conflict in India," 637.

[45]Harjot Oberoi, *The Construction of Religious Boundaries: Culture, Identity and Diversity in the Sikh Tradition* (Delhi: Oxford University Press, 1994), 303.

[46]Archer, *Being Human*, 176.

[47]Robert Woodberry, "The Missionary Roots of Liberal Democracy," *American Political Science Review* 106, no. 2 (2012): 268.

to help unify Indians against the British and Christian imperial power. As a result, Indian Christians were characterized more and more as adherents of a foreign religion that was "unIndian."[48]

Another development that added to the sense of competition and the emergence of the Indian church's otherness was its association with the Dalit castes. This was rooted in the church's early interaction with caste communities. In the mid to late nineteenth century the nature of the Christian community underwent a dramatic change as hundreds of thousands of Dalits became Christian as a result of indigenous mass conversion movements. These movements were initially begun by itinerant Indian Christians who worked independently of any mission oversight and whose "informal agency" mobilized many along family networks.[49] Exponential growth occurred over the coming decades such that between 1881 and 1911 the Christian population throughout India doubled from 0.7 percent to 1.4 percent of the Indian population, with nearly 1.5 million adherents, the majority of whom were from Dalit castes.[50]

The mass conversion of Dalits to Christianity dramatically impacted the character and identity of Christianity in India. Missionaries and the growing church affirmed the unique way in which Christianity could respond to and address the needs of the oppressed Dalits. In addition, with the large numbers of Dalits and their unique social and education needs, missionaries and Dalit Indian pastors oriented their teaching and efforts toward those particular needs. One of the results of this was that the identity of Christianity in these areas became tied to the Dalit community. Because of this close identification of Christianity with the Dalit community, non-Dalit Hindus began to articulate and embrace another competitive contradiction: the missionaries' claim that Christianity was for all Indians versus the non-Dalit Hindu observation that Christianity was the religion of the Dalits. Thus, as missionaries embraced the idea that God was saving the Dalits and

---

[48]Webster, *Social History of Christianity*, 146; Mrinalini Sebastian, "Vamps and Villains or Citizen-Subjects?: Converting a Third-Person Self-Conception of the Indian Christians into a First-Person Narrative," *Studies in World Christianity* 16, no. 2 (2010): 119-20.

[49]Christopher Harding, *Religious Transformation in South Asia: The Meanings of Conversion in Colonial Punjab* (New York: Oxford University Press, 2008), 248.

[50]A. P. Joshi, M. D. Srinivas, and J. K. Bajaj, *Religious Demography of India: A Summary* (Chennai: Centre for Policy Studies, 2003), 8-9.

created churches and efforts that supported this notion, they unintentionally invoked the contradictory message that Christianity was not the religion of non-Dalit Hindus.

There is, of course, much to celebrate in the contemporary Indian church, its practices, theologies, and identity. And the foregoing is a necessarily brief analysis of one aspect of its history and identity. However, the emergent identity of the Indian church as foreign and Dalit is one that continues to shape the church's witness and interactions, bringing with it various goods and evils—that can helpfully be analyzed as the results of complex emergent processes.

SUMMARY: THE CHURCH(ES) EMERGING

Our primarily sociological focus has considered the ways in which churches are emergent: that they arise out of people's interactions with each other in the midst of particular contexts. In North India the church emerged with many relational goods—valued qualities that could only come from the collective commitments and relationships of its people among themselves and with God. However, interactions between groups, whether between missionaries and Indians, or Dalit Christians and non-Dalit Hindus, caused the emergence of various relational logics that were not fully predictable or anticipated. This resulted in an ecclesial identity of the Indian church as foreign and other, an identity that Indian churches still face to this day. In the next chapter we will turn to various case studies, including one from India, where churches and their leaders are seeking to reframe the encounter between Christ-followers and their non-Christian religious communities. In doing so they engage a reverse hermeneutic to reinterpret the nature of the church for their context and counter the existing beliefs and structures of church that have emerged.

4

....

The Church Emerging
Among Other Religions

Case Studies

Up to this point our argument has sought to make two major points. One is that the shape a church takes is deeply influenced by its cultural situation and the values and priorities of that setting, something that we sought to illustrate through the various periods of the history of "church." We have employed the notion of reverse hermeneutic to describe this situation. That is, prevailing notions of human solidarity have, in large part, determined believers' reading of Scripture with respect to how disciples of Jesus form themselves into communities. Of course, Scripture has often pushed back against these ideas, but these prevailing assumptions have provided the necessary starting point and continuing context in which those Scriptures have been read and interpreted. This has been illustrated by the short summaries of developing ideas of church in the West, in chapter two.

The second point of our argument is that the dynamic processes of formation of these communities over time are best understood in terms of emergence theory. This point was developed in chapter three. As people relate to each other and to the gospel from their own cultural situations, there often emerge new entities, including new ideas or understandings, new senses of togetherness and corporate identity, and eventually new social forms or institutions by which to sustain these. As we saw, social groups like churches are reliant on the contributions and perspectives of individual members, but they cannot be reduced to these since these combine to create something that is not always entirely predictable. However, all emergent groups have some general characteristics, including various relational goods, evils, and logics that emerge from their being together. Also, when groups of people relate to each other, whether missionaries and local believers or Christ-followers and their Hindu, Muslim, or other religious family and community, certain new ideas, forms, goods, evils, and logics emerge.

In this chapter we develop both points further by exploring several contemporary situations and the cultural manifestations of church that have emerged, or are emerging, in these places. This exploration also will discover and interrogate ways in which those settings have encouraged or obstructed the emergence of a stable entity that can reasonably be called a church. This review carries forward the assumption we are making that the possibilities for the emergence of church in any place are dependent in large part on reigning assumptions of what human community looks like—its limits and its possibilities.

The discussion in chapter two concluded with the claim that the idea of church that evangelical missionaries took with them was deeply influenced by the notion of communities formed as voluntary societies, which in turn was influenced by the dissenting church tradition whose roots were in the Protestant Reformation. The two aspects of this tradition that we highlighted were the right of private judgment resting on Luther's notion of the priesthood of all believers and the application of this to commitment to a gathered church community, evident in the Radical Reformation—Mennonite, Quaker, and later the free church traditions. These ideas we argued are products of the Reformation and its subsequent history in the West and were taken as normative by evangelical (Protestant) missionaries.

In that chapter we noted some of the benefits that resulted from these ideas in the missionary movement while also calling attention to the drawbacks when the formation of church was believed necessarily to reflect these ideas. We pick up the story in this chapter. While a survey of the emergence of churches worldwide is obviously beyond our scope, it is safe to say that the places where the church is growing the fastest are sites where the notion of church as a voluntary society has taken root—something that is especially evident in the Pentecostal movement of the last century. One thinks, for example, of the burgeoning Protestant churches of the Philippines (except in the south, as we will see), in Africa, and in the house churches of China.[1]

---

[1]Mark Noll, in *The New Shape of World Christianity: How American Experience Reflects Global Faith* (Downers Grove, IL: InterVarsity Press, 2009), develops this connection between the church as voluntary society and the majority churches, as a positive good that allows various people groups

There are clearly places where this model of church has, for various historical and cultural reasons, been resisted, and these places will be the object of our attention in this chapter. As a representative selection, we focus here on Japan, North India, Indonesia, and Mindanao (southern Philippines). In these places alternative assumptions of community and association, mostly based on non-Christian religious traditions, have made the emergence of the church as a voluntary society difficult or, in some cases, impossible. This raises the question we explore in this chapter: What alternative forms of church might be possible, and indeed may be emerging in these places, and what might we learn from their journey to be the church?

THE STRUGGLE TO BE THE CHURCH IN JAPAN

As is well known, Christianity in Japan, after an initial period of success in the sixteenth and seventeenth centuries, has struggled to find a foothold. In contrast to its neighbor Korea, where Protestant Christians make up 15-20 percent of the population, Christians in Japan compose only 1 percent of the population.[2] The earlier success of the Catholic mission led to large numbers of conversions, perhaps as many as 300,000 by the beginning of the Tokugawa period (1603-1637), but eventually this attracted the attention of the shogun, who violently suppressed the Christian movement. This story is best known, both in Japan and the West, from the post-World War II novel by Shūsaku Endō (b. 1923), *Silence*.[3] The popularity of this book and the widespread discussion caused by the Japanese version of the film adaptation have caused some observers to suggest that Japanese disinterest in Christianity has less to do with the person of Christ than with imported forms of Christianity.

It has been widely assumed that this persecution was so severe that it left no trace of Christianity, which did not reappear in Japan until the mid nineteenth century when Admiral Matthew Perry's visit opened Japan to

---

to develop their own expressions of Christianity.

[2]Sung-Sup Kim, "Evangelicalism and Empire: Evangelicals in Korea and Japan Under Japanese Imperialism" (paper presented to Evangelical Studies Section of the American Academy of Religion, San Antonio, TX, November 19, 2016), 1.

[3]Shūsaku Endō, *Silence: A Novel*, trans. William Johnston (New York: Picador, 2016; first published in Japanese under the title *Chinmoku* by Monumenta Nipponica, 1969). This novel was made into a major motion picture by Martin Scorsese, released December 2016.

the West. But this has been recently questioned by Makoto Fujimura among others.[4] Fujimura, an artist trained in Japan in the ancient Nihonga style of painting, came to the Christian faith while studying in Tokyo. He has reflected on the troubled history of Christianity in Japan and argued that Christianity did survive in the form of small groups of "hidden Christians," which nineteenth-century missionaries discovered. But more importantly, he asserts that the violent suppression of Christianity left a scarred memory that constitutes both a continuing tension and an untapped opportunity for religious life in Japan—a tension and an opportunity that Fujimura has himself experienced and explored as a Japanese artist who is also a Christian.[5]

The history that unfolds in Japan, Fujimura argues, is not a pagan culture but a "Christ-hidden culture."[6] This is evident both in the history of hidden Christians and more recently in the large numbers of novelists and culture influencers present in post–World War II Japan. Out of the ashes and suffering of that war, Fujimura sees the potential for Japan becoming the soil that can nurture reconciliation among people, and between people and nature, through the influence of this crypto-Christian presence.[7] But this can only happen, he thinks, if the Japanese people learn to celebrate the Christ already present in their culture and freely respond in a way their history has conspired to block.

Why is it Japanese find Christ so attractive while they resist the structures of Christianity? One answer involves the Western understanding of religion and Christianity introduced by missionaries and Western-educated scholars and the interaction of these concepts with Japanese understandings of Shinto in Japan. When Shinto was established as the national ideology and tradition (*kokutai*) of Japan in the Meiji Imperial Constitution of 1889, it was specifically designated a "nonreligion." That is, though it established the emperor as a god-figure with a royal-priestly role and mandated that all citizens worship at Shinto shrines, these were beliefs and practices that were

---

[4]Makoto Fujimura, *Silence and Beauty: A Faith Born of Suffering* (Downers Grove, IL: InterVarsity Press, 2016). The book is a reflection on the tensions and implications of Endō's famous novel. Fujimura served as a consultant for Scorsese's film.

[5]Fujimura, *Silence and Beauty*, 44-45.

[6]Fujimura, *Silence and Beauty*, 197.

[7]Fujimura, *Silence and Beauty*, 201.

meant to unite all of Japan, reflect a common national heritage, and transcend other religious differences.

Framing Shinto as a nonreligion became particularly important in light
of the recent influence of Western missionaries and scholars. Western missionaries, as was common in other mission contexts, brought with them an
understanding of what a religion was and how it should operate based on
their own Judeo-Christian understanding of religion. But missionaries were
not the only ones to do this. With the Meiji Restoration of 1868 Japan sought
to implement various reforms, many based on Western models. One such
initiative was the establishment of universities featuring Western and
Western-educated scholars. As some of these analyzed Japanese traditions,
particularly those focused on ritual and concepts of the supernatural, they
applied Judeo-Christian categories of religion, similar to what missionaries
were doing. However, traditional Shinto, particularly as understood and
practiced by Shinto priests and authorities, did not directly correspond to
Western categories of a religion with a systematized doctrine and a sphere
of existence that could be separated from government, national, family, or
any other identity.[8]

Another reform of the Meiji Restoration was the promotion of freedom
of religion, something that Emperor Meiji and the Japanese authorities initially saw as important in their overall goal of modernization. This was a
move that Western missionaries obviously also supported as it helped them
frame a choice between Christianity and other religions, including Shinto.
However, as Meiji and Shinto authorities began to understand more fully
the Western notion of religion, they concluded that Shinto was wider and
more encompassing than a religion and that other so-called religions could
theoretically operate within Shinto. As Jun'ichi Isomae points out, the government eventually "recognized the incompatibility between doctrinally
oriented religious concepts and Shintō's own practice-oriented characteristics and, boldly turning the tables, sought to reposition Shintō outside the
scope of the Western concept of religion."[9] Notice that, for these, religion (as

[8]As Isomae shows, Japanese authorities and scholars briefly attempted to systematize Shinto doctrine in the early 1870s but were unable to reach a consensus. Jun'ichi Isomae, "The Conceptual
Formation of the Category 'Religion' in Modern Japan: Religion, State, Shintō," *Journal of Religion
in Japan* 1, no. 3 (2012): 239-40.
[9]Isomae, "Conceptual Formation of the Category 'Religion' in Modern Japan," 239-40.

presented via Western Christian understandings) was primarily about teaching and doctrine, which, in their minds, inadequately captured the essence of Shinto.[10]

This publicly offered reverence for Japanese identity and nationality was framed as public morality whereas religions such as Buddhism and Christianity were understood to reside in the familial and private domain respectively.[11] Christian missionaries, however, contested this interpretation of Shinto and its relation to Christianity. For them, Shinto should be considered a religion on a par with Christianity, which competed for people's loyalty to Christ. Thus, early in the modern period, Christianity as presented by Western missionaries and scholars was perceived to be potentially harmful to Japanese identity.[12] We can see here the presence of a type of competitive contradiction that emerged from the interaction of missionary Christians and the Japanese elite, not unlike the interaction and emergence of a similar contradiction in the Indian context that we discussed in the previous chapter. As in the Indian context, with the growing presence of a foreign-oriented Christian church, there emerged the perception that Christianity was a religion of foreigners that was potentially harmful to Japanese culture and identity.

Following World War II, in conjunction with policies designed to reform Japan along Western democratic lines, General Douglas MacArthur ordered that Shinto, along with its reverence of the Japanese emperor, no longer be considered the national tradition. Shinto was instead separated from the government and reclassified a voluntary religion alongside other traditions, reflecting the prevailing Western view of religions. Despite this, many Japanese have continued to view Shinto as essentially nonreligious,[13] contributing to

---

[10]This is evident in the etymology of the words for *religion, Christianity* and other religious traditions, versus that for *Shintō*. The words for *religion* (*shūkyō*), *Christianity* (*Kirisuto-kyō*), Buddhism (*Bukkyō*), and several of the so-called "New Religions" (e.g. *Tenrikyō*) all contain the suffix *kyō*, meaning "teach," or "teachings." By contrast, the suffix in *Shintō* (*tō*) is usually translated "way." The implication is that Shinto is a tradition to be practiced, not a doctrine to be believed. Our thanks to Dr. Robert Enns for this observation.

[11]Isomae, "Conceptual Formation of the Category 'Religion' in Modern Japan," 237.

[12]S.-S. Kim, "Evangelicalism and Empire," 4, 5. All the while, Kim notes, embracing the Western technology they associated with Christianity!

[13]Aike P. Rots, "Shinto's Modern Transformations: From Imperial Cult to Nature Worship," in *Routledge Handbook of Religions in Asia*, ed. Bryan S. Turner and Oscar Salemink (New York: Routledge, 2015), 132.

what Yoshio Sugimoto summarizes as Japan's "non-exclusivist, eclectic, [and] syncretic" spiritual/religious impulses. In practice, people commonly assume it is possible to pay tribute to Shintoism, visit Buddhist temples, and marry in a Christian church.[14] Perhaps this casual attitude toward religion is best understood in terms of what Sugimoto calls a "friendly authoritarianism," a set of social norms that is not imposed by external institutions but that people learn and internalize and that guides them to view social regimentation as something that is natural. As Sugimoto describes this: "Japanese society has various forms of regimentation that are designed to standardize the thought patterns and attitudes of the Japanese and make them toe the line in everyday life."[15] This means that it is acceptable to see different "religions" as not necessarily in competition with one another but rather as serving different and important functions in life. It also means, he notes, that spontaneous actions, or the free expressions of individuals, are discouraged. Obviously, the idea that individuals can freely choose to join exclusive religious communities would appear difficult or impossible to accept.

So what might a church of Christ-followers look like in such a setting? What are its possibilities? Of course Japanese churches have existed for nearly two hundred years. However, as we have noted, these churches have remained a small, minority religion, often taking the form of various denominations imported from the West. Japanese Christ-followers have explained and sought to address this in two different ways. The first and most prominent has been to compare Japanese Christianity with Korean Christianity, citing the different ways in which each responded to political and cultural institutions. In a recent analysis Sung-Sup Kim, a Korean scholar working in Japan, argues that while evangelicals in Korea, with their separation of church and state, succeeded in siding with the people against the (imperial) authority, they were unable to do this in Japan.[16]

As Japanese preparations for war gathered strength in the late 1930s, the authority of the emperor over religion tightened with the passing of the Religious Groups Act (1939/40), which forced all Christians to join together

---

[14]Yoshio Sugimoto, *An Introduction to Japanese Society*, 2nd ed. (Port Melbourne, Australia: Cambridge University Press, 2003), 256. Sugimoto acknowledges that Buddhist temples are now largely tourist attractions.

[15]Sugimoto, *Introduction to Japanese Society*, 271.

[16]S.-S. Kim, "Evangelicalism and Empire."

in a single United Church of Japan in 1941. Many Christians, anxious for official acceptance by the larger culture, initially welcomed this move as potentially a way of dispelling the foreign identification of Christianity that had emerged over the previous century. But even those within this unified church were not immune to the persecution that followed and were confronted with difficult choices, particularly regarding what it meant to offer allegiance to the emperor.[17] In emergence terms, the existing church's interaction with the imperial cult created a constraining contradiction, central to which was a contradictory understanding of loyalty. As we saw in the last chapter, one of the potential outcomes of this relational logic is a correction of one side or the other. Regarding whether and how to show loyalty to the emperor, most Christians eased the contradiction by agreeing with the Meiji definition of Shinto as a nonreligion involving worshiping at the Shinto shrine.[18] Much like the Christians forced to honor the führer's leadership over the so-called German Church in 1930s Germany, this command to pay tribute carried such weight as to make it a religious observance.[19] Ironically, however, this deference did little to correct the overall perception of Christianity as un-Japanese, for the church continued to define itself as a separate religion and community, albeit one that was friendly to the emperor.

Post-war churches have since criticized this decision as a case of siding with the emperor against the best interests of the Japanese people. In light of this, a growing group of clergy is currently promoting a "theology of Japan," which laments the loss of the prophetic voice during that earlier period.[20] Interestingly, Sugimoto notes that Japanese culture has always tolerated an alternate culture of dissent, groups located on the margin of Japanese culture that challenged the assumed patterns of life.[21] Recent generations of Christians are seeking to claim this space.

---

[17]S.-S. Kim, "Evangelicals and Empire," 7. Kim points out that Japanese Christians earlier had been unable to sympathize with the Korean Christian's struggle for independence from the imperial Japanese rule. See also pp. 1-12.

[18]S.-S. Kim, "Evangelicals and Empire," 10.

[19]Also as in Germany, only a small group of conservative Christians in Japan resisted the emperor's command. Following Christ for this group meant resisting the call to uncritical support for the emperor.

[20]S. -S. Kim, "Evangelicals and Empire," 12.

[21]Sugimoto, *Introduction to Japanese Society*, 261.

But there is another possible response to this situation. Notice how the various Christian responses to Shinto and the emperor accept without question some fundamental assumptions about the nature of religion and church as it relates to Japanese Shinto culture. In this, Christianity and its community (church) are seen as a separate community, based on the Western model of a confessional and free church, which is set against and in tension with Japanese Shinto culture. Whereas some of this tension, such as that created by revering/worshiping the emperor, may have been unavoidable, some Christ-followers have at times challenged these assumptions by pursuing alternatives to traditional forms of church. As early as 1901, a "non-church" movement was surfacing that sought to blend *bushidō* (traditional moral principles) with a Confucian form of Christianity.[22] Around the same time, other new religious movements began to form, seeking to reject Western forms.[23] Prominent among these was Toyohiko Kagawa's Friends of Jesus movement that arose in the 1920s, something widely reported outside of Japan but controversial inside.[24] After a dramatic religious encounter Kagawa devoted himself to the poor and supported his movement through the sales of his popular autobiographical novel. His call was to "start with Jesus and not creeds."[25] Kagawa envisioned a social movement rather than a new church, and the "order" he founded soon spread into all the existing denominations, providing, he hoped, a force for renewal. Soon, however, he realized a social movement alone would have little impact and began to seek converts in a more traditional sense while holding to his social vision. The groups he formed included mutual aid and cooperatives.[26] While he succeeded in attracting large crowds, few actually joined the churches as a result. Kagawa's heritage was tarnished by his autocratic style and, at best, resulted more in a reform and revitalization than in any new form of church.

But one suspects the crowds he drew, like the avid readers of the Catholic postwar novelists, found the person of Christ attractive, even though this

---

[22]See Carlo Caldarola, *Christianity the Japanese Way* (Leiden: Brill, 1979).

[23]A good survey of these movements is found in Mark R. Mullins, "Christianity as a Transnational Social Movement: Kagawa Toyohiko and the Friends of Jesus," *Japanese Religions,* 32, nos. 1 & 2 (2005): 69-87.

[24]Mullins, "Christianity as a Transnational Social Movement," 70.

[25]Mullins, "Christianity as a Transnational Social Movement," 76.

[26]Mullins, "Christianity as a Transnational Social Movement," 81.

did not result in new structures. In like manner, a few Christ-followers in Japan are stepping outside of the institutional church and beginning to fully embrace and participate in Shinto as a Japanese tradition while encouraging fellow Japanese to listen and follow the teachings of Christ.[27] It is too soon to tell what new ecclesial practices and community may emerge from this interaction. Meanwhile, the current model of church in its combination of confessional and free-church structure continues to struggle to find a voice for an effective witness.

CHRIST DEVOTEES (*KHRIST BHAKTAS*) IN NORTH INDIA

In the last chapter we discussed the emergence of the Christian church in India, with a focus particularly on some of the contradictory identities Christianity came to represent in the north. One of these was the perception of Christianity's foreignness and otherness that resulted from its colonial heritage. In response, numerous Christ-followers and churches have sought to correct or constrain the tensions that Christianity experiences in its relationship to other religions. An example of this in North India has emerged in the city of Benares (Varanasi). The Catholic ashram of Matridham, which means "abode of the Mother," lies on the outskirts of the city in the midst of a neighborhood called Christ Nagar (Christ town). The name of the area tells of the Christian presence and activity of primarily Catholic workers since at least the 1950s. The ashram too had its start in and remains a part of a particular Catholic branch called the Indian Missionary Society (IMS).

Many in the Roman Catholic Church in India have long advocated for the inculturation, or contextualization, of its buildings and services.[28] Starting in the 1920s Catholics (and Protestants) began to establish Catholic ashrams, or hermitage retreat centers, designed after the model of the Hindu ashram as inculturated forms of Christian monasteries. This movement

---

[27]This raises the complicated question of ancestors and Japanese identity, which we cannot pursue here. For more on this point see Simon Chan's discussion of Pentecostal-sourced Japanese indigenous church movements that are encouraging prayer and baptism for the dead. Simon Chan, *Grassroots Asian Theology: Thinking the Faith from the Ground Up* (Downers Grove, IL: InterVarsity Press, 2014), 173-74.

[28]*Inculturation* is often used by Catholic scholars as a parallel concept to *contextualization*. Both terms began to be used at the same time in their respective circles in the early 1970s. For a Catholic overview of *inculturation*, see Peter Schineller, "Inculturation: A Difficult and Delicate Task," *International Bulletin of Missionary Research* 20, no. 3 (1996): 109-12.

gained momentum from Vatican II but began to lose its appeal by the 1990s with the rise of Dalit theology and Hindu activism.[29] Though such inculturation efforts dropped off in number and popularity among Catholics toward the end of the twentieth century, some Catholic priests have continued and sustained the work of contextual ashrams, including Matridham.

The vision for Matridham, when it began, was similar to many other Catholic ashrams: to be a novitiate that also fostered experimentation and dialogue around the intersection of the Catholic faith and aspects of Indian Hindu culture. As such, Matridham and other Catholic ashrams, though adapting local and Hindu forms and vocabulary, clearly identified themselves as Catholic. However, starting in the 1990s several people and movements came together such that an altogether different type of ecclesial expression began to emerge at Matridham.

Part of the backdrop to this new expression of church was evangelism, undertaken by various Indian Catholic, Protestant, and Pentecostal missionaries and pastors in the surrounding villages. The people in the villages had begun to learn of the Christian message from some of these missionary/pastors even though many of the villagers did not fully accept the message or come to gatherings.[30]

A further influence, mentioned above, was the leadership given by Catholic priests who were concerned that Christianity should look more authentically Indian. Though not all indigenizing Catholics were evangelists or motivated by evangelism, those that came to Matridham clearly were, and they began visiting villages to get to know the inhabitants, to pray for them, and to share the gospel with them.

A third factor was the arrival of charismatic Catholics. In October 1993 a group of Catholics from The Divine Center, a charismatic Catholic center in Kerala, South India, conducted a three-day convention regarding charismatic spirituality. In partnership with Pentecostal Protestants, they

---

[29]For a history of the ashram movement and analysis of its decline, see Xavier Gravend-Tirole, "From Christian Ashrams to Dalit Theology—or Beyond?: An Examination of the Indigenisation/Inculturation Trend Within the Indian Catholic Church," in *Constructing Indian Christianities: Culture, Conversion and Caste*, ed. Chad M. Bauman and Richard Fox Young (New Delhi: Routledge, 2014), 110-37.

[30]Kerry P. C. San Chirico, "Between Christian and Hindu: *Krist Bhaktas*, Catholics and the Negotiation of Devotion in the Banaras Region," in Bauman and Young, *Constructing Indian Christianities*, 31.

held prayer meetings for the sick at Matridham and at the nearby cathedral. People came from the nearby villages, many of whom received healings, and the word spread among the villages about what was occurring at the ashram.[31]

The following year one of the leaders of that team, Father Anil Dev, became the *acharya*, or guru, of the ashram. Since that time, under his leadership and that of the other priests, the ashram has developed prayer and worship services that emphasize healing, preaching about Jesus, and reading from the Bible, utilizing the forms and vocabulary of Hindu devotional spirituality (*bhakti*).

Though these influences help to make Matridham nearly unique among other Catholic ashrams, it is one particular practice—or, to be more accurate, the absence of a particular practice—that sets it apart: that of baptism. For a variety of reasons Matridham priests refuse to baptize people, unless they submit to a lengthy process, which few are able to complete. We will explore the reasons for this in a moment, but what emerges from this is a blurring of religious lines. Since baptism in India represents for many the social and legal marker signifying a change of religions,[32] those who come to Matridham for prayer and worship, and even worship Christ in their homes, are considered Hindus, both by the Indian government and by the priests themselves.[33] This combination of charismatic worship with Hindu devotional spirituality—around the person of Jesus but without the attendant pressure or requirement to "convert," or change religions—attracts upwards of five thousand *Khrist bhaktas*, or Christ devotees, to come to Matridham for worship services each week.[34]

---

[31]San Chirico, "Between Christian and Hindu," 35.

[32]Hindus, Muslims, and Christians have separate civil laws pertaining to marriage, divorce, guardianship, and succession. At birth each person is placed into a civil religious category for legal purposes. Persons who undergo Christian baptism are required to notify the government (or, in many states, to notify the government before being baptized) to change their legal religious status.

[33]For the *Khrist bhaktas* themselves and their immediate neighbors their identity is perhaps more fluid. *Bhakta* families sometimes keep symbols such as pictures of Jesus or crosses in prominent places in their houses and wear a cross or rosary. In these ways they identify and are perhaps identified as somehow not fully Hindu. However, they also often have Hindu priests conduct their marriages and in other ways identify with the Hindu community. Ciril J. Kuttiyanikkal, *Khrist Bhakta Movement: A Model for an Indian Church?: Inculturation in the Area of Community Building* (Berlin: Lit Verlag, 2014), 167, 82.

[34]Father Prem Antony, a priest with the Indian Missionary Society, estimates that 3,000-5,000 come for the Sunday gatherings and approximately 7,000 attend the monthly daylong *satsang* with its

Despite this blending of religious identities, Matridham itself and its priests still maintain a clear Catholic identity as seen in many of their symbols and rituals, including the Eucharist. In this way Matridham is unique from other movements we review here and that have been discussed in some of the literature on "insider movements," who often maintain few if any formal links to established Christian churches.

Yet, by the estimation of the *bhaktas* themselves and the priests who lead them, Matridham shares many characteristics of other "insider" groups who want to see a new model for church emerge in their context, one that eschews the contradictions that have hampered its growth in the past. In their studies on Matridham, Kerry P. C. San Chirico and C. J. Kuttiyanikkal identify some of what Father Anil Dev and others at the ashram hope for. First, the fathers have a desire for their people to experience a vibrant spirituality and faith. One way to do this, in their estimation, is to de-emphasize baptism.[35] It is interesting to note that they do not explain this de-emphasis primarily on the basis of contemporary debates about conversion, which are often quite heated. It is not, they argue, that they want to avoid being persecuted by more fundamentalist Hindus who oppose religious conversion. Rather, the fathers are disheartened by the nominalism of some in the Catholic Church and see the *Khrist bhaktas* as having a "genuine faith" that challenges the Catholic Church in a positive way. While not anticipated, the relationship of charismatic worship and Hindu bhakti devotion has allowed a vibrant faith to emerge that does not precisely fit the social categories of Christian church or Hindu sect. It occupies a space between these, intersecting and drawing from them while representing something new.

Interestingly, the priests do not see the lack of baptism as a hindrance to becoming part of the church. As Kuttiyanikkal summarizes the viewpoint of one priest, "For him [the priest], although they [*Khrist bhaktas*] are not the body of Christ through sacraments, they are his body through faith. He wants to consider this movement as a Church with a difference. For him, it

---

focus on lengthy worship and healing prayer. Prem Antony, "The Khrist Bhakta Way: A New Way of Being the Church," in *The Emerging Challenges to Christian Mission Today*, ed. S. M. Michael and Jose Joseph (New Delhi: Ishvani Kendra and Christian World Imprints, 2016), 235-36.

[35]Kuttiyanikkal, *Khrist Bhakta Movement*, 156; and San Chirico, "Between Christian and Hindu," 38.

is the Church of the future."[36] Here again devotionalism, so typical in the Hindu *bhakti* tradition, becomes a type of sacrament that, though not officially endorsed by the church, is seen—when guided by the Holy Spirit—to serve an ecclesial function similar to baptism.

Second, and related to this, the priests are strongly motivated by evangelism. This motivation was not always found in other Catholic ashrams, which were often established out of a desire to model a new type of Christian faith and to foster interreligious dialogue in the midst of a shared ascetic/monastic context. But even these have been subject to intense criticism by more conservative Hindus, charging that Catholics are appropriating Hindu symbols in order to lure in and convert unsuspecting Hindus.[37] The Matridham fathers hold these realities in tension; they adamantly and truthfully refute accusations that they are converting people since they do not readily baptize and thus allow their people to remain Hindu. But, they also hold evangelism—the proclaiming of Jesus and his message—to be of highest importance and want people to become devoted to him.[38] In emergence terms, the fathers are acknowledging the presence of a tension or contradiction in their context; the gospel is a message that calls for people to make a decisive turn to Jesus and that some may find threatening to Indian-Hindu identity. The purpose of their ashram, they would acknowledge, is to encourage people to become Christ-followers. However, they refuse to let the contradiction become competitive (where one side "wins" against the other) and instead seek to correct aspects of both arguments. Following Christ does not mean leaving one's Hindu family and tradition, and Hinduism can fully include those who fully devote themselves to Christ.

Third, the priests see their work not only in terms of its impact on people's faith but also as a way of preserving their Indian heritage. As they observe the moral, technological, and cultural changes that are occurring across India, many driven by increased internationalization, the priests view

---

[36]Kuttiyanikkal, *Khrist Bhakta Movement*, 156; see also San Chirico, "Between Christian and Hindu," 39-40.

[37]Sita Ram Goel, for example, accused the Catholic ashrams and their gurus of being "swindlers" who designed ashrams in order to convert Hindus. Sita Ram Goel, *Catholic Ashrams: Sannyasins or Swindlers?*, 2nd ed. (New Delhi: Voice of India, 1994).

[38]Kuttiyanikkal, *Khrist Bhakta Movement*, 173; and San Chirico, "Between Christian and Hindu," 33-34.

Matridham as providing strength to Indians in general and to *Khrist bhaktas* in particular to resist forces that would undermine traditional Indian values and culture.[39] Thus they see themselves not only as evangelizing people to Jesus but as evangelizing the culture back to its Indian roots and heritage.

The church that emerges from this unique relationship of Hindu devotionalism and charismatic Catholic spirituality has several unique features. One, as we have begun to note, is an aesthetic devotionalism focused on Christ but immersed in Hindu-style poetry, images, and rituals. Many of these same aesthetics and rituals also echo Catholic elements. For example, the ritual of procession is one familiar to both Hindus and Catholics. Thus, on Good Friday thousands of Hindus come to Matridham to take part in a *parikrama*—a Hindu procession that circumnavigates a holy area. But in this case the procession follows an image of Christ around the ashram, periodically stopping for healing prayer in Christ's name.[40] In addition, though Matridham in some ways looks similar to the voluntary-society model of church that we have seen in so many places, it also functions in ways that are more traditionally Hindu, even allowing those who desire it to maintain a Hindu communal identity. For example, it is common for families to have their *ishta devata*, or preferred deity, and to frequent temples where that deity is featured. However, many Hindus do not see themselves as "members" of those temples. Even in the case of Hindu guru devotionalism, where persons become devoted to a guru because of his or her spiritual teaching, powers, and identity, the commitment is to the guru and not always to a particular institution or community. In a similar way, many of the *Khrist bhaktas* of Matridham are making Christ their *ishta devata* and participating in the ashram and in other associated village gatherings. In this way these groups reflect a uniquely Hindu ability to hold onto several potentially competing loyalties within the context of an overall sense of Hindu communal identity.

The future of this movement is hard to predict. As San Chirico has surmised, it could remain an in-between community whose lively Christ-centered spirituality continues to challenge Hindus and nominal Catholics to become devoted Christ-followers.[41] It could also be that the movement's

---

[39]Kuttiyanikkal, *Khrist Bhakta Movement*, 157.
[40]Antony, "Khrist Bhakta Way," 237.
[41]San Chirico, "Between Christian and Hindu," 39.

deity (Jesus) and other devotional figures (the Virgin, saints) become diffused throughout the local area and join the localized expressions of Hindu spirituality. A third possibility is that the movement identifies more fully with its charismatic leanings, making more and more links, formally and informally, with other Pentecostal/charismatic Christian churches and becoming identified as such. Given the current pressures, from both Hindus and Christians, to create religious boundaries and polarity, the latter is quite probable. In the meantime it is evident that a new ecclesial expression has emerged that challenges existing norms in many ways.

JAVANESE CHRISTIANS (*KRISTEN JAWA*) IN INDONESIA

From the beginning of Dutch presence in Indonesia in 1605, generations of Dutch missionaries, tightly controlled first by the Dutch East India Company and later by the colonial government, labored to form the Protestant Church of Indonesia (a.k.a. *Indisch Kerk*). As late as the middle of the nineteenth century this consisted of small groups of believers drawn largely from tribal non-Muslim groups.[42] The situation was to change dramatically when in the 1870s an Indonesian evangelist, Sadrach Surapronata (c. 1835–1924), began work among Javanese Muslims. Soon thousands of Javanese Muslims became followers of Christ in a movement that offers important lessons for reflection on the church.[43]

A unique set of social and political circumstances faced Dutch missionaries working in nineteenth-century Java. But what appeared as obstacles to foreign missionaries were seen by Sadrach to offer a special opportunity. The island of Java at this time was largely poor and socially stratified. The local elite followed centuries-old indigenous traditions and strongly resisted the control of the colonial powers. Islam in Java consisted of an amalgam of Muslim and indigenous beliefs and practices. The missionaries for their part looked on the Javanese as "children of nature," worldly and sensual, in need of the civilizing influence of Christianity.[44] Small wonder that most Javanese

---

[42]See David Garrison, *A Wind in the House of Islam: How God Is Drawing Muslims Around the World to Faith in Christ* (Monument, CO: WIGTake Resources, 2014), loc. 717.

[43]In addition to Garrison's work, we are extremely fortunate to have a doctoral dissertation on Sadrach's movement by Sutarman Soediman Partonadi, *Sadrach's Community and its Contextual Roots: A Nineteenth-Century Javanese Expression of Christianity* (Amsterdam: Rodopi, 1990).

[44]This description is drawn from Partonadi, *Sadrach's Community*, 11-18.

resisted the *Indisch Kerk* as a foreign entity that was allied with the colonial government. Ironically, beginning in 1851 a Christian community that included a number of indigenous believers began to form, but since these believers came from the lower classes, they were never fully accepted by the missionaries or the *Indisch Kerk*.[45]

It was out of such a group that Sadrach began his unique work. Sadrach, or Radin as he was originally called, was raised a Muslim and trained in a Qur'an school. In the 1860s he was surprised to learn that his former guru, Pak Kurmen, had converted to Christianity after losing a debate with a Christian named Tunggul Wulung.[46] In 1867 at the age of thirty-two Radin was baptized in the *Indisch Kerk* and took Sadrach as his Christian name. From his mentors, Wulung and Kurmen, he learned that he did not need to leave behind his Javanese culture but could make use of Javanese customs in his own developing discipleship and ministry. Though still considering himself a part of the *Indisch Kerk*, in 1870 he set out on his own to evangelize his people.[47] As David Garrison notes, Sadrach intended "to retain yet transform for Christian purposes, as many Javanese customs as possible."[48]

Sadrach consciously took on the role of *kyai* (traditional guru) and followed the accepted pattern of public debate as his primary means of evangelism. He was soon known as a powerful guru, not only for his ability in debate but for his ability to control the evil spirits that haunted the dark places of Javanese culture. Soon large numbers of Javanese were converted, many of whom Sadrach personally trained as *kyais*.[49] By 1890 these groups consisted of almost 7,000 believers from 411 villages.

Especially notable for our purposes was Sadrach's attempt to gather new believers together in ways compatible with traditional customs (*adat*). Believers were called *Kristen Jawa* (Javanese Christians), and their church was called a *mesjid* (lit., "gathering"), the same term used by Muslims for their mosque. Their modest church structures of bamboo and palm fronds followed the pattern of Javanese mosques, though the symbols inscribed on these spaces were uniquely Christian. A three-tiered roof spoke of the Trinity;

---

[45]Partonadi, *Sadrach's Community*, 29-30, 48.
[46]Garrison, *Wind in the House of Islam*, loc. 725.
[47]Partonadi, *Sadrach's Community*, 58, 65.
[48]Garrison, *Wind in the House of Islam*, loc. 740.
[49]Partonadi, *Sadrach's Community*, 65-66.

the crescent was replaced by the *cakra*, a symbol taken from Javanese lore, with its Hindu and Buddhist roots. The *cakra* was the weapon used by Sri Krisna, incarnation of the mighty Wisnu, here taken over and reinterpreted as a symbol of the gospel "to pierce even the most obstinate of human hearts."[50]

Significantly, meetings of the *Kristen Jawa* resembled traditional religious gatherings. Genders were separated, and women wore head coverings; Muslim practices were followed as much as possible. Creeds and confessions were rewritten and not simply translated. For example, since the Qur'an refers to Jesus as the Spirit of God, their statements read: "*Yesus Kristus ya Roh Allah*" (Jesus Christ is the Spirit of God). In their Thursday evening gatherings they repeated this phrase, beginning softly and gradually increasing the volume until finally they reached a state of mystical trance.[51] Their music made use of *tembang*, a traditional (Javanese and Sundanese) musical form. Worship services were held twice on Sundays, led by an imam (leader) who began the service with a prayer of thanksgiving (or perhaps the Lord's Prayer), followed by a Javanese hymn and Scripture readings interspersed with singing. A brief exposition of the passage or a testimony followed, and the service closed with congregational singing.[52]

Though Sadrach's believers initially were baptized by pastors of the *Indisch Kerk*, these communities were effectively independent of the control of the church authorities. This served Sadrach's purposes well since, as an indigenous movement, they were not subject to the strict controls the colonial government had placed on the *Indisch Kerk*. And since Sadrach himself was not ordained for some time, these groups often went without baptism and Eucharist altogether, even as they continued to make use of traditional customs such as burning of incense and sprinkling flowers on the water.[53] They valued their freedom highly, calling themselves a free Christian group.[54] Still, while much of their practice was indistinguishable from their Muslim neighbors, they were careful to exclude those practices they believed inconsistent with their new faith, such as prayers for the

---

[50]Partonadi, *Sadrach's Community*, 210.

[51]Partonadi, *Sadrach's Community*, 136.

[52]Partonadi, *Sadrach's Community*, 133.

[53]Partonadi, *Sadrach's Community*, 69, 210.

[54]Partonadi suggests this nonviolent expression of freedom played a constructive role in developing indigenous notions of political independence. Partonadi, *Sadrach's Community*, 76.

dead or celebration of the birth and death of Muhammad.[55] Partonadi's summary is apt: "Sadrach developed a style of leadership and form of community which were not only rooted in and inspired by traditional Javanese values and customs, but were also critically corrective of those same values and customs."[56]

Despite the continuing relationship with the *Indisch Kerk*, relations with the missionaries soon became troubled. Partonadi notes that ideas of separation of church and state had come to be widely accepted in Holland. This together with the evangelical revivals of that time sparked the formation of voluntary mission societies, which sponsored many of the missionaries in Indonesia in Sadrach's time.[57] A few missionaries continued to support and mentor Sadrach, but sadly most of the leadership grew suspicious of these new methods. The missionaries were deeply concerned that Sadrach's method, since it did not reflect their ideas of the separation of church and state, led inevitably to syncretism.[58] Behind this conviction however, Partonadi argues, lies some guiding assumptions about missions and the preferred form of the church that predetermined their response to Sadrach's movement. In the first place, missionaries held the conviction that the Reformed Church with its structures and confessions was not only the primary agent of missions but the model to be implemented. In this model, described for example by Abraham Kuyper as *kerklijk zending* (ecclesiastical mission), missions becomes an essential part of the church structure, and local churches are charged with extending mission work.[59] Meanwhile, missionaries, influenced by the evangelical revivals, stressed the need for individual conversion involving a transformation of pagan lifestyles into a higher Christian morality, making them suitable to becoming a part of the institutional church as the missionaries understood it. Basically, Patronadi argues, missionaries understood their work to be the establishment of Reformed churches in Java as the true church of Christ.[60]

---

[55]Partonadi, *Sadrach's Community*, 151.

[56]Partonadi, *Sadrach's Community*, 203.

[57]Partonadi, *Sadrach's Community*, 31.

[58]Partonadi, *Sadrach's Community*, 90.

[59]Partonadi notes however that Kuyper was open to allowing the local form to be adapted by believers, showing some sensitivity to issues of contextualization. Partonadi, *Sadrach's Community*, 169.

[60]Partonadi, *Sadrach's Community*, 173.

Missionaries, for their part, quickly concluded that Sadrach's communities were taking shape in vastly different ways. Soon accusations were made that Sadrach was putting himself in the place of Christ, spreading false teachings, and aggrandizing himself at the expense of *Indisch Kerk* church authorities. After much debate, in 1893 formal ties with the mission were severed.[61] As intended, this move undermined the viability of Sadrach's efforts. As an independent movement Sadrach's communities were put into direct competition with the Dutch missionaries and the *Indisch Kerk*. As in the case of India, a constraining contradiction was allowed to become competitive. Partonadi notes: "It was impossible to try to compete with the ZGKN [Dutch mission] in terms of funds, equipment and skills."[62] This, along with the weakness of the leadership that succeeded Sadrach, led finally to his movement being re-absorbed into the *Indisch Kerk* in 1933.

It is important for our purposes to highlight the essential elements of Sadrach's program. What made his movement so attractive to so many Javanese people, and what began to emerge in this context? First, as Partonadi notes, Sadrach was raised in a strong *ngelmu*-seeking tradition. The highest concern of such a seeker was the "essence and meaning of life itself, the objective being the perfection of life."[63] Equally important, such quest called for a true *panutan* (mediator). This called for more than an ordinary *guru* because a true *panutan* had to be perfect, that is, someone demonstrating true moral perfection. To Sadrach the gospel represented the highest *ngelmu*, a superiority that called for demonstration in debate and also in the lives of Jesus' followers. Accordingly, teaching in Sadrach's movement focused on Jesus' resurrection and on his purity of life and ethics, especially as seen in Matthew's Sermon on the Mount (Mt 5–7): Jesus was the true *panutan*. Partonadi concludes: "Was not Jesus in fact the truly pious guru who fulfilled God's law unto death? Was not Jesus the powerful guru whose ministry included healing and exorcism? *To follow in the steps of Jesus* as *guru* and *panutan*, the perfect, pious exemplary figure . . . was the essence

---

[61]Partonadi shows how most of these accusations were based on cultural misunderstandings and, in some cases, jealousy. See Partonadi, *Sadrach's Community*, 174-86.

[62]Partonadi, *Sadrach's Community*, 104.

[63]*Ngelmu*: traditional spiritual knowledge. Interestingly, Partonadi notes here the possible confirming influence of Dutch pietism brought by the missionaries. Partonadi, *Sadrach's Community*, 218.

of Sadrach's Christology."[64] Clearly Sadrach found these emphases missing from the *Indisch Kerk*, and so he sought to form communities of followers gathered around gurus who sought to model the life of Jesus, the Spirit of God. Much of this was no doubt conscious and intentional. But it is also probable that Sadrach, along with those in his community, naturally brought together what missionaries understood as separate. For him, the qualities of the *panutan*, along with the various symbols and their related cognitive categories, could and should relate to aspects of the Christian teaching and tradition as presented by *Indisch Kerk* and his own reading of Scripture. What emerged from this relationship was an ecclesial community that affirmed and enhanced the people's cultural heritage as well as the relevance of the Christian message for that setting. It is not hard to understand why this proved so attractive to the people of Java, nor why it sparked the incomprehension of the missionaries. Sadly, what could have become a generative process that recognized the new possibilities of following Jesus, and a fresh movement of the Spirit of God, was misunderstood, and the opportunity was lost. The church in Indonesia struggles to this day to recover the insights of this rich heritage.

FOLLOWERS OF CHRIST IN MINDANAO

In southern Philippines, in the region now called Bangsamoro, over the last three generations there have formed groups of followers of Christ who insist on remaining within their Muslim culture.[65] In this unique setting these believers have found a way to follow Christ while remaining Muslim people. But this same context has also made it impossible for these believers to consider joining (or forming) a Christian church. To understand why this paradox exists, it is necessary to review a bit of their history.

During the Spanish period the colonial rulers followed a policy of indirect rule that recognized Muslim customary law. In 1914 the American authorities abrogated this policy, which was interpreted by the people to mean that the Christian government in Manila was refusing to "respect

---

[64]Partonadi, *Sadrach's Community*, 224 (emphasis original).

[65]The following is dependent on the thorough study of E. Acoba [pseud.], "Towards an Understanding of Inclusivity in Contextualizing into Philippine Context," in *The Gospel in Culture: Contextualization Issues in an Asian Context*, ed. M. P. Maggay (Manila: OMF Literature/ISACC, 2013), 416-50.

Muslims for being Muslims."[66] Consequently, the people of Bangsamoro experienced a strong sense of "unbelongingness" to the Philippine nation. They felt that only Christian Filipinos were "deemed entirely trustworthy and considered non-ethnic"; non-Christian Filipinos were ethnic and suspect, attitudes perpetrated and elaborated through the educational system and the dominant narrative of Filipino history.[67] The process of Filipinization of the south, where large numbers of Christians were relocated (often on confiscated tribal lands), has been seen as a virtual crusade, in which lawless Muslim tribes needed to be civilized by Christian Anglo-Saxon civilization.[68] In October 2012, after years of peace negotiations interspersed with outbreaks of violence, a Framework Agreement of Bangsamoro was signed, which, after four years of transitional preparations, promised a nonsubjugated Muslimhood. At the time of this writing, this process is in the hands of the newly elected President Rodrigo Duterte, who is himself from the south and boasts a Muslim heritage.

Under these circumstances, what possibilities exist to form a community of believers whose identity is firmly ethnic and religious but who refuse to identify either as Filipino or as Christian? Interestingly, E. Acoba points out that this ethnic identity, in its Muslim form, makes room for an understanding of community as inclusively diverse, that is, made up of various tribal groupings.[69] This is not pluralism in the Western sense but embraces differences within a larger solidarity, that in turn finds it final form in the *Ummah*—the larger inclusively diverse Muslim community.

This unique context poses the question: How might this embrace of difference allow for formation of particular groupings of followers of Jesus (*Isa al Masih*)? The four original leaders who had become followers of Jesus believed that this was possible, and they came together to form what they called Indigenous Movement Communities (IMC), that is, those communities who seek to follow Jesus and his teachings while guarding against

---

[66] Acoba, "Towards an Understanding of Inclusivity," 421.

[67] Acoba, "Towards an Understanding of Inclusivity," 419.

[68] See Melba Padilla Maggay, Rey Corpuz, and Miriam Adeney, *Raja Sulaiman Was No Carabao: Understanding the Muslim Question* (Diliman, Quezon City: Institute for Studies in Asian Church and Culture, 2001), 10, 11.

[69] Acoba, "Towards an Understanding of Inclusivity," 417.

practices associated with the Christian church.[70] Particularly striking is their decision to call their small communities *da'wahs*. *Da'wah* in Arabic comes from the verb meaning the act of preaching, or what one does as a result of preaching, but these believers have made this into a noun: a *da'wah* is a community of Jesus followers.[71] In a recent colloquium the leaders of these groups asked those in attendance to formulate a working definition of *da'wah*. After some discussion the participants agreed to define *da'wah* as "inviting others to the way of righteousness."[72] Thus, they chose to define themselves not as a fixed entity but in terms of practices that issued from following the teachings of *Isa al Masih*, preserving the verbal sense of this Arabic word. For them this new identity, as those formed by the teachings of Jesus, does not cancel their Muslim identity but allows them to rise above their history of subjugation. They are consciously creating a new space where their newly liberated voices will be welcomed within their continuing Muslim identity.[73]

In this troubled and fraught setting, these believers are bringing into close relationship their Muslim community and heritage and the teachings of Jesus and his followers. Out of this, as we have seen with other groups, emerges a unique ecclesial expression that resists the narrative of the evangelical missionaries and that deeply reflects the life and history of these new believers. But notice that this is not simply a contextualization strategy for them. Rather, their ecclesial shape, including the people's developing practices and insights, reflects the unique matrix of religious and cultural relationships as well as those that they exclude (Filipino Christian) because of the recent history of ethnic and religious tension.

Acoba in a recent conversation has brought this emergent process up to the present. These groups, while meeting together over a meal, are currently in the process of translating the book of Acts into their local language— sensing the deep resonance of their experience with that of the communal identity of Jewish followers of Christ in that book. Recently, the local imam visited the home of one of the leaders and noticed the transcript of this

---

[70] Acoba, "Towards an Understanding of Inclusivity," 424.
[71] This move was described to me in personal conversation with E. Acoba, in Manila, October 24, 2016. This conversation is also the source of comments in the following paragraph.
[72] Acoba, "Towards an Understanding of Inclusivity," 424-26.
[73] Acoba, "Towards an Understanding of Inclusivity," 432.

translation and asked about it. When they described what they were translating, the imam found it so interesting that he asked if he could use it in his teaching at the mosque! In a further development, they have now decided that they can recover an older name of *jemaah* (Arabic for "meeting") for their groups. Previously, Muslims in Southeast Asia had resisted using this term because of its recent connection with terrorist groups, but these believers now feel this better expresses an impulse that connects with their own heritage, even as it constructs a trajectory that transcends this.

These believers have found a place in their community where they can live out their new identity as followers of Christ.[74] The communal character of this ecclesial project calls attention to a new communal hermeneutic in which the meaning of these texts emerges out of a dialogue among different perspectives and voices. Acoba has called attention to the presence of multiple sets of hermeneutical approaches and even exegetical methods in these communities, suggesting a different application of their understanding of community as inclusively diverse.[75] This suggests a strikingly different understanding of pluralism than is prevalent in the West, but one that finds a parallel in the emerging ideas of freedom in early modern Europe that we described in chapter two. Living in a communal culture, one cannot expect to have complete freedom of choice or assembly. Still, as was the case of the various principalities that made up early modern European society, there are spaces for various liberties to emerge and allow believers to express their newfound freedom in Christ.[76] While not designing church in a form familiar to Westerners, these believers are able to exploit the possibilities inherent in their solidarity to join together and live out their witness to Christ.

It is difficult to specify either the character or the direction of this project because it is an emergent process with an open future. But there is a clear sense to these believers that God is present in a living way as they gather and invite others to the way of righteousness. And specific structures of ecclesial practice are emerging. The notion of church as a voluntary society, in which

---

[74]An adapted version of the following two paragraphs also appears in William Dyrness, "Can We Do Theology from Below? A Theological Framework for Indigenous Theologies," *International Journal of Frontier Mission* 35, no. 2 (Summer 2018): 1-9.

[75]Acoba, "Towards an Understanding of Inclusivity," 424-26.

[76]See Peter H. Wilson, *The Heart of Europe: A History of the Holy Roman Empire* (Cambridge, MA: Harvard University Press, 2016), 265.

members freely choose to join or not, is an inadequate model for their emerging notion of church, nor is it one with which they engage in their context. But at the same time their assumptions about community as inclusively diverse provides spaces for them to come together around a study of Scripture as they seek guidance in their commitment to follow Jesus in the midst of their newly liberated Muslim identity.

CONCLUSION

These various examples offer some evidence for our claim that cultural contexts influence how communities are understood and formed, and how these in turn determine how the church will emerge (or not) in those places. Some, like Japan, have proved highly resistant not only to traditional forms of church but also to new possibilities. Others, as in India and Indonesia, while sometimes resistant to traditional forms, have found cultural spaces for emergent forms that express traditional values. In the Philippines, cultural and historical factors have effectively precluded followers of Christ from identifying with traditional Christian structures—at least publicly. These differences constrain us from seeking generalizations about what forms the church will or ought to take in a given setting. No doubt some readers will wonder, Are there not theological values that Christians carry with them because of their commitment to the authority of Scripture? What models might we find there to guide our understanding and assessment of the differences we have discovered? These are good questions, and we turn to them in the following chapter.

5

. . . .

Biblical Metaphors for Church

After seeing these diverse permutations of communities of Jesus followers, alert readers are likely to observe that, whatever we might think of these new forms of community, there is still a biblical mandate for thinking about the church in particular ways. Specifically, they might wonder, Does the New Testament not articulate normative metaphors or images of the church? Paul Minear, in his classic study, argued a half century ago that, while there are many images of the church in the New Testament (he claims a total of 96), four image-clusters are dominant: people of God, new creation, fellowship of faith, and the body of Christ.[1] By images he means imaginative forays that are suggestive in expressing the new thing that God is doing in Christ. While he does isolate these central images, which we will focus on as well, he hesitates to call any one of them determinative. In a judgment consistent with our focus on emergent qualities, he concludes that amidst this diversity of imagery "no figure dominates the stage," and none imply tightly bounded entities.[2] Still, significant images, or what we will call metaphors, emerge in the New Testament, metaphors that capture our attention and call for explanation. In this chapter we will focus in particular on three of these—the people of God, the community of the Spirit, and the body of Christ—and examine their significance for our study.

What about Minear's reference to the new creation? Here we need to bear in mind the argument of the first chapter. The work of God represented by the life and work of Jesus the Christ, we have argued, did not centrally focus on the forming of a community that became the church. Christ's preaching extended more broadly to what he called the kingdom of God. This program,

---

[1]Paul S. Minear, *Images of the Church in the New Testament* (Philadelphia: Westminster, 1960), 20-23. The four he singles out are more accurately thought of as constellations of imagery. See p. 67.
[2]Minear, *Images of the Church*, 222, 225.

as it is further elaborated in the New Testament, included the restoration and renewal of the whole of creation, all that had been fatally damaged by Adam's sin. This story began with the calling of Abraham and the formation of a people who would be his heirs and would be as numerous as the stars in the sky (Gen 15:5). It continued with the divine deliverance of Abraham's heirs from Egypt and their settlement in the land promised to Abraham, but it also envisioned, in the prophets, a new order of creation, what God calls in Isaiah "new heavens and a new earth" (Is 65:17). The idea of a new creation is picked up by Paul in the New Testament (2 Cor 5:17), and though it includes a particular "peoples," its scope is larger than this, encompassing eventually nothing less than the resurrection of all things (Rev 21–22). As the great Catholic scholar Louis Bouyer puts this, the Pauline mystery "is basically the secret of God's eternal plan for the salvation of the universe and especially the salvation of mankind, which he created."[3]

This more comprehensive perspective is important to keep in mind because, as we argued in the first chapter, God's purpose in calling out a people finds its importance within the larger program of redemption that includes a new order of righteousness and justice. This new order, called the reign (or kingdom) of God, formed the centerpiece of Jesus' ministry. And his purpose in calling disciples to follow him, a band that many have seen as a precursor of the church, was to make them a part of his ministry of announcing (and embodying) the reign of God and its world-shaping character. (See Mt 10:7-8, where Jesus empowers and sends them out to extend his own ministry.) So the church is for the sake of the kingdom, not the other way around. As Jürgen Moltmann reminds us, the church is a part of the history of God. His assessment is worth recalling:

> It is not the Church that has a mission to fulfill to the world; it is the mission of the Spirit and the Spirit through the Father that includes the Church, creating the Church as it goes on its way.[4]

Nevertheless, even if the church is not the focus of Christ's work and ministry, neither is it something secondary or unrelated to these larger purposes.

[3]Louis Bouyer, *The Church of God: Body of Christ and Temple of the Spirit*, trans. Charles Quinn (Chicago: Franciscan Herald, 1982), 159.
[4]Jürgen Moltmann, *The Church in the Power of the Spirit: A Contribution to Messianic Ecclesiology*, trans. Margaret Kohl (New York: Harper & Row, 1977), 64.

In fact, in Colossians 1 Paul connects the creation of all things in and for Christ with a striking image of Christ as "head of the body, the church" (Col 1:18). Such images then demand further reflection.

What does it mean to call these expressions metaphors or images? Calling something an image or metaphor underlines the unique rhetorical status of the figure of speech in question. That is, the expression does not function as a literal description of something but proposes an image suggestive of something that is difficult (or sometimes impossible) to express literally.[5] Jesus' parables often function in this rhetorical way. When Jesus compares God to the unjust judge (in Lk 18:1-8), he does not mean that this judge was exactly like God but that there were similarities that help us imagine something about God: If a judge who did not fear God would respond to the cries of people, how much more would God avenge his people? Metaphors and images become more central in biblical attempts to describe something God is doing because this work often has no human analogy. The description of this new community in the New Testament is such a thing; it is stretching the bounds of all that we know about human communities. So these images are "imaginative forays" that show us something about this community that we cannot grasp by more literal expressions.[6]

At the same time these images, even if they are not definitive, are normative for believers. Since we are persuaded the Spirit of God moved these writers in special ways, these images have an authority that cannot be discarded. We might say the images we explore in this chapter help us understand the theological ontology of the church. That is, they express the special way God is present and working in and through these communities, despite their very diverse cultural expressions.

THE PEOPLE OF GOD

By all accounts, calling believers in Christ "the people of God" constitutes a central biblical image. Paul Minear notes that the focus of this image is on

---

[5]A helpful description of this use of language is found in E. L. Mascall, *Words and Images: A Study in the Possibility of Religious Discourse* (London: Libra Books, 1957), 112.
[6]Minear, *Images of the Church*, 20-23.

its corporate nature and its roots in the First Testament people of God.[7] The notion of the people of God begins with the calling of Abraham and the promise that his seed will number as the stars in the sky (Gen 15:5), but they are not formally constituted as a people until their deliverance from Egypt. God was the first to use this term when he tells Pharaoh to "let my people [Heb. *ammi*] go" (Ex 5:1), and in Deuteronomy, in Moses' final address, Moses says God brought Israel out of Egypt to become "a people of [God's] very own possession" (Deut 4:20). In the Psalms the Lord is asked to bless his people with peace (Ps 29:11), will not cast off his people (Ps 94:14), and takes pleasure in his people (Ps 149:4). The most moving reference to this image is embodied in God's call for the prophet Hosea to marry a prostitute. When she bears Hosea a son, God tells Hosea to name him Lo-ammi, meaning "not my people," explaining that because of their unfaithfulness Israel is not God's people, and he is not their God (Hos 1:9). But immediately after this God recalls the promise to Abraham that eventually the seed of this people will be as the sand of the sea, which cannot be measured, and though they had been called "not God's people," they will one day again be sons and daughters of the living God (Hos 1:10). In that day God will say to the ones who were not God's people, "You are my people" (Hos 2:23). Despite Israel's infidelity, God could not forget the promises to Abraham. And because he is God, he would not execute his anger upon them (Hos 11:8-9). This promise that God would one day reconstitute his people is emphasized also in Jeremiah. There God promises a "new covenant," not like the old covenant, which Israel broke, but a new covenant that will be kept. For in that day, God promises: "I will put my law within them, and I will write it on their hearts; and I will be their God, and they shall be my people" (Jer 31:33). The continual focus on the days that are coming (Jer 31:31) implies that the final realization of this people of God lies in a future that God will bring about. And the parallel emphasis on a law written on their hearts points to the transformation that God intends to bring about.

This future is inaugurated in the coming of Jesus to restore or, better, reconstitute God's people. In the New Testament, in the very first chapter of

---

[7]Minear, *Images of the Church*, ch. 4. Louis Bouyer's study of the church as the people of God also begins his account with Abraham and the deliverance of Israel from Egypt. Bouyer, *Church of God*, 175-179.

Matthew, the connection between Christ and the people of God and the significance of names are both affirmed when the angel tells Joseph that he is to name his son Jesus, "for he will save his people [Gk. *ton laon autou*] from their sins" (Mt 1:21). The author of Hebrews makes explicit the connection with the prophecy of Jeremiah by means of a long quote from Jeremiah 33: in those days, "I will be their God, / and they shall be my people" (Heb 8:10). This has been realized, the author goes on to say, in the new covenant brought about by Jesus' death and resurrection, events that render the old covenant obsolete (Heb 8:13). Peter similarly addresses the exiles of the dispersion, those who have been called by God into the "spiritual house" founded by Christ (1 Pet 2:5), and calls them "a chosen race, a royal priesthood, a holy nation, God's own people." But what is noteworthy in this designation is its purpose: "In order that you may proclaim the mighty acts of him who called you out of darkness into his marvelous light" (1 Pet 2:9). This is followed by a quote from Hosea that you who were once not a people are now God's own people (1 Pet 2:10). Clearly, those called to follow Christ have been initiated into a community whose purpose is to give witness to the mighty work of God in Christ, whether this is by their words or by (and with) their very lives. However rich these suggestions of a peculiar people are, the Scriptures resist identification of the people of God with some particular ethnic group or some particular (social or political) location. In the First Testament, Genesis 1–11 challenges all such limitations by announcing God's rule over all of creation. This narrative demonstrated how a particular people, Israel, could be in relationship with God, even as it insisted God's rule extended beyond this people. Indeed, God has to remind Israel that they were not a people but had become a people of God; similarly, Christ has to remind the Pharisees that God could raise up children of Abraham from the stones (Mt 3:9). And though they will number as the stars or sand, and will come from the east and the west, in every case they respond to the call of God that constitutes this people.

Here it is fitting to recall the conclusion of Louis Bouyer's discussion of the people of God. Significantly, he points out, Jesus appropriates the Passover meal to offer a new form of the Jewish blessing (*barakah*) pronounced on that occasion, substituting his death for all previous sacrifices, thus separating "his church, the *ekklesia theou* of the latter days from the people of the sons of Abraham. . . . The church is the People of God, promised in Abraham . . . who have gone through total renewal, which only the image and death and resurrection, introduced by the great vision of Ezekiel, can adequately describe."[8]

This image of God's people has been picked up frequently in Christian history, but nowhere more centrally than in the Second Vatican Council of the Roman Catholic Church (1961–1965). In the second chapter of the "Dogmatic Constitution of the Church, *Lumen Gentium*," the people of God are defined: "At all times and among every people, God has given welcome to whosoever fears him and does what is right."[9] The new covenant has birthed this "new people of God" with Christ as its head: "The heritage of this people are the dignity and freedom of the Sons of God in whose hearts the Holy Spirit dwells as in his Temple. Its law is the new commandment to love as Christ loved us."[10] Significantly, this new people extends itself to all people bearing witness to Christ "by means of a life of faith and charity," even those not formally linked in full communion with the church.[11]

The significance of the placement of this emphasis on the church as the people of God in the second chapter of "*Lumen Gentium*," ahead of the mention of the hierarchy of the church in chapter three, has engendered a great deal of debate. After the initial draft of this document was circulated, many voices were raised in support of including centrally the image of the people of God, which subsequently was inserted as chapter two.[12] The fact that this precedes the chapter on the hierarchy has led observers to see a revolution in thinking on the church, from a structured institution to a pilgrim people. Richard McBrien, for example, has argued that this represents a revolution in understanding of the church, which is not the only agent bringing about the values of the kingdom. The church then needs to abandon the illusion "that she is the ordinary means of salvation and that all people

---

[8]Bouyer, *Church of God*, 230, 235.

[9]"*Lumen Gentium*," in *The Documents of Vatican II with Notes and Comments by Catholic, Protestant, and Orthodox Authorities*, ed. Walter M. Abbott, trans. ed. Joseph Gallagher (New York: Guild Press, 1966), 24.

[10]"*Lumen Gentium*," 25.

[11]"*Lumen Gentium*," 29. The document extends this to those who have never heard but who "moved by grace, strive by their deeds to do his will as it is known to them through the dictates of conscience." "*Lumen Gentium*," 35.

[12]Cf. Bouyer, *Church of God*, 166, 167.

are invited to belong to her."[13] The modesty and focus on the people rather than the hierarchy pleased some theologians and displeased others. Ernst Käsemann liked the focus on the pilgrim people of God en route to its eschatological destiny; Joseph Ratzinger (later Pope Benedict) regretted that this imagery was not sufficiently connected to the sacraments. Traditionalists resisted any revisionist understanding of the church. Avery Cardinal Dulles, for example, has argued that Vatican II was not a revolution of thinking on the church but a recovery of authentic newness that characterizes the Word of God. Interpreters like McBrien, he thinks, depart substantially from the proper teaching of "*Lumen Gentium*," which insists that the kingdom "grows in and through the Church." Rather, Dulles thinks, the chapter on the "People of God" focuses on the "personal freedom and responsibility of each member" over against the imagery of the "Body of Christ."

Though the debate continues, a focus on the people of God has changed the conversation for both Catholics and Protestants with respect to the nature of the church. Though our brief review of biblical references to the people of God highlighted the call of God as constitutive of this people, the conversation issuing from "*Lumen Gentium*" has stressed "the responsibility of each member." Whereas the one reminds us of God's sovereign call, the other reflects a modern focus on personal agency. Princeton Seminary theologian Ellen Charry's description of the church goes some way toward restoring the balance between these themes when she describes the church as "those who have been taken into God's cosmic drama of salvation, made known in the redemption of Israel from Egypt and in the cross of Christ."[14]

The people of God then are those who share in the new covenant inaugurated by Christ's death and resurrection and which he celebrated with his disciples in the Last Supper. Sharing in this blessing constitutes believers as people of God. Simply put, as Louis Bouyer argues, "Whoever hears this word, whoever believes in it, whoever agrees to give himself to it, with and in Christ, *belongs thereby to the Church*."[15] This is certainly true whatever

---

[13]Richard P. McBrien, *Do We Need the Church?* (New York: Harper, 1969), quoted in Avery Dulles, "Nature, Mission, and Structure of the Church," in *Vatican II: Renewal Within Tradition*, ed. Matthew L. Lamb and Matthew Levering (New York: Oxford University Press, 2008), 29-31. Discussion which follows is indebted to Dulles's discussion.

[14]Ellen T. Charry, "Sacramental Ecclesiology," in *Community of the Word: Toward an Evangelical Ecclesiology*, ed. Mark Husbands and Daniel J. Treier (Downers Grove, IL: IVP Academic, 2005), 204.

[15]Bouyer, *Church of God,* 239 (emphasis added).

and whoever this people may be as an ethnic or tribal body, or indeed whatever particular form the celebration of this blessing may take. That is the point of the particular celebration Christ initiated during that Passover meal. His disciples, though Jewish, were being made part of a new people without losing their identity as Jewish people. Soon Gentiles, Romans, Parthians, and people from every nation under heaven (Acts 2:5-11) would be celebrating this passage to a new people, though in every case without losing their location as people from these particular nations.

THE BODY OF CHRIST

Of the main images that we are highlighting perhaps none has received such diverse interpretations as the "body of Christ," not least because of the various ways in which the New Testament writers use the phrase in 1 Corinthians, Romans, Colossians, and Ephesians. In 1 Corinthians 12 and Romans 12, Paul uses this image to address the church's disunity and the different but interrelated functions of various ministries.[16] Paul's description of the body in 1 Corinthians 12:12-27, for example, follows his appeal in 1 Corinthians 10 to not "partake of the table of the Lord and the table of demons" (1 Cor 10:21). This table of the Lord was the Eucharist—the bread and cup, through which the church shared in the blood and body of Christ. Sharing together in this "one bread" makes those who are "many" into "one body" (1 Cor 10:17). Paul returns to this image in 1 Corinthians 12, where diverse people—Jews, Greeks, slaves, free—are baptized into one body and "made to drink of one Spirit" (1 Cor 12:13). This unity has social implications, he goes on to say, as God gives gifts to people and arranges them within Christ's body, or the local church, as he chooses (1 Cor 12:18). Notice that in 1 Corinthians 10 and 12 being a part of Christ's body consists of relations between people and Christ and among themselves, which in turn shape the local Christian association into something wholly unique. As Paul summarizes, "Now you are the body of Christ and individually members of it" (1 Cor 12:27).

---

[16]It is apparent that Stoic literature used the body as a metaphor for the cosmos and for society in general, and was thus a familiar image. The New Testament writers, however, used the term in wholly unique ways. Robert J. Banks, *Paul's Idea of Community: The Early House Churches in Their Cultural Settings*, rev. ed. (Peabody, MA: Hendrickson, 1994), 66.

Paul uses a similar phrase in Romans 12, saying, "So we, who are many, are one body in Christ, and individually we are members one of another" (Rom 12:5). Though speaking to a very different church context, Paul seeks to make a similar point: because the Roman church members together are Christ's body, no one among them should "think of yourself more highly than you ought to think" (Rom 12:3). This highlights another important feature of this metaphor, present in both 1 Corinthians and Romans: being a member of Christ's body not only signifies an elevated identity for the fellowship but requires of the members an elevated standard in its practices and ethics.[17]

Whereas Paul refers to local churches as the body of Christ, the writers of Colossians and Ephesians employ the metaphor in a more expansive way, though still using it to counter wrong tendencies and establish a new modus operandi for the church. In Colossians the believers become Christ's body, his church (Col 1:18, 24), by "putting off the body of the flesh" through baptism (Col 2:11-12). Through this transformation the believers enter into "a new mode of existence."[18] And, similar to Romans, this new existence has ethical implications, including the challenging of social divisions (Col 3:9-13). As Minear observed, "The image of the head and its body was thus used to attack . . . the world's way of dividing mankind into competing societies, whether religious, racial, cultural, or economic. The image of the body of Christ thus served as a way of describing a social revolution."[19]

For the writer of Ephesians the body of Christ is again wider than any one assembly and is the nexus for reconciliation, particularly between Jews and Gentiles (Eph 2:11-16). The writer also uses it to bring guidance to the church's unity and use of spiritual gifts, this time emphasizing that the gifts are important for "building up the body of Christ" (Eph 4:12). Believers are portrayed as not only a part of the body but intricately involved in its well-being. The body of Christ is thus simultaneously an eschatological reality headed by Christ and one in which the members actively participate. As the

---

[17]Thus, as Colin Miller has argued, the sections following Paul's description of the body (Rom 12:9–15:13) provide guidance on various issues of conduct and should thus be seen as extensions of what it means to be a part of Christ's body. Colin D. Miller, *The Practice of the Body of Christ: Human Agency in Pauline Theology After MacIntyre* (Cambridge: James Clarke & Co., 2014), 137-38. This point holds whether or not one supports Miller's argument that Romans 12:9-15:13 specifically refers to conduct in the church's *agapē* or Eucharistic meals.

[18]Minear, *Images of the Church*, 209.

[19]Minear, *Images of the Church*, 211.

writer says, believers are continually in the process of growing up "in every way into him who is the head, into Christ" (Eph 4:15).

As this overview highlights, the body of Christ helps convey, among other things, that the church is a collective (locally and regionally) that edifies and serves all its members, breaks down social divisions, and finds its core identity in Christ as its head. But what else might this metaphor be seeking to convey about the nature of the church and its relation to Christ? On the one hand, many scholars and traditions have interpreted the metaphor as showing the elevated status of the church in God's economy and as a guide for the social relations of the church.[20] This has been a particularly important theme for scholars and leaders who have sought to argue for a more egalitarian or democratic view of the church, particularly from Protestant and free church traditions.[21]

On the other hand, Catholic and Orthodox traditions, following after Augustine, have interpreted the body imagery from a more concrete standpoint.[22] This body, though mystical, is nonetheless a unit composed of Christ and the church. Augustine calls this the "whole Christ," in which Christ willingly joins with his church—locally, globally, and across ages—in order to be one with it.[23] This notion was reiterated in chapter one of Vatican II's "*Lumen Gentium*" and again in 2000 in "*Dominus Iesus*" under the guidance of then-Cardinal Ratzinger. In the latter declaration it says, "And thus, just as the head and members of a living body, though not identical, are inseparable, so too Christ and the Church can neither be confused nor separated, and constitute a single 'whole Christ.'"[24]

---

[20]For example, see Banks, *Paul's Idea of Community*, 59-63.

[21]However, as Gary Badcock has shown, body imagery did not automatically convey egalitarianism. Though Paul no doubt sought to admonish the "stronger" to have regard for the "weaker," it does not follow that Paul necessarily meant to flatten social hierarchies. "To say that the weaker parts of the body have functions indispensable to the rest is to make a case, not for the equality of the parts, but rather for the indispensability of the weak, who need to be kept in their place for the good of the rest." Gary D. Badcock, "The Church as 'Sacrament,'" in Husbands and Treier, *Community of the Word*, 195.

[22]Badcock, "Church as 'Sacrament,'" 195.

[23]Augustine, "Sermon 341," in *Sermons on Various Subjects 341-400*, part 3, vol. 10 of *The Works of Saint Augustine: A Translation for the 21st Century*, trans. Edmund Hill, ed. John E. Rotelle (Brooklyn, NY: New City Press, 1995), 26.

[24]Congregation for the Doctrine of the Faith, "Declaration '*Dominus Iesus*': On the Unicity and Salvific Universality of Jesus Christ and the Church," June 16, 2000, 4.16, www.vatican.va/roman_curia/congregations/cfaith/documents/rc_con_cfaith_doc_20000806_dominus-iesus_en.html.

What does this mean for a local church? Is it a church in and of itself? The Catholic interpretation would suggest that local churches can be understood to be the "body of Christ" insofar as they are manifestations of the universal (Catholic) church, though Vatican II did allow that other churches may be a part of this. Protestants, on the other hand, have been wary of the universalizing hierarchies, which this interpretation has historically allowed. Miroslav Volf, for example, interprets the metaphor of body not as an organic collective identity but rather as a "particular kind of personal communion between Christ and Christians."[25]

Though metaphors are multivalent by nature, Volf illuminates a perspective that resonates with the emergent nature of the church that we are presenting. Agreeing with Heon-Wook Park, Volf argues that the "body of Christ" should be interpreted from the perspective of the man and woman becoming one body (1 Cor 6:12-20; Eph 5:22-33; cf. Gen 2:21-24). By this understanding the new body is not an organic entity (even if mystical in nature) but rather a body constituted through the relations or communion of persons.[26] For Paul, being "united in the same mind and for the same purpose" (1 Cor 1:10) is not about being a part of the same ecclesial body but rather about being in communion with Christ and each other.[27] As we saw in our discussion of emergence in chapter three, through the relationship of a husband and wife emerges a new entity called a marriage that includes many relational goods. This, as we argued, is a very real entity that is dependent upon but not reducible to the parts (husband and wife). In a similar way a new entity or "body" emerges as (1) local believers relate to each other and Christ and (2) Christ and the various churches, across regions and across time, join together through the bond of the Spirit. But this latter does not make the local church any less a church. For Volf, each local church is a church and is connected to the entire communion of those "in Christ" as an anticipation of "the eschatological gathering of the entire people of God."[28] Thus, the local

---

[25]Miroslav Volf, *After Our Likeness: The Church as the Image of the Trinity* (Grand Rapids: Eerdmans, 1998), 143.

[26]Volf, *After Our Likeness*, 141-42; and Heon-Wook Park, "Die Vorstellung vom Leib Christi bei Paulus" (PhD diss., Tübingen, 1988).

[27]In fact, in the first chapter of 1 Corinthians Paul argues against the sense of belonging to a particular grouping, whether associated with Paul, Apollos, Cephas, or even Christ (1 Cor 1:12). Yung Suk Kim, *Christ's Body in Corinth: The Politics of a Metaphor* (Minneapolis: Fortress, 2008), 2.

[28]Volf, *After Our Likeness*, 145.

church in its local communion is the body of Christ, which creates for its members certain goods, privileges, and obligations such that to be a part of "one body" is consonant with sharing in the common good of that body.[29]

THE COMMUNITY OF THE SPIRIT

Another primary image of church that Minear discusses is what he calls "The Fellowship in Faith." For Minear this phrase brings together a constellation of related images describing the church as a "fellowship" that consists of "holy ones" who are connected through the Holy Spirit. It is an image that seeks to "illuminate the fabric of human relations within the church," particularly because of its fellowship (*koinōnia*) in the Holy Spirit.[30]

When the Apostles Creed declared a belief in "the communion of saints," it was reflecting numerous New Testament references to saints or "holy ones" (*hagioi*), verses such as Romans 1:7—"to all God's beloved in Rome, who are called to be saints"—or 1 Corinthians 1:2—"to the church of God that is in Corinth, to those who are sanctified in Christ Jesus, called to be saints." The designation of people as "holy," upon first glance, would seem to draw from the First Testament language of holiness. Though this is true, the connection is not straightforward. For, in the First Testament, it is almost always God who is holy (such as in Lev 11:44) and occasionally, by strong association, the holy of holies, the temple itself, or angels. Only once (Ps 16:3, "as for the holy ones in the land") is holiness ascribed to people. Thus, holiness is originally and principally a quality of God's own divinity, only selectively attributed to his temple and angels. However, in later First Testament literature, in the Septuagint, and finally in the New Testament, the word is gradually used to refer to God's people, particularly as those who stand in close relation and proximity to God. There is thus a developed and extended use where, as A. K. M. Adam says, "the language of holiness began at the heart of the Temple, and was extended to apply to the people and material objects within the Temple; and gradually came to include the people who came to worship at the Temple."[31] This development and the context in which it is found help

---

[29]Minear, *Images of the Church*, 181.

[30]Minear, *Images of the Church*, 138.

[31]A. K. M. Adam, "Saint-Spotting in Scripture: Οἱ Ἅγιοι in the New (and Old) Testament" (paper presented at the Saints Without Borders: 47th International Ecumenical Seminar, Strasbourg, France, July 3, 2013), 3.

to shed light on why it was so important for Paul, and the writer of Hebrews, to designate the church believers in Jerusalem, Corinth, Rome, Philippi, and elsewhere as "holy ones." First, doing so reinforced Paul's conviction that Gentiles were now included with Jews in the community of those designated and marked by God's holiness. But second, and reflecting the First Testament background of its usage, Paul (and Hebrews) is highlighting the proximity and place in God's cosmic order that each of these church communities now occupies. To call them "holy ones" brings attention to "a sense of the world whose centre is God, surrounded by a court which reflects God's own identity, peopled by 'holy ones.'"[32]

Our reflection on the community of holy ones can extend into other areas as well. For the church to be characterized by God's own distinctive quality brings to the church a responsibility. As Minear says, reflecting on 1 Peter 1:16 ("You shall be holy, for I am holy"), the gift of being holy ones brings with it "the gift of a task."[33] The expectation is clear that the church of believers should be characterized by conduct, in relations with each other and with those outside of the church, that befit and reflect the status of those called holy. This focus on conduct highlights that, in our phrase, this group of holy ones is a communion or fellowship. The Greek word *koinōnia* has at its root the idea of sharing in "common." The sense is that God, as the one who brings the church together, calls it to a special type of reconciled community, one where normal social differences are transcended and overcome because of the quality of holiness to which they are called and aspire.

Much more could be said on this quality of fellowship, but we want to give attention to another key part of this phrase. The church is a community of holy ones that is empowered by the Holy Spirit. On the day of Pentecost, Jesus' promise to the disciples in Acts 1:8 was fulfilled when the Holy Spirit came upon them and all the men and women gathered to pray in the upper room. It would not be correct to call this event, as many have done, the "birth of the church" since the church as a gathered community around the person of Jesus existed before this. Neither would it be accurate to say that the Holy Spirit was not at work prior to this day. However, when the disciples

---

[32]Adam, "Saint-Spotting," 7.
[33]Minear, *Images of the Church*, 138.

experienced the baptism of the Holy Spirit on that day, they interpreted it as a special fulfillment of the Spirit of prophecy, as foretold by the prophet Joel (Joel 2:28). What was the purpose of this gift? The gift of God's Spirit was certainly meant, as was seen on that day, as an empowerment for witness for Jesus. But, as Max Turner has shown, it is something more. The gift of the Holy Spirit to Jesus' followers was not only the "fuel for mission" but also the power of God that would purge and restore his community.[34] Peter has in mind this quality and work of God in Acts 5:3 when he tells Ananias that he has lied to the Holy Spirit about the actual amount he received from the sale of his property. In a dramatic way God punishes Ananias, and then his wife Sapphira, with death to symbolically show the type of purging and holiness that he commanded through his Spirit in the church.[35] And, as Acts shows, this restoring work, though beginning with Israel, was also meant to restore and bring Gentiles into God's holy proximity. After Cornelius obeys God and receives the Holy Spirit, Peter later reflects on this act as "cleansing their [the Gentiles'] hearts by faith" (Acts 15:9).

There are numerous other related analogies and images that relate to the church as a community of the Spirit.[36] Our overview, however, illustrates the way in which particular scriptural images regarding a community of holy ones, indwelt by the Holy Spirit, help believers to conceive of the nature of relations within and outside of the church. Within, the church displays the marks of re-stored and restructured relationships. This quality of relationship in turn impacts its witness among those outside of its community such that they "may see your honorable deeds and glorify God when he comes to judge" (1 Pet 2:12). However, despite its high calling, the church must not regard itself more highly than it ought. As Moltmann reminds us, the holiness to which the church is called "does not divide the church and Christians substantially from sinful humanity." Rather, the church is holy "precisely at the point where it acknowledges its sins and the sins of mankind and trusts to justification through God."[37]

---

[34]Max Turner, "The 'Spirit of Prophecy' as the Power of Israel's Restoration and Witness," in *Witness to the Gospel: The Theology of Acts*, ed. I. Howard Marshall and David Peterson (Grand Rapids: Eerdmans, 1998), 345.

[35]Turner, "'Spirit of Prophecy,'" 346.

[36]Minear, *Images of the Church*, ch. 5, for example, includes in his section discussions of "the justified," "the disciplined community," "slaves of God," and the "household of God."

[37]Moltmann, *Church in the Power of the Spirit*, 353.

These three metaphors of the church—people of God, body of Christ, and community of the Spirit—are three prominent and, we have argued, normative images describing the work of God in and through the church. Their purpose in Scripture is not to circumscribe the limits of what God is doing but rather, as images, to evoke imaginative descriptions of his work among his people. The church is a new people, rooted in but also transcending their particular cultural communities, bound together through their relationships with each other and Christ, and brought near to God through the Holy Spirit. This "high" view of the church means its identity is always more than a social or religious gathering. Reflection on these images leads one to conclude that they have no necessary connection to any particular social or political structure. However, the church is also a social gathering that, because of its unique relationship to God, is called to display in its relationships a new ethic reflecting God's own holiness.

This last point calls for further elaboration. The church, as a social gathering, displays its ethic, worship, and life together in particular ways. These are what we can generally call practices, which every social group develops and shares together. What's more, the practices of social groups contribute in substantial ways to the emergent identity and qualities of those groups. Churches have, through the centuries, developed particular *ecclesial* practices, such as baptism, Communion, worship, preaching, and many others, and have normally turned to Scripture to guide them on questions regarding these practices. And, as we saw from chapters two and four, churches have historically and currently developed widely diverse interpretations regarding which practices are essential and the correct way to practice them. With such diversity, how are we to regard ecclesial practices and their relationship to the church? It is to this that we turn next.

6

. . . .

Theological Practices of Church

W e have seen from reviewing the biblical evidence in the last chapter that
the purposes of God in creation and re-creation embrace the work of renewal of all things begun in Christ's resurrection and the pouring out of the
Holy Spirit. This renewing work is often expressed as the reign of God in
human history and its culmination in the new heaven and earth. Though
this cosmic program includes forming a community, or rather multiple
communities, of people from every kindred, tongue, and nation who, according to the vision of John, will eternally sing praises to the Lamb that was
slain (Rev 5:9, 12), we argue these communities are not to be equated with
the institutional Christian church even if there is significant overlap between
the two. Indeed, we argue that this community is not about institutions at
all, but in the words of Dietrich Bonhoeffer, are about "using social connections to extend God's rule."[1]

Such social connections, as we have seen, can take numerous forms,
ranging from formalized institutions with long histories to informal and
temporary groups sharing meals and Bible studies. As we showed in the last
chapter, there is no single biblical form, or metaphor, that could be seen as
determinative.[2] To understand the inherent possibilities and limitations of
such forms, in this book we are using emergence theory to better understand their dynamic and fluid characteristics. In this chapter we add another
dimension to this approach to understanding church. If the ecclesial identities are an emergent phenomenon, then one important way to understand

---

[1]Dietrich Bonhoeffer, *Sanctorum Communio: A Theological Study of the Sociology of the Church*,
German ed. Joachim von Soosten; English edition trans. Reinhard Krauss and Nancy Lukens
and ed. Clifford J. Green (Minneapolis: Fortress, 1998), 230.

[2]Recall Paul Minear's conclusion: "No figure dominates the stage." Paul S. Minear, *Images of the
Church in the New Testament* (Philadelphia: Westminster, 1960), 222.

them is in terms of characteristic practices that express this identity—what we will call ecclesial practices. We saw in the chapter on historical forms of church (chap. 2) that their essential nature was often described in terms of multiple functions that expressed their identity as church. These were termed "marks" or "practices" that were deemed essential to their nature as church—preaching, praying, celebrating sacraments, and so on. If the previous chapter sought the theological ontology of biblical notions of church, this one will define that nature in terms of practices—what believers in Christ do as individuals and groups to express and embody that reality.

In the first instance, what believers do to embody the new creation is what we call their "worship." In a very real sense this chapter will argue that it is the worship—baptism, celebrating Communion, hearing the word, praise, and prayer—that constitutes the life of the community gathered in Jesus' name. As J. J. von Allmen says in his classic study of these practices, worship is the "sphere *par excellence* where the life of the church comes into being, and that the fact of the church first emerges. It is there that it gives proof of itself, there where it is focused, and where we are led when we truly seek it, and it is from that point that it goes out into the world to exercise its mission."[3]

This chapter is entitled "Theological Practices of the Church" to emphasize that the functions with which we are concerned, insofar as they express some aspect of church, are theological practices. That is, the communities we examine do things together that they believe are theological. By this we mean things freely engaged in by human actors, which are at the same time things in which God is fully present and engaged.[4] When believers offer praise, God is present: God, says the psalmist, is "enthroned on the praises of Israel" (Ps 22:3). When Christians pray, the Spirit prays with and for them. Paul notes that, since we do not know how to pray as we should, the Holy Spirit inspires the believer's prayer with "groanings which cannot be uttered" (Rom 8:26 KJV; cf. "sighs too deep for words," NRSV). Such ecclesial practices, then, are an intrinsic part and extension of God's creative and re-creative work in Jesus Christ, as this is applied and energized

---

[3]J.-J. von Allmen, *Worship: Its Theology and Practice* (New York: Oxford University Press, 1965), 44.
[4]For a fuller expression of this notion of theological practices as central to the church and its worship, see William A. Dyrness, *A Primer on Christian Worship* (Grand Rapids: Eerdmans, 2009), chap. 1.

by the Spirit. So when believers in Christ gather to hear the word of God preached or taught in some way, when they pray or praise God, or when they perform certain prescribed rituals as an expression of their faith in Christ, the Spirit is also present and working. And insofar as God is indeed present and working, we are justified in claiming that these acts have become ecclesial in the sense we intend.

But here it is important to keep the role of practice in proper perspective. These practices in and of themselves do not create the church. What the church does as people called by God, it does not in its own strength but as people empowered by the Spirit. Jürgen Moltmann, elaborating on a point cited in the last chapter, insists:

> It is not the Church that administers the Spirit as the Spirit of preaching, the Spirit of the sacraments, the Spirit of ministry. . . . [Rather,] the Spirit administers the Church with the events of word, and faith, sacraments and grace, offices and traditions.[5]

In this chapter, then, we consider the faith, sacraments, offices and traditions. The underlying question that our argument has raised, and that this chapter seeks to address, is this: Given the multiple cultural forms—insider, emergent, and non-church movements—what particular practices might reflect the "ecclesial" character of these? That is, what functions might God be using to move ecclesial movements, by the Spirit, toward the eschatological purposes God has for all things?

THE ORIGIN OF ECCLESIAL PRACTICES

Often at this point in a discussion of the church, specific normative practices are outlined as determinative of the Christian church. We discussed some of the historical examples of these in chapter two. We recall that Calvin famously argued that wherever the word of God is preached and heard and the sacraments are rightly administered, there God is forming the church. Starting with such a definition, we might find it easy to assume that these practices are characteristic of the Christian church universally. Such assumptions lie at the root of all the unsavory arguments in the history of

---

[5]Jürgen Moltmann, *The Church in the Power of the Spirit: A Contribution to Messianic Ecclesiology*, trans. Margaret Kohl (New York: Harper & Row, 1977), 64.

Christianity about whether baptism is properly performed by immersion or by sprinkling—with appropriate marshaling of biblical evidence, or historical precedent, however sketchy this may be.

But the practices that appear in the biblical text did not drop from heaven; they represent preexisting cultural practices that have been incorporated into the life of God's people and, in the process, have taken on new meanings for these people. Here we need to remember that every culture, from time immemorial, has had rituals of initiation and inclusion that mark their social identity. Often these center on table fellowship, as we see in the graphic account of Abraham entertaining three strangers, who turn out to be angels of God (Gen 18:1-10; 19:1). Or they may include various rituals of cleansing, as with Elisha and Naaman (2 Kings 5:10). In both cases, inherited social practices have been embraced in a larger narrative of God's redemptive program. These practices in themselves are not formally sacraments as theologians understand them, but they provide the raw materials, the social situation as it were, in which sacraments, properly speaking, emerge.

Occasionally we learn how such practices become part of the Christian tradition—how they have become sacraments. For example, in the Last Supper with his disciples Jesus makes use of the Passover meal, which was itself a Jewish appropriation of table fellowship, to inaugurate what came to be called Communion, or Eucharist. But often the origin of Christian rituals is impossible to know with any precision. For example, baptism does not make an appearance in the First Testament, but it suddenly appears in the Gospels when John appears baptizing people in the Jordan River. Apparently this represented a practice of purification associated with the Jerusalem temple worship and service, as well as practices of cleansing adopted by the Jewish sects, especially the one centered in Qumran that had influenced John. Whatever its source, Jesus himself accepts John's baptism (Mk 1:9), and with Paul this practice becomes a sacrament—a central symbol of the believer's union with Christ's death and resurrection (Rom 6:1-5).

But here is the central question we raise in this chapter: Is the theological meaning of the practice Paul recommends necessarily connected to the cultural practice of cleansing that he inherited? Or is this connection a contingent and historically situated connection? We argue in this book that these connections are contingent, and reflect God's purposes to transform people (and ultimately the created order) by adopting and adapting common social customs and making them into vehicles of his redemptive program. The contingency lies not in the theological reality that is represented—the believer's incorporation into the death and resurrection of Christ—but in the social practice that is taken to mark this event. This is significant because such inherited practices often express the social identity of people, and this identity, so we argue, God intends to enhance and transform but not overturn. Let us call this a contingent liturgical process that takes on theological meaning. While there could be others, in this chapter we focus on five prominent practices: baptism, Communion, teaching the word of God, praise, and prayer.

Before turning to this discussion, it may be appropriate to say a word about the notion of offices in the church. It is often noted that a characteristic pattern of the Christian church is the appointment of leaders who become bearers of offices, ordinarily understood as authorities appointed to order the worship and life of the community, such as pastors or priests, or deacons and elders.[6] But in the New Testament these offices are seen, initially at least, as functions not of individual office holders but of the community as a whole, which is meant to embody the functions implied in the offices, whether this is preaching (*kerygma*), service (*diakonia*), fellowship (*koinōnia*), or witness (*martyria*). These functions, it is true, were soon assigned to particular persons, as is seen for example in Acts 6:1-7 when specific persons had to be designated to handle the daily food distribution to needy widows. This community service (*diakonia*) was assumed, but as a practical matter, it required specific individuals to implement. However, the function of the community, that is, its embodying of God's program of renewal, preceded and determined the appointment of individuals, who, on the basis of their various giftedness, were called to carry out the various "offices" of the community. This order of things is stressed especially in Ephesians 4:11-13, where the multiple gifts of the body, which themselves express the victory of the risen and ascended Christ (cf. Eph 4:9-11), are given for the sake of building up the body, the community of Christ. We see already in the New Testament that, as the church developed its institutional form,

---

[6]Bonhoeffer, *Sanctorum Communio*, 231-38. The church, he notes, is the bearer of the offices. He lists preaching, orderly administration of sacraments, pastoral care, and priestly mediation.

these functions of the body became enshrined in particular (and eventually professionalized) roles. While this is not a bad thing, the process should not obscure the proper order of things: the functions of the offices belong to the body, and whatever their form, they exist to promote the health of that body as the agent of God's renewing purposes in the world. What are normative, then, are not the contingent forms these offices took in their first-century setting (or in their later setting in church history); rather, the offices or functions developed as needed for the health and growth of the body, whatever culturally appropriate (and contingent) form they might take.

Since the community of Christ lives in history, it must take on some social and cultural shape. And it does this, we argue, not by introducing "Christian" practices that have developed in the history of the church but by adapting itself to the social (and even religious) customs on the ground and forming from these, by an emergent process, a new community of faith and practice. These various customs can be taken up into the worship life of the community in the same way the Jewish (and Roman) customs were taken up and reinterpreted by believers in the first century. But, as we have argued, the contingent origin of liturgical practices of various kinds offers no limitation to their eventual theological meaning; in fact, it may enrich this process.

This process of adaptation and embrace is important to note because it is often assumed that, since a particular social practice was embraced by Jesus and Paul, it has now become incumbent on believers—resulting in the endless attempts and arguments seeking to discover how the early Christians baptized or performed what became the Eucharist. Even if this should be discovered, why should that first-century (contingent) practice necessarily be determinative for believers living two millennia later, in vastly different settings? Since a certain variety is evident already in the New Testament, why should we not allow similar variety of forms within ecclesial practice today? What is authoritative in the teaching of Jesus and Paul is the theological meaning ascribed on those practices, not the specifics of those practices, which are mostly impossible for us to recover in any case.

Surely many readers will find the designation of received Christian practices as "contingent" troubling. This is because Western Christians, the primary audience for this book, have mostly lost sight of the historical (and cultural) development of their various ritual orders and have come to consider their current form somehow privileged. As to the first aspect, we have too often undervalued the contribution of the received cultural meanings in our own development of worship practices. Contingency then should be taken not as something arbitrary or meaningless but as representing the symbolically textured cultural situation in which communities of faith take shape. As Rowan Williams writes, "Representation is what it is in virtue of relations between symbols that constitute it, in such a way that what may seem contingent aspects of it are in fact significant."[7] Appropriating the symbolic meaning of cultural objects taken up into the worship life of believers, Williams implies, can allow us more fully to inhabit our humanity and be open to spiritual transformation.

As to the privileging of our received worship practices, surely this is a product of the continuing influence of "Christendom" thinking on our discussion of church. This is especially true in the mission situation this book addresses. For, as Jehu Hanciles points out, "The western missionary enterprise was marked by the dye of Christendom in its fundamental assumptions, operational strategy and long term objectives."[8] That is, it has too often been allied with the mentality of territorial expansion, pursued with the collusion of political power, and framed, often unconsciously, in terms of spreading Christian civilization around the world. Most missionaries today eschew such triumphalism, but we still need to heed the conclusion that Hanciles draws: "If the Christendom notion of one normative expression of the faith belongs to a passing era, perhaps no concept is more definitive of the new epoch than *diversity of forms and expressions*."[9]

Nowhere is this transition more problematic than in the forms and practices of the community of Christ. Here the influence of Christendom continues. Hispanic scholar Carlos Cardoza-Orlandi, in a response to a recent collection of articles by young Asian theologians, noted that these scholars consistently referred to *church* in abstract terms, as though everyone understood what this means. He went on: "This generic reference to the

---

[7] Rowan Williams, *The Edge of Words: God and the Habits of Language* (London: Bloomsbury, 2014), loc. 3990 (p. 191). Cf. Charles Kraft notes that the Christian meaning may need to be subordinated to "larger traditional events so that people understand the significance and importance of the ceremonies." in Kraft, "Dynamics of Contextualization," in *Appropriate Christianity*, ed. Charles Kraft (Pasadena, CA: William Carey Library, 2005), 173.
[8] Jehu J. Hanciles, *Beyond Christendom: Globalization, African Migration and the Transformation of the West* (Maryknoll, NY: Orbis, 2008), 96.
[9] Hanciles, *Beyond Christendom*, 111 (emphasis original).

'church' assumes a static and triumphalistic ecclesiology—what I call a typical 'Protestant micro-Christendom.'" This view, Cardoza-Orlandi says, is a legacy of the Western missionary movement and may actually impede the development of "unique Asian ecclesiologies, grounded in the interplay between mission and what it means to be the church on Asian soil."[10]

The point here is that the adoption of emergent practices and reinterpretation of biblical examples, so clearly evident in Christian history, suggests a posture of openness to the development of new Christian rituals and liturgies today. Indeed, as we have noted, it is often impossible to specify the exact lineage of Christian practices that have become part of our historical liturgies. Stephen Neill has pointed to the fourth century as a creative period for the development of the great liturgies but reminds us that "all classical liturgies are anonymous. We do not know who the writers were . . . [, and] all give evidence of a long process of development."[11] This process of development surely embraced a wide variety of social practices that were later enshrined in formal liturgies and confessional statements. The patristic formula *lex orandi, lex credenda* ("the law of prayer [is] the law of belief") implies that the practices of faith, of which prayer is arguably central, precede and often inform intentional and formal belief. Indeed, emerging forms of prayer and praise may even herald and lead to new understandings of faith, as was often true during the patristic period of the Christian church.[12] All believers pray, or sing their praises; not all of them reflect on theological texts. Indeed, most do not, nor in many cases are such texts available or accessible to them. Nevertheless, their prayers and praise can fuel new practices that may eventuate in more formal statements of faith.

And this development continues to this day. Consider a modern example of liturgical development described by the Mennonite John Yoder.[13] Yoder

---

[10]Carlos F. Cardoza-Orlandi, "An Invitation to Theological Dialogue," in *What Young Asian Theologians Are Thinking*, ed. Leow Theng Huat (Singapore: Trinity Theological College, 2014), 132.

[11]Stephen Neill, *A History of Christian Missions*, ed. Owen Chadwick, 2nd ed. (New York: Penguin, 1986), 41. This is not to say such exploration is impossible or ill advised, just that it is usually difficult and therefore should not be determinative for contemporary practice.

[12]This is a fundamental argument of J. N. D. Kelly, *Early Christian Creeds*, 3rd ed. (London: Longman, 1972). He notes, for example, that creeds grew out of earlier baptismal confessions.

[13]John Howard Yoder, "A People in the World," in *The Royal Priesthood: Essays Ecclesiastical and Ecumenical*, ed. Michael G. Cartwright (Grand Rapids: Eerdmans, 1994), 65-101. See the discussion

describes this development in terms of what he calls "social practices." (Though he admits they are often called sacraments, he worries about the mechanical and superstitious overtones of this more formal term.) These practices include binding and loosing (mutual forgiveness in the body, Mt 18:15-18), breaking bread together, the fullness of Christ (charismatic ministry of the whole body, Eph 4:11-14), baptism, and the rule of Paul (dialogue as the preferred means of congregational decision making, 1 Cor 14). Yoder underlines the fact that these practices are performed not by the clergy but by the whole congregation on behalf of and for the sake of the larger community. In other words, these ecclesial practices of the community that embody God's work in Christ are meant to have social impact beyond the gathered community. All of them, moreover, represent various contingent customs, adopted during the development of these peace churches, that have taken on transformative meaning in their new setting among God's people in the world. Their social origin offers no handicap to—indeed, it potentially enriches—their use in service of God's people and their ministry in the world.

Yoder's practices will to a certain degree be familiar to Christians residing in the West. Christians in the majority world, however, should be expected to adopt other social customs in their emergent worship experience. Yoder notes that Willem Visser 't Hooft, the great ecumenical leader and missiologist, proposed witness, service, and Communion as the most appropriate marks of the church. Stephen Neill wanted to add to the Reformation marks of the church those of missionary vitality, suffering, and nobility of the pilgrim.[14] These functions are characteristic of the whole body of believers and not simply the clergy and, moreover, speak to the special situations of majority-world believers in Christ and the practices that may be taken up into Christian liturgical practice, a process that may eventuate in new forms expressive of old functions.

This leads to a final point we need to make before discussing specific practices. On the one hand, while rituals and practices are contingent, and flow out of our cultural situation, they are not determined by that location. As we discussed in chapter three, we do not subscribe to a version of cultural

---

of these social practices in Craig A. Carter, "Beyond Theocracy and Individualism," in *The Community of the Word: Toward an Evangelical Ecclesiology*, ed. Mark Husbands and Daniel J. Treier (Downers Grove, IL: IVP Academic, 2005), 173-87, from which the following is taken.

[14]Yoder, "A People in the World," 75.

determinism but acknowledge that people exercise choice and agency when deciding on their liturgies. On the other hand, in making our choices we do not examine every possible option, were that even possible. Rather, our cultural situation constrains and presents to us a certain set of choices that, for us, make most sense and seem most "natural." That set of possible choices will differ between communities such that, for example, one church's choice on how to celebrate baptism may look markedly different from another's.

Not only does our cultural community present to us particular choices but, as we know from the history of the missionary enterprise, power can also impact the ability to choose. Often without fully realizing it, Western missionaries brought with them a set of opinions about which practices were appropriate for a new church. When these missionaries were not able to acknowledge their own underlying presumptions, the "receivers" of the gospel were told how they should pray, praise God, implement teaching, and so on—their choices were sifted and approved by the missionaries. Though usually well meaning, Western Christians have thus constrained and enabled the set of choices available to new churches. This is where many of the newly emerging movements that we highlight in this book are seeking to expand their repertoire of practices by opening up new possibilities that may have been previously rejected. In light of this, we now turn to more concrete examples of baptism, Communion, teaching, praise, and prayer and ask, How might such practices be understood and evaluated in the current situation of the global church?

BAPTISM, PRACTICES OF INITIATION INTO CHRIST

We have argued that normative theological meaning has taken multiple forms in the long development of various liturgical practices. Consider the practices of baptism. The theological content of baptism that Paul highlights in Romans (6:3-4) stresses that the practice of baptism, whatever shape it takes, is meant to signify the believer's identification with Christ's death and resurrection. The actual practice of baptism in the New Testament, as we have seen, represented an adaptation of the baptism that apparently arose among Jewish sects around the time of Christ, and that John had adopted and practiced. But this heritage and adaptation, interestingly, is nowhere explored in any detail—it is rather taken for granted. This received social practice was then taken up and made into a central image of the Christian's identification with Christ. What Paul emphasizes in baptism, after all, is not a particular social practice but the identification of the believer with Christ's death and resurrection. The specific ritual chosen to symbolize this is left open; it is nowhere specified in the New Testament. And Christians have taken a variety of positions on the question. Some, like the Salvation Army and Quakers, consider this a spiritual reality that need not be connected to any ritual while others, like the Roman Catholic and Eastern Orthodox communions, have developed highly detailed rituals for the practice.[15]

To illustrate, consider the case of the *Khrist bhaktas*[16] in Chennai, South India, as described by Jonas Jorgensen, along with insights by Dayanand Bharati, a Hindu *Khrist bhakta* leader and spokesman.[17] The *Khrist bhaktas* are followers of Christ from Hindu backgrounds who, as a part of their ritual life together, incorporate a Hindu practice of initiation known as *guru diksha* (guru initiation). This they link to the biblical practice of baptism. From the Hindu perspective, this connection between *diksha* and baptism is meaningful and significant for at least two reasons.

First, many Hindus often understand rituals in general as ways to create new possibilities and realities for the person partaking in them. That is, Hindus do not generally engage in rituals first and foremost to symbolically reflect a doctrine or truth. Rather, as Hindu scholar Joyce Flueckiger says, they participate in rituals to tap into their agentive power to effect human transformation, create new identities, and identify and sustain social

---

[15]John Jay Travis notes that some Muslim-background believers in Asia are similar to the Salvation Army and Quakers in not emphasizing baptism or Communion. John Jay Travis, "Insider Movements Among Muslims, A Focus on Asia," in *Understanding Insider Movements: Disciples of Jesus Within Diverse Religious Communities*, ed. Harley Talman and John Jay Travis (Pasadena, CA: William Carey Library, 2015), 139. The attempt to mediate these differences has made what can only be called spectacular progress over the last half century leading to the publication of *Baptism, Eucharist and Ministry* (Geneva: World Council of Churches, 1982), which stresses the theological and biblical ground of the various (historical and cultural) practices that have developed in the church.

[16]*Khrist bhaktas* are followers of Jesus who retain their identity as Hindus. The *bhakti* traditions of Hinduism, from which the term *bhakta* derives, dates to the medieval period. The poets and teachers of these traditions often depict God as a personal being to whom people can be personally and inwardly devoted as a way of becoming one with God.

[17]Jonas Adelin Jorgensen, *Jesus Imandars and Christ Bhaktas: Two Case Studies of Interreligious Hermeneutics and Identity in Global Christianity* (New York: Peter Lang, 2008); and Dayanand Bharati, *Living Water and Indian Bowl: An Analysis of Christian Failings in Communicating Christ to Hindus, with Suggestions Toward Improvements* (Delhi: ISPCK, 1997).

communities.[18] Of course, for a Hindu to engage in a ritual often implies a certain amount of agreement with some doctrine or belief, such as the efficacy of a deity's power or the importance of the ritual for maintaining their family's tradition and community. However, Flueckiger points out that, for Hindus, the function of rituals is often not primarily to reflect back and make a statement about a prior commitment but rather to look forward to what the ritual promises to open up for the person.

Second, the particular ritual of *guru diksha* is one where a guru, or teacher, gives the grace of initiation into the *parampara*, or tradition, that the guru espouses and promotes. Within many Hindu traditions the guru is held in high esteem and accepts *shiyas*, or students, to learn from him or her. Any person can listen to and learn basic teachings from gurus without taking initiation. However, when a person desires to learn more deeply from the guru, and when the guru invites and accepts the person to come under his or her teaching and join the guru's community, that guru administers *diksha*. In so doing, the disciple receives the privilege of sitting at the guru's feet, submitting to and learning from the guru, and receiving the guru's blessing. The form of this ritual varies, but often the initiates receive new names and practices that immerse them more deeply into the *parampara*, or pathway, they have chosen. From a social standpoint, such gurus and their communities are often understood to be part of the wider Hindu social community. An initiate partaking in *guru diksha* is seen as choosing a particular path within the wide array of Hindu pathways and, thus, still remains Hindu.

As is often the case, particularly within Hindu traditions, rituals such as *guru diksha* can have a variety of meanings and assume an array of forms. Because of this, Bharati, a *Khrist bhakta*, says that such practices "are flexible enough to be adapted for conveying biblical meanings."[19] Since the object and means of the *guru diksha* initiation ritual are flexible, Hindu *Khrist bhaktas* link it to their interpretation of baptism. Consequently, some fellowships administer *guru diksha* by immersing initiates in a river or pond while reciting *shlokas* (verses) from the Sanskrit Bible.

But notice how the *Khrist bhaktas'* Hindu framework interacts with their reading of Scripture, providing a reverse hermeneutic through which they

---

[18]Joyce Burkhalter Flueckiger, *Everyday Hinduism* (Oxford: Wiley Blackwell, 2015), 191.
[19]Bharati, *Living Water and Indian Bowl*, 115.

interpret the significance of baptism for them and their community. For them, baptism is both a symbolic statement about their submission to Jesus as their guru as well as an agentive practice that seeks to appropriate God's grace for their lives.[20] Though the latter is shaped by a particularly Hindu understanding of practice, it also begins to reflect a Catholic understanding of baptism as sacrament, or as a practice that facilitates God's grace.

As is evident, the *Khrist bhaktas* have interpreted baptism via a Hindu practice but have also transformed the Hindu practice in significant ways. In particular, whereas *guru diksha* often signals a disciple's commitment to a human guru and ultimately to a deity or divine presence via the guru's teaching, the *Khrist bhaktas* become disciples of the divine Jesus himself, not a human intermediary. Notice how the transformation of this ritual has a striking parallel to the early Christian struggle with eating meat offered to idols (1 Cor 8). First, Paul pointed out that this offering could be understood in a variety of ways and valued for various reasons, including simply as food created by God. Second, Paul adapted this to be a part of the Christ-followers' practice of table fellowship, where this meat could be received with thanksgiving as a gift of God's good creation (as Paul describes in 1 Tim 4:3-5).

Notice too that interpreting baptism through the framework of *guru diksha* helps the *Khrist bhaktas* avoid certain connotations of baptism common in India, such as joining a traditional Christian church, joining the Christian "religion," or changing sociolegal status. Instead, the ritual seeks to administer Christ's grace and power to his devotees in a way that does not destroy the person's Hindu identity and family connections but rather affirms these within the framework of devotion to Christ.

Of course, as we have noted, what emerges from the interaction and adaptation of practices cannot always be predicted, and believers should evaluate the relational goods and unintended evils that may result. Paul drew attention to the way in which the Corinth believers, in their consumption of food offered before idols, could also "become a stumbling block to the weak" (1 Cor 8:9). As Paul indicates, not everyone understands that idols do not exist or will be willing to revalue food in the way the believers were doing (1 Cor 8:7). Indeed, there are times when specific rituals and

---

[20]Jorgensen, *Jesus Imandars and Christ Bhaktas*, 374.

adverse power and spirits are so closely connected in the understanding and experience of others that the performance of those rituals would actually become a stumbling block for following Christ or significantly distort what it means to follow him. As we noted in chapter four, Christians' uncritical acceptance of the role of the emperor in Japan when the Religious Groups Acts was passed in 1939/40, and of the role of the führer in the German Church during the 1930s, had many unfortunate consequences. But Paul's careful discussion seems to suggest we should not allow such concerns to keep us from critical interactions with and adaptations of the gifts and opportunities our cultural traditions have made possible.

What is needed in every case is a careful evaluation of the emergent goods, evils, and tensions that arise as biblical texts and practices are interpreted via the cultural context. Thus, the social impact of notions of baptism call for careful scrutiny. Notice that adapting Hindu ceremonies of initiation did not involve a break from one social community and an initiation into another. This troubles many observers. Shouldn't baptism recognize this social transition from one community (cf. Hindu) into another (cf. Christian)? It could be, and often has been, interpreted as such. But why should that necessarily be the case when the communities in question are largely understood in social (and familial) terms?

The two critical issues need to be disentangled: the cultural and the theological. First, it is characteristic of Christ-followers in Hindu and Muslim communities to de-emphasize baptism as a ritual of social disruption. We noted the way it is interpreted via *guru diksha* in some Hindu settings. In the Muslim world, as Mazhar Mallouhi points out, there is no ceremony that calls for entrance into the Muslim community. As with many parts of the world, one is born a Muslim or a Hindu. As a result, Mallouhi notes, though born a Muslim and now a follower of Jesus: "Muslims need never publicly or personally appropriate faith as is expected in the Christian tradition of baptism or confirmation, but on the contrary must take decisive action if they want to remove themselves from community."[21] As a result, there are no rituals of initiation that correspond to the idea of baptism as a movement from one religious community to another.[22]

---

[21]Mazhar Mallouhi, "Comments on the Insider Movement," in Talman and Travis, *Understanding Insider Movements*, 117.

[22]In Hindu settings in India, fundamentalist Hindus have in recent years promoted *ghar wapsi*

Here the theological meanings of baptism become relevant. In the New Testament baptism did not involve leaving one religious community (Jewish) and joining another (that is, Christian). Rather, it meant sharing in the death and resurrection of Christ and determining to follow Christ and walk in that resurrection life (Rom 6:3-11). This did not mean leaving one's community; rather, it meant entering the community more deeply with the reframed understanding of allegiance to Christ. Notice that this idea of following after Christ more deeply within one's community is similar to what Hindu *Khrist bhaktas* understand as they interpret baptism via *guru diksha*. One might be prompted to ask: If changing one's social location was not the intention of New Testament baptism, how did it come to have this meaning for many Christians today? In response, we would recall our discussions in chapter two regarding the believers' churches initiation of a legacy of adult baptism, which became the primary sign of one's "conversion" to faith and of joining the "true church." We also noted how the idea of church taken overseas by American missionaries was too often understood as a voluntary society, which individuals make free decisions to join or not. Is this then an unintended consequence of that way of thinking—that individuals must make free choices to join (or not to join) a religious community? We also challenged the universality of such assumptions and noted the existence of many cultures where cultural solidarity is thought to preexist and thus determine individual identity. And we saw in the chapter of case studies how believers in Bangsamoro have reinterpreted community in ways that are consistent with their identity as Muslims but that resist the missionaries' Christendom narrative.

This diversity of settings raises another possibility that calls for comment. What if specific cultural assumptions suggest a wider application of practices like baptism that might extend their theological reach in those places? A possible example is cultures of Africa and Asia, where ancestors are considered part of the living community. They might ask, Why cannot baptism be extended to them? Apparently some Christians in Japan, as we noted in an earlier chapter, are rethinking the possibility of baptism on behalf of the dead. For Western Christians immersed in the ideology of individualism, such notions are inconceivable. We believe each of us must be baptized for

---

(homecoming) ceremonies to reconvert Christians and Muslims back to Hinduism. This is, however, a recent and uncommon practice.

ourselves, whether as infants or adults. But here is where people in other settings find our assumptions confusing. For these Japanese believers, and for many other people, the separation between the past and the present, and between the individual and the community, is not fixed in this way. According to Peter Wilson, when Christian missionaries preached to the Slavs during the Middle Ages, "the refusal of Christian priests to baptize ancestors made no sense to Slavs."[23] How could baptism be rethought in such a setting?

EUCHARIST, COMMUNION, REMEMBERING CHRIST'S DEATH

Rituals growing out of Christ's initiation of the cup and bread, which are to be taken as a memorial of his death and an anticipation of his return, have surely been central to Christian practice over the years. Indeed, along with baptism, this practice points to the central reality of believers' incorporation into Christ's death. Jesus, a Jewish rabbi dining with his Jewish disciples, appropriated the Passover celebration in instituting a ritual representing the new covenant sealed by his blood. His First Testament background, including the deliverance from Egypt, the blood sacrifices of the sacrificial system, and the prophecies of the prophets about a new covenant, all contributed to the significance embodied in Jesus' blessing of the bread and wine. Like other ceremonies, the Eucharist carries multiple meanings: the theological meaning, the broken body and shed blood as representative of a new and final sacrifice; the actual ritual practice, the taking and blessing of bread and wine and distributing to the disciples; and finally the meaning expressed in Jesus' words: "This is my body that is for you. Do this in remembrance of me" (1 Cor 11:24).

As early churches spread beyond their Jewish origins, they adapted to new situations. In the Greco-Roman tradition of banquet meals, the cup and wine was given a new setting.[24] It is important to note in this regard that, in Jesus' initiation of it and its ongoing practice among the churches, the Eucharist was not a part of a worship service involving a set of token symbols but was part

---

[23] Peter H. Wilson, *The Heart of Europe: A History of the Holy Roman Empire* (Cambridge, MA: Harvard University Press, 2015), 78.

[24] Dennis E. Smith. *From Symposium to Eucharist*, 133-72. Smith also shows that, though Jewish meal traditions had unique origins and characteristics (such as dietary restrictions) by the first century CE, they had been highly influenced by and reflected the wider Greco-Roman banquet practices and ideologies.

of a full meal. Church leaders were certainly aware of the symbolic nature of bread and wine, and even offered special thanksgiving prayers. But these were offered and celebrated in the midst of a meal itself; it was only much later that the Eucharist would become an event distinct from a meal gathering.[25]

Additionally, the bread and wine apparently had more than one meaning for early churches. Jesus' (and Paul's) association of the bread and wine with the body and blood of Jesus was of course very important for the early churches. But early Christian leaders also seemed to associate the Eucharist with God's work of gathering his church. One of the earliest Communion prayers from the Didache says, "Just as this broken bread was scattered upon the mountains and then was gathered together and became one, so may your church be gathered together from the ends of the earth into your kingdom."[26] Though the association of Christ and his death is no doubt close to the surface in this prayer, no explicit mention is made of Christ's body and blood. Rather, the breaking of bread is interpreted in terms of its being brought back together again as a church (Christ's body) from all parts of the earth.

Our point again is that the practice and purpose of the Eucharist have changed over time according to various cultural situations. This is no less the case currently, and an examination of the multiple practices globally raises the question: What can be done by those seeking to follow Christ's teaching whose cultural and religious context seriously conflicts with the social and religious context of the New Testament?

The southern Philippines provides an important instance, both of the challenge and of the possibilities of cultural appropriation as this has been recently described by Filipino theologians. Among the Manobo people in Davao del Norte, malevolent spirits called *busow* are believed to search for blood to satisfy their cravings.[27] During indigenous religious rituals, the spirit priest drinks the blood of sacrifices on behalf of good spirits that offer protection against the *busow*. When the missionaries began teaching about the death of

[25] Andrew B. McGowan, *Ancient Christian Worship: Early Church Practices in Social, Historical, and Theological Perspective* (Grand Rapids: Baker Academic, 2014), 37-39.
[26] Didache 9.4, from *The Apostolic Fathers in English*, trans. Michael W. Holmes, 3rd ed. (Grand Rapids: Baker Academic, 2007).
[27] Brian Powell, "Manobo Blood Sacrifice and Christ's Death," in *Christologies, Cultures and Religions: Portraits of Christ in the Philippines*, ed. Pascal Bazzell and Aldrin Peñamora (Manila: OMF, 2016), 87, 88.

Christ and the practice of drinking his "blood" the people were shocked. Was God a *busow*, they wondered? Would they be possessed by an evil spirit by drinking Christ's blood? As a result, Brian Powell has written, "local congregations [of Christians] rarely, if ever, celebrated the Lord's Supper."[28] The local practice resisted appropriation of a positive image of sharing in Christ's new covenant as this was encouraged in the New Testament.

In other cases appropriation is natural. For instance, incorporation into Christ's new covenant framed as a messianic banquet can be used to celebrate a newfound unity. Elsewhere in Bangsamoro, *sandugo*, an ancient Moro ritual in which participants wound themselves and drink each other's blood, creating a new community of one blood, has been appropriated as a ritual of Christ's love "characterized by responsibility for others."[29] Some followers of Christ have sought to appropriate this ritual for Christian communities.

In the article that discusses this possibility, Aldrin Peñamora raises the larger question these cases pose for the surrounding Christian churches. He proposes they reconsider this ritual as anamnesis, a remembering of Christ's death in such a way that believers are challenged to offer their lives that others may live. This participation in the death of Christ, called by some theologians in the Philippines a "theology of struggle," seeks to identify with the Moro people in their struggle by emphasizing the suffering of Christ (*Pasyón*, Passion of Christ), showing the determination of God to identify with the worst human wretchedness.[30] This accepts the marginalization of the Moro people as a Christian problem and not simply a Muslim problem. For it was a Christian government that instigated the policies of immigration by Christian settlers from the north that deprived the Moros of their homeland.[31] Can Matthew 26:28, "This is my blood of the covenant, which is poured out for many for the forgiveness of sins," be interpreted as the call to Christians to share in the suffering of their neighbors?

Recalling Yoder's insistence that these sacramental practices are also, and perhaps inevitably, social practices suggests that one value of reflection on the variety of rituals is to return to our own traditions with fresh understanding

---

[28]Powell, "Manobo Blood Sacrifice," 90.
[29]Aldrin M. Peñamora, "The Christ of the Eucharist and Moro-Christian Relations," in Bazzell and Peñamora, *Christologies, Cultures and Religions*, 178.
[30]Peñamora, "Christ of the Eucharist," 172.
[31]Peñamora, "Christ of the Eucharist," 174.

for what God is doing with people who seek to follow Jesus. And it may include reflection on the social impact, not only of our worship practices but also of our teaching.

TEACHING THE WORD OF GOD

If remembering Christ, or Eucharist, in whatever form it may take is an important practice, various forms of teaching or preaching the Scripture are also central practices of Christ-followers. But what emerges in a study of various churches, and insider groups especially, is the way the teaching embodied in Scripture is always placed in conversation with inherited religious texts. New Buddhists in eastern Thailand read Scriptures against the background of the teachings of Buddha; believers in Christ in southern Philippines read Scriptures along with the Qur'an and the Hadith. As we saw in a previous chapter, the Filipino experience of teaching Scripture has recently involved a communal work of translating the book of Acts into their own language so they can better understand the emergent experience of their community against that of believers in the early church.

Many Christians in India are discouraged from reading or ascribing value to Hindu, Sikh, or Muslim scriptures. However, some Sikh followers of Jesus have a high regard for the Sikh scriptures, the Guru Granth Sahib. This is a compilation of the prayers and poetry of the various Sikh gurus, as well as other Hindu and Muslim poets whose thoughts about devotion to God were similar to the Sikh gurus. Among the Sikh gurus, the person and stories of the first founder of the movement, Guru Nanak, are often most highly revered. For example, a popular story regards a trip Guru Nanak made to the Muslim holy site of Mecca. Upon arriving, he rested himself by sitting at the base of a tree and extending his feet out toward the sacred Kaaba. In many cultures, to extend the bottom of your feet toward a person or sacred object can be interpreted as a sign of disrespect. Such was the reaction of a local Muslim when he saw Guru Nanak's posture. After the Muslim chastised him, the guru said, "Pick up my feet and place them where there is no God." The Muslim moved the guru's feet, but, as he did so, the Kaaba moved and followed to wherever the guru's feet were placed. This showed the Muslim that God was indeed not limited to a particular location and that the guru had extraordinary knowledge of God. To the Sikh followers of Jesus who share this story, it emphasizes a truth they see from the Bible that is also expressed and reinforced via their own Sikh religious heritage. As one Christ-follower expressed it, "We tell our people that from this story Guru Nanak is saying that God is in every place. Everywhere. So let's search for that God who gave spiritual children to Guru Nanak."[32]

Notice how, for this Christ-follower, the founder of Sikhism is not someone who led people down a wrong path. In fact, Sikhs affirm that his "children" (the Sikhs) have at their foundation an impulse to know about the true God. This desire to know God, expressed so beautifully in many of their scriptures and prayers, comes to its fulfillment in Christ. For them it does not matter that Christ's revelation came chronologically before Guru Nanak; Christ still fills and completes the longings that have been expressed through the Sikh gurus and those that followed.

Many Western Christians probably at this point wonder where the line should be drawn with regard to utilizing and respecting the scriptures and figures of other religious traditions. Though Christ-followers in other contexts do not always think in terms of a line, many do ponder the type of relationship their religious heritage has with Christ and the Bible. For example, Gaurav, a leader of Hindu and Sikh Christ-followers, distinguishes between *respect* and *worship*. Hindus and Sikhs bow down and touch the feet of their parents and others they seek to honor, but this is not worship. In like manner, a person can offer respect to Guru Nanak and the scriptures without worshiping them.[33]

As another example, John Jay Travis explains how, among Muslim Christ-followers, Muhammad and the Qur'an are "revalued" in relation to Christ and the revelation of the Bible. Aspects of Muhammad's teaching and the Qur'an that are in line with the Bible and point to God's truth are retained. In this way Muslim Christ-followers can refer to Muhammad as a prophet insofar as he denounced the polytheism of his day, warned of an upcoming day of judgment, and affirmed the Bible as the Word of God. The relative place of Muhammad and the Qur'an, however, is superseded by Jesus and the Bible since the person and revelation of Christ now provide the main frame of reference for their understanding of God's ways and purposes.[34]

---

[32]John Jay Travis, personal communication with Darren Duerksen, April 15, 2010.
[33]Many orthodox Sikhs make the same distinction; they bow down and revere the gurus and scriptures but save worship only for God.
[34]John Jay Travis, personal communication with Darren Duerksen, July 11, 2017.

These examples may again strike many Western Christians as strange and threatening. But let us recall our discussion in the last chapter: even in the Bible God's work was often described against the backdrop of the religious traditions and practices of local cultures. At times God's revelation challenged these practices and teachings, but at other times the latter helped to illuminate and make clear to a people the nature of God and his work. Teaching is never given in a cultural or religious vacuum.

PRAISE

A further example of the way in which practices emerge out of religious contexts exists in areas of worship styles and music. When the *Khrist bhaktas* in India gather, they love to sing *bhajans*, a style of music widely popular in Hindu and Sikh *bhakti* traditions.[35] *Khrist bhaktas* stressed that this music was part of their heritage and intrinsic to their family and social memories. Singing *bhajans* is central to Hindu worship and is considered an act of praise to the devotee's preferred deity. For believers in Christ, it became a suitable vehicle of praise to God. The *bhakti yoga* featured *bhajans* in order to foster love for deities like *Rama*; *Khrist bhaktas*, "in the singing of the *bhajans*, . . . realize the qualities of Jesus and enter into a loving relation" with him.[36]

All these practices, including those incorporating music, are both ecclesial and social. That is, they shape the church in its theological identity and vision, and also orient it in relation to its wider social context. In this way the practices in general, and music in particular, are part of an emergent process of identity formation. On an ecclesial level, music provides the cultural language by which Christ-followers individually and corporately connect with and worship Christ. In this sense it orients the church community and its cultural context within the narrative of the gospel. Music also helps to bring that same biblical narrative into their particular religious community. The composition and singing of *bhajans*, for example, give expression to a corporate faith in Christ and relate that faith with the poetic narratives and musical aesthetics of Hindu and Sikh *bhakti* traditions. What

---

[35]Darren Todd Duerksen, *Ecclesial Identities in a Multi-Faith Context: Jesus Truth-Gatherings* (Yeshu Satsangs) *Among Hindus and Sikhs in Northwest India*, American Society of Missiology Monograph 22 (Eugene, OR: Pickwick, 2015), 74-75.
[36]Jorgensen, *Jesus Imandars and Christ Bhaktas*, 374.

emerges, then, is an ecclesial community that witnesses to the presence and continuity of Christ within their own setting. For example, the following is a *shabad* (Sikh devotional song) written by a Sikh Christ-follower:

Open the eyes of your heart O man
The God that you seek is near you O man
God is a friend of the pure
The fortunate ones get a vision of God
Join your heart with him O man
The God that you seek is near you O man
Read and meditate on God's word
Hold on to Jesus
There is no other way to heaven
The God that you seek is near you O man
Open the eyes of your heart O man
You have sought everywhere
You have bowed at every dwelling
With all your efforts you failed to find God
The God that you seek is near you O man
Open the eyes of your heart O man
Neither in the churches nor in the temples
God is in your heart
O Noor [the songwriter] receive him in faith
The God that you seek is near you O man
Open the eyes of your heart O man[37]

Of particular interest is the way that this song's style, as well as its lyrical themes, reflect the *bhakti* tradition out of which the Sikh tradition arose. For example, compare the themes of this song, and particularly the last two stanzas, with a well-known poem of Kabir, a fifteenth-century Hindu *bhakti* poet, some of whose work is featured in the Sikh scriptures. Kabir writes,

O Servant, where dost thou seek Me?
Lo, I am beside thee,
I am neither in temple nor in mosque:

---

[37]Noormallu Walia, "Open the Eyes of Your Heart," Sikh Punjabi Music Video (English subtitles), (India/Pakistan: Create International, 2010), www.indigitube.tv/video/sikh-punjabi-music-video-engsub.

I am neither in Kaaba nor Kailash [Varanasi].
Neither am I in rites and ceremonies,
nor in Yoga and renunciation.
If thou art a true seeker, thou shalt at once see Me:
Thou shalt meet me in a moment of time.
Kabir says: O Sadhu! God is the breath of all breath.[38]

In this famous poem Kabir expresses a sentiment shared by many medieval *bhakti* poets—God is near, even beside us, and cannot be found in the most sacred sites. In this he cites two of the most famous locations: the Kaaba in Mecca (for Muslims) and Kailash, or Varanasi (for Hindus). Even the various rituals are empty for the purpose of finding God, and it is only the true seeker who will find him. The parallels between this and the Sikh Christ-focused song above are numerous and are obviously intentional. Religious institutions (including the institutional church!) are inadequate for finding God, who is always near and made manifest through Christ. But this is not simply an individualistic faith. The medium of the *shabad* itself, a call-response song, presupposes and invites the gathering of a corporate (ecclesial) community to join together and affirm God's closeness to them through Christ. To do so it draws on an ancient narrative of Hindus and Sikhs longing after God and ties this into a biblical narrative that accentuates Christ.[39]

PRAYER

Practices of prayer offered to gods and spirits make up a central practice for all religions. In Nigeria, traditional Igbo morning prayers are offered by the head of the household, who, after a ritual washing, squats in the center of the compound and greets God as a way of sanctifying the new day:

Obasi [creator God] who dwells above
Glorious and powerful King
The incomprehensible and ineffable One.
Unfathomable waters
King of the Heavens

---

[38]Kabir, *One Hundred Poems of Kabir*, trans. Rabindranath Tagore, assisted by Evelyn Underhill (New York: Macmillan, 1915), 1.
[39]Noor, the songwriter of the contemporary song quoted above, also uses the *bhakti* convention of speaking to himself at the end of the song, calling himself to do what he is telling others to do.

The King who dwells above and is above all
And yet whose garments reach the earth
The immanent one.
I submit entirely to you in homage
We are still here
The land and place you allotted to us
And in the condition you last met with us . . .
Give us life, worthwhile life (Igbo: Ezi Ndu).[40]

Cyril Okorocha argues that this prayer for a "worthwhile life" becomes for the Igbo a sign of the new life that Christ brings to his people. The traditional Igbo prayer is thus inscribed with a new Christian meaning.[41]

In Korea the large Christian community has come to be known by its central emphasis on communal prayer in a variety of forms—from daily early morning prayer services to weekend retreats at mountain retreat centers. Though this is widely known and admired as reflective of Korean spirituality, recent research has shown that these practices existed in indigenous traditions of Korea. The early morning prayer meetings, for example, are thought to have been started by Kil Sonju during the 1907 revival in the northern part of Korea. Kil had been converted from Taoism in 1897, and Taoist practice involved early morning prayer to the Jade King. Sung-Deuk Oak has recently argued that Kil appropriated a variety of Taoist practices— dawn prayer, fasting, audible incantation, all-night prayer meetings—and relocated them to the Christian church.[42] Here, practices preexisting the arrival of Christianity have been taken over and reinterpreted in a Christian setting so as to deepen their communal and spiritual, and Korean, identity.

Some Native American Christ-followers have reached into their own traditions to find ways in which to pray and worship God. For example, Richard Twiss describes how he and others have utilized the traditional sweat lodge as a place for prayer. The lodges are constructed using the traditional materials and design typical for a given tribe and reservation but are considered "sacred

---

[40]Cyril Okorocha, "The Meaning of Salvation: An African Perspective," in *Emerging Voices in Global Christian Theology*, ed. William A. Dyrness (Grand Rapids: Zondervan, 1994), 67, 68.

[41]Okorocha, "The Meaning of Salvation." 72-73

[42]Sung-Deuk Oak, "Major Protestant Revivals in Korea: 1903–1935," *Studies in World Christianity* 18, no. 3 (2012): 270-72. He argues that evidence like this suggests the major indigenous influences were Taoist rather than Shamanist as is sometimes argued.

places of worship and intercession in the Spirit of Jesus."[43] After the lodge is made hot with steam, participants are led by an elder through four rounds of prayer, singing, and sharing. In some cases the leader burns sage or sweet grass to symbolize their prayers ascending to and being heard by God. The hot, sweaty setting is not comfortable but, as Twiss says, creates a setting for reflection on how "the Holy Creator helps us face the frailty of our humanity, and pours grace, forgiveness, healing and love on a willing recipient in the name of Jesus."[44]

Another important aspect of the sweat lodge is the use of stones, sometimes called "grandfather stones."[45] Many native languages use a word for stones that indicates they are animate objects. Since these are known by the tribes to be some of the more ancient objects in a given context, the tribes sometimes see these as similar to grandfathers or ancestors. As such, the stones, in a sense, speak to and remind the community of their connection to the land, and they also hear the prayers and stories of the people. Though the prayers are to God, an ancient spiritual witness is also present and available as support.

Similar to the other practices discussed, prayer is a normative theological practice but one whose expression is highly contingent on the community's cultural context. As church communities have done and continue to do, they draw from a selection of concepts and practices and reinterpret these for the development of new Christian ritual and liturgy.

Though the practices we have discussed are normative, our list is not exhaustive. One might add to these and discuss the practices of testimony, evangelism, patience, hospitality, and fellowship, to name a few. We have not attempted to be comprehensive but have tried to illustrate the ways in which normative practices, such as various liturgical practices of worship, are appropriated and given theological meaning in contingent ways. This creates an emergent process whereby God enhances and transforms, but does not overturn, the community's social customs and identities. Ecclesial practices like these are uniquely able to locate the community's own cultural narrative

---

[43]Richard Twiss, *Rescuing the Gospel from the Cowboys: A Native American Expression of the Jesus Way* (Downers Grove, IL: InterVarsity Press, 2015), 146.

[44]Twiss, *Rescuing the Gospel*, 148.

[45]We are grateful to Randy Woodley for added information and clarification regarding these practices.

within that of the gospel and in turn to identify the presence of the gospel within the community's historical and ongoing cultural narrative. This dual movement—people locating themselves in the ongoing biblical story and recognizing God's presence and work within their own community's narrative—allows the emergence of new church communities that will be both in continuity with and distinct from their social context.

....

7

Markers of the Transformative Church

The neighbors begin to arrive slowly, coming to the house as the North Indian heat starts to lessen ever so slightly with the approach of evening. They are generally upper-caste and affluent Hindu and Sikh families, many around retirement age. Though Padman has only lived in their neighborhood for four years, they have gotten to know him through his visits to them, his involvement in local civic work, and his willingness to offer legal advice and counsel when needed. They also know that he and his family are upper-caste Arya Samaj, a branch of Hinduism that prioritizes the ancient Vedas and associated rituals.

Padman has invited them to participate in a *satsang* (truth gathering), which he hosts periodically dependent on his own schedule as a lawyer. He knows and has practiced the Arya Samaji rituals well and adapted them according to his own devotion to Christ. He has thus translated portions of the New Testament into Sanskrit, which he recites during the *satsang*. He also sings *bhajans*, some of which have been composed by other devotees of Christ. He is careful, however, not to use the name Jesus, preferring to use the name Charitosh since *Jesus* instantly brings to mind colonial and other unhelpful connotations with his educated, high-caste neighbors.

Padman's fellowship is occasional, including people with varied understandings of Charitosh and his teachings, and in many ways it is only the beginning of what we may call a church. Indeed, many would be hesitant to say that a church has even yet begun since Padman and his family and friends do not (yet) have some of the practices and marks that form what many would call a church. Throughout history, as we have seen, various combinations of such marks have been suggested. For example, for Luther the church was "the assembly of all believers among whom the gospel is purely preached and the holy sacraments are administered according to the gospel."[1] Calvin agreed with these but placed greater emphasis on correct faith and the disciplined Christian life. Menno Simons, contemporary to Calvin, added four additional marks: holy living, brotherly love, unreserved testimony, and suffering.[2] Though these leaders differed slightly, all three were reacting against the Roman Catholic Church's definition of the church as a perfect society (*societas perfecta*) marked by a clear sacramental system and institutional structure that included holy orders, episcopacy, and the papacy.

Markers such as those proposed by the Reformers and Anabaptists continue to characterize the ecclesiologies of these and other Christian traditions today. These markers also provide the framework by which these churches evaluate other churches and gatherings such as those occurring in Padman's house. However, as we saw in chapter two, such practices, theologies, and marks of the church have always emerged out of particular historical circumstances, and often in response to perceived excesses or problems in other churches. Though a historical study such as ours shows this to be the case, quite often the particular expression of an ecclesial marker becomes frozen in time, disassociated from the cultural, social, and political influences that generated its emergence. Over time, the context in and through which those markers gained their particular salience fades from view, and the practices themselves come to be seen as pure markers of the church.

While it is important for churches to define what they mean by *church*, we are arguing that it is wise and important for churches to recognize the cultural milieu in which their particular ecclesiology and ecclesial markers have emerged, and in which they continue to have relevance. Some perhaps resist this, fearing that such a project makes those ecclesiologies less biblical or true. Others may resist because they fear such acknowledgment will only further divide an already fragmented global church. But must this be the case? Rather than seeing such diversity as undermining the work of God or creating greater division, we suggest that the diversity of the global church in general

---

[1] Augsburg Confession 7.1, in *The Book of Concord: The Confessions of the Evangelical Lutheran Church*, ed. Robert Kolg and Timothy J. Wengert, trans. Charles P. Arand (Minneapolis: Fortress, 2000), 42.

[2] For summaries on these see Veli-Matti Kärkkäinen, *An Introduction to Ecclesiology: Ecumenical, Historical & Global Perspectives* (Downers Grove, IL: InterVarsity Press, 2002).

and of insider groups in particular are gifts God has provided his people. These gifts of diversity provide all churches with the opportunity to critically reflect on their own beliefs and practices and affirm, modify, or repent of those things that do not conform to God's purposes for them. In addition, when a church views its distinct understanding and practice of church as a gift, this understanding should remind them that their practices ultimately derive from God and his work among people. As Allen Verhey says, "This language of 'gift' should be enough to keep us from claiming moral superiority for Christians or for ourselves in comparison with other Christians."[3]

In the midst of diversity, what is it that holds churches together across time and place? Of the various markers that can be and often are highlighted, there are several that we, in line with the argument of this book, contend are normative and particularly important in this age of church diversification. Our choices are determined by the belief that, as an integral part of God's overall work of re-creation, the church is meant to be a transformative presence based on the life and work of Christ, as made present by the Holy Spirit. We have at various points alluded to this principle, particularly in chapter one, where we drew attention to the overall work of new creation that God is shaping by his Spirit. The church, we have said, is neither the sum total of nor peripheral to that new creation. Rather, the church is an active agent called to participate in the transformation that is presently occurring through the ongoing work of Christ, which will ultimately culminate with the worship of the Lamb in heaven. In the final chapter we will look more closely at this eschatological reality and how the church figures into it. In this chapter, however, we discuss several markers that signal the transformative presence of the church. The question we want to pursue here is this: If the practices and forms of church are varied and contingent, what might we say are normative markers of the church, common across time and location, and how might these elucidate the quality of its transformative presence? The following are five particular markers—and more could well be added—that flow from our discussions of church thus far. We will express these as a series of qualifications:

---

[3]Allen Verhey, "'Able to Instruct One Another': The Church as a Community of Moral Discourse," in *The Community of the Word: Toward an Evangelical Ecclesiology*, ed. Mark Husbands and Daniel J. Treier (Downers Grove, IL: InterVarsity Press, 2005), 168.

- Wherever the story of Christ is heard and obeyed

- Wherever a community forms around this story

- Wherever this community responds to this story in prayer and praise

- Wherever this community seeks to live in peace with each other and their wider community

- Wherever an impulse drives this community to witness to Christ and the transformation the Spirit has brought about

- There, we can say the emergent dynamic of the church is present.

In this chapter, then, we discuss each of these ecclesial markers in turn. We will consider in particular how these together create a distinctive missiological witness drawing people toward and transforming them into a local community of Christ-followers and an eventual gathering of every tongue, people, and nation who will worship God.

Context Matters: Space, Presence, and Embodiment

Before we discuss each of these ecclesial markers, it is important to recall the contextual character in which these markers necessarily emerge. (1) The marks of the church all draw attention to the way in which the church occupies space—social, historical, and symbolic/aesthetic.[4] Churches are usually aware of social space. Many of our conceptions of church include the idea of gathering in a location, which includes social components. Churches are also conscious of occupying a social space when they seek to navigate cultural changes or take seriously their call to witness to and reshape their contexts. In these instances they become acutely aware that their community creates a social space of conversation that is in turn in conversation with other social entities, whether that be families, social and political institutions, other churches, mission agencies or nonprofits, or other religious communities. Quite often churches, particularly evangelical churches, become protective of their social space, seeking to guard it against what they perceive as the unhelpful, or threatening, influence of others. While this posture is an understandable response for those who feel threatened or attacked, it can

---

[4]See William A. Dyrness, "Spaces for an Evangelical Ecclesiology," in Husbands and Treier, *Community of the Word*, 251-72.

also reflect an inadequate view of the way in which God is present within the space of the church, as well as in the other spaces with which it interacts.

(2) The marks of the church presuppose actual presence. By this we mean two things. First, we recognize the presence of God with his church. The Orthodox tradition captures this idea of presence in the space of the church building itself. For many Eastern Orthodox traditions, the church building represents an important window or conduit through which God relates to people, and people to God. Of course God is not restricted to the building, but neither is the building purely symbolic. Indeed, the Orthodox understanding of presence is not unlike how the Jews experienced God via the tabernacle and temple in the First Testament, or even how other religions currently understand the role of physical space. God inhabits and is present in space.

Such ideas arouse Protestants' suspicions and recall the excesses to which such teachings have previously led. Luther, following the scholastic movement, strongly reacted to the centralizing tendency and the propping up of hierarchical structures to which such understandings of presence and space could lead. This was not new. Already in Acts 7 Stephen debated the Hellenist Jews who had settled in Jerusalem in part because of the importance and value they placed on the Jerusalem temple. In response, Stephen draws on Isaiah 66:1-2, stating, "The Most High does not dwell in houses made with human hands" (Acts 7:48). This follows on his review of select vignettes of Jewish history, including the recollection that at Mount Sinai they had made a calf, offered sacrifices to it as to an idol, and "reveled in the works of their hands" (Acts 7:41). Specifying a space and location for divine presence has always held the risk of idolizing or valuing that space over the One who occupies it. But denying God's physical presence risks the opposite danger of Docetism, which sees Christ's incarnation and continuing presence by the Spirit as ultimately unreal. Though challenging the emphasis given to the temple, Stephen does not deny Godly presence. Rather, he affirms it and relocates it to the places that the Hellenistic Jews had themselves left—the places outside of the Holy Land! And he emphasized that God's presence was active—not passive—as seen through his speech to and actions on behalf of his people. In all the episodes of the First Testament, such as Abraham's encounters with God in Mesopotamia or Moses' conversation with an angel via a burning bush in the Mount Sinai wilderness, God was working to bring about his purposes.

Another aspect of presence is that which occurs between people—the presence of people to and with each other. This relates to a third characteristic that underlies our ecclesial markers. (3) God's encounter with people, and theirs with each other, is, as Willie Jennings has reminded us, an encounter with and between actual bodies. In our tendency to emphasize the verbal, social, and spiritual aspects of the ecclesial encounter, the Western church has sometimes lost sight of the physicality that is involved.[5] Jennings makes this point in reference to Acts 2:42-47, where the early church community engaged in various activities, including selling their possessions for mutual benefit. Jennings observes that such giving was not new and that, while important, in the First Testament God specified his desire for people, not possessions. Regarding Acts 2, Jennings explains,

> A new kind of giving is exposed at this moment, one that binds bodies together as the first reciprocal donation where the followers will give themselves to one another. The possessions will follow. What was at stake here was not the giving up of all possessions but the giving up of each one, one by one as the Spirit gave direction, and as the ministry of Jesus made demand.[6]

Possessions were not disembodied commodities but were connected to the identity of the believers themselves. An exchange of goods was preceded by physical presence, of people encountering each other in the experiences and historical realities of their lives. Because of this embodied presence, objects could become symbolic of the new life they were being called to live. Possessions could be shared to express the new mutuality that Christ has made possible by the Spirit; table fellowship could become a symbol both of God's loving presence and of our presence to and for each other—what the New Testament calls *koinōnia*.

---

[5] As Jennings has shown in *Christian Imagination*, the Western colonial church's misunderstanding of physicality, including land and bodies, resulted in a long history of displacing bodies in various ways and re-categorizing them, particularly along the lines of a racialized and nationalized imagination. In other words, the church was seen through the overlay of national and racial identities, profoundly distorting the New Testament's witness to the Spirit's role in joining this new communion vision. See Willie James Jennings, *The Christian Imagination: Theology and the Origins of Race* (New Haven, CT: Yale University Press, 2010).

[6] Willie James Jennings, *Acts* (Louisville, KY: Westminster John Knox, 2017), 39.

Much more could be said regarding each of these. But our point is that
these three interrelated aspects of church provide a framework and corrective for what is sometimes missed or forgotten by Western Christians—
influenced as they are by a long heritage of Platonism—and particularly
Protestants, but often not by believers of other contexts. For believers such
as Padman and his community, and those of our other case studies in chapter
four, space, presence, and bodies are often integrally connected in their experience of religious community and life. In addition, and in line with our
understanding of the church's emergent character, each of these provides an
important basis for the emergence of a church's unique identity and qualities,
dependent on its own unique cultural and historical heritage. The persons
of the church relate to each other and to God in the midst of their created
space—that is, their situation in God's created order and what they have
made of these gifts (i.e., their culture). Out of this particular situation unique
expressions of ecclesial markers will emerge. While none of these factors is
an ecclesial marker in itself, they all deeply influence the shape of the theological markers that we will review.

HEARING AND OBEYING CHRIST

As we turn to our discussion of ecclesial markers, the first draws attention
to those spaces where the story of Christ is heard and obeyed by a people.
Protestants may hear in this the echoes of Luther and Calvin, both of whom
specified that the church is the gathering wherein "the gospel is purely
preached." The church, as is famously described by Reformed theologians,
is a "creature of the word" (*creatura verbi*). As is apparent in the way this
marker was described, the practice of preaching was the prominent method
by which the Word would be made known. This Word is of course more
than the sermon itself; it is the promise of God, his living gospel.[7] However,
what remained central for Luther and other Reformers was that it should be
proclaimed. Thus, this marker helped to identify the church as an event or
as "something *going on* in the world."[8] This is to not to say this story could

---

[7]Barth, developing this more fully, understood the Word of God to be in three related forms: the
person of Christ, Scripture, and the preaching of the Word. See *Evangelical Theology: An Introduction* (Grand Rapids: Eerdmans, 1979).
[8]Eric W. Gritsch and Robert W. Jenson, *Lutheranism: The Theological Movement and Its Confessional*

not also be "proclaimed" in media other than simple preaching or teaching. Many people first see the gospel as it is lived out by others, or represented in a dramatic form or ritual, or even in a movie (for example, in the *Jesus* film[9]). But in whatever form, the central truth of God's work in Christ will be seen, heard, and obeyed.

As we have previously seen, the Reformers' view of church as a Word-event emerged as they read Scripture and sought to counter Catholic doctrines and practices of church. This reverse hermeneutic helped them clarify what other traditions had also emphasized, though perhaps not to the same degree: the church emerges out of people's interpretation of and response to the living gospel. Though this seems to be a shared marker across many traditions and contexts, we want to shift the emphasis from preaching or proclamation alone to hearing *and* obeying. In the mid twentieth century Eugene Nida helped usher in a significant shift in the missionary understanding of communication. Up to his time the dominant paradigm among mission practitioners was a "cargo" mentality of communication, whereby the message was packaged according to the presenter's understanding and the receivers were educated so that they could properly understand and receive it. Nida shifted the paradigm to one of receptor-oriented communication. Though still focused on delivering a "package," the latter was attentive to matching the meanings of the source with the meanings of the receptor.[10] More recently, cognitive theories have swung the spotlight away from a focus on the package to that of the process—the "cognitive apparatus" that processes ideas.[11] As R. Daniel Shaw has shown, both of these—attention to the "package" and to the communication process—highlight important aspects of the communication experience.

In light of this, we suggest that church is marked not only by the proclamation of the Word in message form but equally by the hearing, or processing, of the Word that occurs. With the Reformers we would affirm that the church

---

Writings (Philadelphia: Fortress, 1976), 131. Emphasis added.

[9]*Jesus*, directed by Peter Sykes and John Krish, produced by John Heyman (Burbank, CA: Warner Bros. and Campus Crusade for Christ, 1979).

[10]R. Daniel Shaw, "Beyond Contextualization: Toward a Twenty-First-Century Model for Enabling Mission," *International Bulletin of Missionary Research* 34, no. 4 (2010): 209.

[11]Shaw, "Beyond Contextualization," 211.

is formed by a Word-event that originates outside of itself.[12] However, as we learn from Acts and Paul, the event is more than proclamation. It is rather primarily concerned with what the receivers do with the Word, recognizing that many who hear do not necessarily respond positively. In Acts, for example, Luke often wants his readers to differentiate between those who responded favorably to the disciples' message, thus becoming or remaining part of God's people, and those who rejected that message. Insofar as a church-forming event is taking place, the event is not so much the proclamation as it is the positive reception and interpretation of the Word by people.

What does this "positive reception" look like? Here the theme of obedience, and obedient discipleship, becomes important. In the First Testament Abraham is the paradigmatic example of a response that initiated God's work, not only in Abraham but for the formation of his people. Seen through the New Testament book of Hebrews, Abraham was commended for his faithful obedience (Heb 11:8). Similarly, throughout the First Testament, obedience to God and his covenant was the primary sign of whether Israel was in alignment with its covenant and identity as God's people. Obedience and identity as God's people went hand in hand.

The theme of responding to God's Word with obedience as a sign of being part of God's people and kingdom continues in the New Testament. A prominent text, particularly for evangelical missions-oriented Christians of the last 150 years, has been the Great Commission of Matthew 28:18-20. They have often focused on the first part of Jesus' instructions to his disciples to "go therefore and make disciples of all nations." The emphasis on going to the nations is not misguided. However, as David Bosch points out, it has often eclipsed the second half of Jesus' instructions, to teach them to "obey everything that I have commanded you."[13] Far from being a postscript, Jesus' instruction regarding obedience is central to Matthew's Gospel. Discipleship, or the process of submitting to the will of God, was for Matthew a primary sign of whether and how a people were truly "hearing" God's Word and

---

[12]For a helpful discussion and critique of the Lutheran teaching of Word-event, see Cheryl M. Peterson, "Who Is the Church?," *Dialog: A Journal of Theology* 51, no. 1 (2012): 24-30.

[13]Bosch shows how the emphasis on going to all nations reflected, and reflects, the Western evangelical desire to counter more relativistic theologies and reinforce the importance of preaching salvation to people who would otherwise remain eternally "lost." David J. Bosch, *Transforming Mission: Paradigm Shifts in Theology of Mission* (Maryknoll, NY: Orbis, 1991), 340-41.

participating in God's kingdom. As Bosch describes it, "Discipleship involves a commitment to God's reign, to justice and love, and to obedience to the entire will of God."[14] Though discipleship, in Matthew's view, is not simply an invitation to join a church, neither can discipleship and church be divorced from each other. The Matthean ideal is that every church member should be a true disciple, obeying the commands of Jesus.

Thus a key ecclesial marker is hearing and obeying the Word so as to be formed as disciples of Christ. But this is never envisioned as an individual activity or process. Rather, the hearing and obeying of God are done within community, which leads to our next marker.

COMMUNITY

When Robert Schuller began to host church gatherings in a Southern California drive-in theater in the 1950s, some questioned whether this was still church. Of concern was the individualistic nature of the event—that people could "come as you are in the family car," listen to music and a sermon, and drive away without interacting with others. Of course Schuller did encourage people to come together in other settings, but at issue in the discussion was the nature of a key marker of the church—the formation of a community around the story of Christ.

The question of what it means for the church to be a community stretches back to the New Testament itself, in which, as we have seen, there are a variety of references and metaphors. Many references assume or address actual, local groups of people. For example, Paul refers to churches as specific groupings, often using the word *ekklēsia* ("to the church of God that is in Corinth," 1 Cor 1:2). The character, relationships, practices, and doctrines that these local groups shared constitute a common theme throughout the New Testament. As we have discussed, in Acts 2:44-47 (and also Acts 4:32-35) the early disciples developed community in practical ways, sharing possessions and coming together for shared rituals and meals—summed up in the New Testament focus on *koinōnia*. It was in and through these local church communities that individual and corporate discipleship in Christ was thought to occur. In Luke-Acts, for example, the process of conversion and

---

[14]Bosch, *Transforming Mission*, 81.

discipleship was, as Joel B. Green says, "a reconstruction of one's self within a new web of relationships."[15] For New Testament writers, and particularly Luke, reconstruction does not happen in isolation. Rather, the life of the converted receives new meaning and clarity of trajectory in the midst of ongoing relationships with the church community.

While the New Testament gives much attention to the identity and character of the local church community, it also suggests, particularly in Ephesians and Colossians, that the church has a wider and more expansive identity—a community that spans across locations and incorporates all those believers who have come before and who will follow after (Eph 1:20-23; 2:19-22; 3:10; 5:22-33; Col 1:18). The church is not only rooted in local communities but is a part of a cosmic plan and identity that transcends cultural and regional particularities.

These two visions—the local church and the universal church (often denoted with a capital C)—certainly communicate important visions of what it means to be a church community. And it has been common for churches in various times and locations to emphasize one or the other in light of their cultural contexts. For example, in the mid- to late-twentieth-century African theologians such as John S. Mbiti, Christian Gaba, and Kwame Bediako developed what Anthony Balcomb has called "theologies of being."[16] These theologies were attentive to the religious, cultural, and linguistic particularities of specific tribal groups in Africa.[17] Though these scholars saw the importance of a more general, pan-African Christian identity, they pursued this by valuing the church as a community located within particular tribes, each of which worships and theologizes within their particular language and culture. As such,

---

[15]Joel B. Green, "Conversion in Luke-Acts: The Potential of a Cognitive Approach" (paper presented to the Consultation on the Use of Cognitive Linguistics in Biblical Interpretation, Society of Biblical Literature, Washington, DC, November 2006), 19.

[16]Anthony Balcomb, "From Liberation to Democracy: Theologies of Bread and Being in the New South Africa," *Missionalia* 26, no. 1 (1998): 54-73.

[17]Mbiti focused on eschatology among the Akamba of Kenya. John S. Mbiti, *New Testament Eschatology in an African Background: A Study of the Encounter Between New Testament Theology and African Traditional Concepts* (Oxford: Oxford University Press, 1971). Gaba analyzed concepts of salvation in the scriptures of the Anlo of Ghana. Christian R. Gaba, *Scriptures of an African People: Ritual Utterances of the Anlo* (New York: NOK, 1973). Bediako examined Christology and ancestor veneration among the Akan of Ghana. Kwame Bediako, "Jesus in African Culture: A Ghanaian Perspective," in *Jesus and the Gospel in Africa: History and Experience* (Maryknoll, NY: Orbis, 2004; first published 1990 by Editions Clé, Yaoundé, Cameroun), 20-33.

each church has its own experience of Christ and should express this to the wider church, African and global. This focus on and empowerment of local churches and theologies was, and remains, an important countermovement to Western colonial impulses that did not value the perspectives of such churches.

More recently, however, African theologians have been seeking to address the ethnic and tribal divisions that have caused much distress and pain in various African contexts. In doing so they are emphasizing more universal ecclesiologies. This emphasis received a strong focus from the Roman Catholic Church during and following the Synod of Bishops' Special Assembly of Bishops for Africa in 1994. In response to the many expressions of racism, ethnocentrism, and various forms of violence, the synod renewed the image of the "Church as the Family of God." In light of sectarian divides, they said, "Christ has come to restore the world to unity, a single human Family in the image of the trinitarian Family."[18] In a similar way, African leaders and theologians such as Paul Mbandi and Kuzuli Kosse have been articulating ecclesiologies that seek to transcend and transform ethnic difference by appealing to the church's universal nature.[19] For example, in a reflection on the unity of believers, Kosse acknowledges the importance of the local church but goes on to say:

> But the local church is only one link in the unity of the universal church. The unity that God brings extends to all believers of all nations, denominations and times. Tribalism, ethnicity and denominationalism are hindrances to the unity of God's people and must be resisted. Of course, each ethnic group or tribe has its place in the church, but only as links in a long chain.[20]

For these leaders and scholars the church should be marked by a superordinate communal identity, one that does not forsake other social identities but integrates them under a common identity.

These and other theologians suggest that the church exists in both forms; they are always and everywhere rooted in the visible assembly of believers,

---

[18]Synod of Bishops, "Special Synod of Bishops for Africa, Message of the Synod, English text released May 6, 1994," para. 25, www.ewtn.com/new_evangelization/africa/synod/message.htm.

[19]For an overview of these works, some of which have not been widely published, see Stephanie A. Lowery, *Identity and Ecclesiology: Their Relationship Among Select African Theologians* (Eugene, OR: Pickwick, 2017).

[20]Kuzuli Kosse, "Unity of Believers," in *Africa Bible Commentary: A One-Volume Commentary Written by 70 African Scholars*, ed. Tokunboh Adeyemo (Grand Rapids: Zondervan, 2010), 1314.

but there also exists a universal church that reminds those believers of a wider identity, a "family," that crosses particularities. As Miroslav Volf expresses it, the church has two "partially overlapping entities," the local and the universal, that are united in their common relation to the Spirit of Christ and in their "anticipation of the eschatological gathering of the entire people of God."[21] Because of this, "every local church can also be *completely* the church even though it encompasses only a part of the universal church."[22]

WORSHIP

The focus on obedience of Christ and the formation of a community around his story finds its counterpart in the next marker: the response of the community in prayer and praise, or communal worship. It is important, however, that we make clear what we mean when we say that worship is an ecclesial marker.

First, starting from a biblical perspective, we need to remember that worship for the early church did not simply refer to an event ("Sabbath worship") or a specific set of practices (such as prayer, singing, Eucharist, etc.). As Andrew B. McGowen states, worship "was not about services, but service; not about gestures that signaled belief or allegiance, but about allegiance itself."[23] Though worship and liturgy have in modern times come to be associated with specific rituals and practices—an event—which we will focus on as well, it is important to remember that the biblical communities always understood these as part of a wider, holistic orientation of service, obedience, and allegiance to God.[24] As such, worship is connected to and flows from the marker of obedience, and can be understood as those rituals that "embody proper reverence and service toward God."[25]

Second, the biblical writers always portray worship as a response to the actions of God on behalf of, among, and through his people. There is no more profound example of this than in the very choice of *which* people with

---

[21]Miroslav Volf, *After Our Likeness: The Church as the Image of the Trinity* (Grand Rapids: Eerdmans, 1998), 141.

[22]Volf, *After Our Likeness*, 141. Emphasis original.

[23]Andrew B. McGowan, *Ancient Christian Worship: Early Church Practices in Social, Historical, and Theological Perspective* (Grand Rapids: Baker Academic, 2014), 261.

[24]McGowan, *Ancient Christian Worship*, 5.

[25]McGowan, *Ancient Christian Worship*, 7.

whom God decided to covenant. As Walter Brueggemann shows, First Testament texts such as Deuteronomy 7:6-10, 9:4-5, and 10:14-15 make abundantly clear that Israel had no quality that raised them above others in God's estimation. Ultimately, the answer as to why God chose Israel above others— the "scandal of particularity"—defies explanation and "can only be understood as a divine impulse of affection."[26] The same can be said of the people later chosen to be a part of the emerging Christ movement, the church.[27] Though the modern enlightenment sensibilities of Western Christians may cause them to emphasize the role of individual agency in following Christ and becoming a part of the church, and though this is an important theme that can be supported by Scripture, the countertruth about the God who chooses is equally strong and should always provide the foundation for the community's worship.

We see indications of worship as an ecclesial marker in the early days of the Christ-following movement as narrated in Acts. Following the day of Pentecost and Peter's speech, Luke portrays two subsequent responses of the people. The first is the acceptance of Peter's message by and baptism of more than three thousand people, adding them to the community of Christ-followers. The second response is a list in Acts 2:46-47 of several activities: devotion to the apostles' teaching, fellowship, the breaking of bread, and prayers. Though this list was most likely not a description of the early church's liturgy, it is nonetheless an indication that the early church, in addition to remaining a part of worship in the temple, also employed rituals that expressed their own growing identity as Christ-followers. They are practices that flow from and reflect accepted modes of worship but that also receive a "makeover" into, as Joel Green summarizes, "patterns conforming to those of the new community" where "thinking, feeling, believing, and behaving are transformed."[28]

In Paul's letters we continue to see the importance of worship in characterizing the community. This is perhaps why Paul is concerned about worship gatherings that, in his estimation, have ceased to express gratitude

---

[26]Walter Brueggemann, *Old Testament Theology: An Introduction* (Nashville: Abingdon Press, 2008), 198.

[27]Brueggemann, *Old Testament Theology*, 199.

[28]Joel B. Green, *Conversion in Luke-Acts: Divine Action, Human Cognition, and the People of God* (Grand Rapids: Baker Academic, 2015), 132.

to God and instead are reinforcing social hierarchies and selfish impulses, as in 1 Corinthians 11:17-34. In these instances worship, and specifically the practice of the Lord's Supper, was no longer displaying the church's root-edness in the work of Christ. The church's identity as a "body of Christ" had become distorted, and the people needed to be reminded of the obligation to God and each other that comes with eating the bread and drinking the cup of the Lord's death. In other words, worship gives continual testimony to the One who gathers and constitutes his people.

As we pointed out above, much of our understanding of worship reflects an "event" understanding of church, including activities such as praise, prayer, the Eucharist, singing, kneeling, standing, silence, shouting, dancing, and so on. These activities are responses to the story of Christ, expressed in ways congruent with the worshipers' sense of what it means to approach and interact with the divine. Churches often form these into liturgies, or orders of worship. Though the word *liturgy* is most often used among high-church traditions, it is a truism that all churches, even the most spontaneous and "free" in style, establish liturgies or commonly expected repertoires and order.

But worship liturgy does its ordering work in other ways as well. In this it creates order, not just in the practical sense of an order of worship events but in that it seeks to reorder perspectives within individuals and the group as a whole. For James K. A. Smith, in his series on liturgical theologies of culture, liturgical practices "educate" or re-form the community of be-lievers.[29] They do this not simply by reaffirming cognitive beliefs—a common emphasis in Western Protestant and evangelical traditions. Of course, worship does reflect and reinforces important theological beliefs. However, drawing on Pierre Bourdieu, worship also works at an uncon-scious level, shaping within people a *habitus*—a way of navigating the world that often operates unconsciously.[30]

Worship practices are not unique in this. Many of our daily practices operate out of a type of *habitus*, including those that are quite mundane. These, however, do not work on people's formative identities in the ways that

---

[29]James K. A. Smith, *Desiring the Kingdom: Worship, Worldview, and Cultural Formation* (Grand Rapids: Baker Academic, 2009); and idem, *Imagining the Kingdom: How Worship Works* (Grand Rapids: Baker Academic, 2013).

[30]J. K. A. Smith, *Imagining the Kingdom*, 80-84.

Smith claims for worship. What, then, causes worship practices to have a deeper and more long-lasting impact on believers and the church community than other practices? Smith distinguishes between "thin" and "thick" rituals.[31] The former are those regular routines that are mundane, utilitarian, and do not deeply impact our identity (such as brushing teeth). Thick rituals, on the other hand, are practices and liturgies that are meaning-full. These are "rituals of ultimate concern that form identity, that inculcate particular visions of the good life."[32] These rituals help to shape individual identity. But they also help to create a corporate sense of identity—a sense of we-ness, with a sense of a micro- and macro-story in which the people participate and into which they join.

Though Smith provides a helpful description of how the thick rituals of worship shape individual and corporate identity, he does not provide a strong account of the source of such rituals. How do churches develop their worship practices, including thick rituals? For Smith, it seems, these come through and from the church community itself, and often stand in contrast to other rituals. They provide what he calls a "counter-formation" process by which liturgy overturns or supersedes the formation proceeding from other rituals in which people partake.

Though churches certainly shape their own practices, might Smith's concept of counterformation potentially overemphasize the discontinuity and boundaries between the practices of the church and those of the wider social context? Smith unfortunately fails to recognize or at least discuss what we have presented throughout this book: that the ecclesial character and practices of the church are always drawn out of the church's particular cultural situation. Worship practices are meaningful and have the power to form individuals and community precisely because they reflect peoples' cultural identities and values, many of which are derived from the cultural context itself. Of course, ecclesial communities modify practices to express their devotion to Christ, and we would agree with Smith that these have formative causal powers. However, where these new values and narratives contrast with those of the wider culture, we might say they are providing a "re-formation." In this, rather than working against or countering a cultural context, certain rituals

---

[31] J. K. A. Smith, *Desiring the Kingdom*, 82.
[32] J. K. A. Smith, *Desiring the Kingdom*, 86.

serve to re-form or re-create that which has been marred by our fallenness as people.[33] This also agrees with and follows on from our earlier analysis of biblical practices, positing that many ecclesial worship practices emerged out of and reflected particular religious and cultural contexts.

Worship, and the re-formation it helps to instill, is thus a powerful emergent property arising out of the interaction between people through their liturgical activities. Worship cannot be reduced to the sum of the parts (a particular order of events), but neither is it divorced from these. Rather, worship emerges as people interact with one another and with God using commonly agreed upon rituals. And, as happens with other emergent properties, worship in turn works back on the parts that make it happen, forming in them dispositions that further their journey of discipleship.

LIVING IN PEACE (SHALOM) TOGETHER AND WITH THE WIDER COMMUNITY

We discussed above the importance of community as a mark of the church. Our fourth marker is related to this notion of community but expands on it and offers an additional characteristic. That is, the church exists where its people seek to live in peace with each other and, by extension, with their wider community.

Church creeds and formulations have often stated the importance or ideal of unity. This focus on unity, as we saw in chapter two, was often a response to threats to the doctrinal or structural unity of the church. The Nicene Creed, for example, as we discussed in chapter two, was created to address the doctrinal threat posed by Arian and Donatist churches in parts of Constantine's empire. To preempt further division and promote the unity of the church, and to in turn bolster the unity of the Roman Empire, Constantine convened and sponsored the Council of Nicaea, producing the creed declaring the church to be one, holy, catholic, and apostolic. This did help promote the political unity Constantine and others desired. However, because it was sometimes enforced by violence, it did not always encourage shalom with minority groups or those outside the empire.

---

[33]Smith acknowledges that Christian worship practices are best understood "as the restoration of an original, creational desire for God," though practically they function to counter the "misinformation of secular liturgies." J. K. A. Smith, *Desiring the Kingdom*, 88.

Churches throughout history have affirmed and interpreted this creed and its call for unity in their own ways. That the church should be "one" was often supported by Scriptures such as Jesus' prayer in John 17:20-21 that those who believe in him would "all be one." Insofar as church unity has been understood to be structural, such oneness has eluded the church at least since the Schism of 1054 between the Eastern Orthodox and Roman Catholic Churches and particularly since the formation of Protestant churches in the sixteenth century. Doctrinal unity too, from the earliest days in the book of Acts, has eluded the church. Taking into account this history, many have asked and continue to ask, What does it mean to affirm unity or oneness as a mark of the church? And what does this mean in an age of increasing globalization and diversification?

Such questions were strongly pursued and debated in the latter half of the twentieth century, resulting in what many have called Communion ecclesiology. Coming to prominence through Vatican II and subsequent World Council of Churches (WCC) and other church conferences, Communion ecclesiology emphasizes the Trinity as a model or basis for church unity. As Dennis M. Doyle summarizes, "To say that the Church is a 'communion' is to emphasize that, although certain (aspects) of its institutional structures remain essential, it finds its ultimate basis in relationships among human beings with God through Christ and in the Holy Spirit."[34]

In light of this we suggest that the church should not be characterized so much by unity, since this carries with it perhaps more institutional and doctrinal burden than it can and should bear as an ecclesial marker. Rather, a more helpful way of framing this is a focus on living in peace (shalom) together and, where at all possible, with the wider community.

A focus on relational shalom as an ecclesial marker suggests several things. Though the concept of shalom implies justice and equity among people, the First Testament points to a more fundamental quality of relationship. As Wolterstorff explains, "In shalom, each person enjoys justice, enjoys his or her rights. There is no shalom without justice. But shalom goes beyond justice. Shalom is the human being dwelling at peace in all his or her

---

[34]Dennis M. Doyle, "Henri de Lubac and the Roots of Communion Ecclesiology," *Theological Studies* 60 (1999): 211.

relationships: with God, with self, with others, with nature."[35] In the New Testament, and particularly in the book of Acts, this quality of community is characterized in part by being "together" (*homothymadon*), which also indicates one mind, accord, or passion. This word *homothymadon* indicates more than a collection of people who happen to be together. Rather, at the various times it is used (Acts 1:14; 2:1, 46; 4:24; 5:12; 15:25), the church exhibits a unique quality and unity of fellowship. Thus, in Acts 2:46 (and Acts 5:12), for example, the community is of one mind in purpose and focus, helping to distinguish them in the midst of the wider Jewish community.

But this quality of living in peace was something that, though experienced uniquely by the church, was also meant to extend to all people and all of society. God's people were and are pictured as a primary locus whereby shalom, relational shalom, is extended into the world. This shalom is meant to counter sin and human brokenness in all its forms, the "relational evil" and violence that emerged as a consequence of Adam and Eve's sin in Genesis 2. Because of this evil, creation has continually experienced a variety of "poverties" that mark the absence of shalom. As Bryant Myers has described, human poverties in all forms (material, relational, spiritual, etc.) are characterized by "relationships that do not work, that are not just, that are not for life, that are not harmonious or enjoyable."[36] In light of this, the church is called not only to experience shalom for itself but to model and extend into its context relationships that do work so that others can experience the human flourishing that was lost. There are two particular implications of this marker, when and where churches embrace and embody it.

First, relational shalom means that the church relates to its context in peaceful, nonviolent ways, particularly when it is in conflict with its context. For example, at various points throughout Acts the disciple community conflicted with the authority claims of various power structures. The community challenged the supremacy of Roman imperial authority by applying the words *Savior* and *Lord*, particularly *Lord Jesus*, thus denouncing and challenging others who would be called savior and lord, including the

---

[35]Nicholas Wolterstorff, *Until Justice and Peace Embrace* (Grand Rapids: Eerdmans, 1983), 69.
[36]Bryant L. Myers, *Walking with the Poor: Principles and Practices of Transformational Development*, rev. and exp. ed. (Maryknoll, NY: Orbis, 2011), 143.

imperial powers. Paul, too, came into conflict with and resisted the authority of the Jewish and Roman structures, for instance, at his trial before Festus in Acts 25:8-12.

But what is not often recognized in these and other examples is that, though the church chastised and challenged its context at times, it did so nonviolently. Because a violent response would have been so out of keeping with the example of Jesus and the character of the new community, it would be easy to forget that violence was nonetheless an option that was open to them and other groups. As Witherington shows, violent movements were common, and the Roman authorities were quite aware of and concerned over any leader or movement that might violently rebel against their rule.[37] Violent resistance was an option for the church community but one they did not choose. Where violence does occur, as in Jesus' crucifixion, it is perpetrated by those who respond negatively to the gospel.

The second implication of living in shalom with the wider community can be framed via a question: To what degree should the ecclesial community interact with and be "yeast" that permeates its social context, and to what degree should it be wholly distinct and set apart from all other communities? The answers to this vary across time and place, often in relation to the exigencies of the context. As we saw in chapter two, when some sixteenth-century Anabaptists failed to gain the approval and endorsement of many in ecclesial and civic authority, this rejection provoked the emergence of a separatist ecclesiology that viewed the church as set apart from "the world." Many contemporary believers who have been rejected by their Muslim, Hindu, Sikh, or other families come to a similar understanding—the church must be completely separate from those religious communities.

But, as we saw above, while the Scripture is clear that the church is to be marked by community and provides many examples regarding its communal character, it is often less concerned with defining clear, universal boundaries between the ecclesial community and other communities. As Joel Green shows, even texts such as 1 Peter 1:1 and 2:11, which envisions

---

[37]Ben Witherington III, *The Acts of the Apostles: A Socio-Rhetorical Commentary* (Grand Rapids: Eerdmans, 1998), 661.

believers as "exiles" and "aliens," also presuppose their ongoing engagement with and honorable conduct within their context.[38]

Regarding the relation of the ecclesial community to that of other religious communities, one suggestive case study is Saul's turn to Jesus in Acts 9. How did this event, and his subsequent participation in the ecclesial community, (re)shape his relationship to his Jewish tradition? We may begin by cautioning against the use of the word *conversion* to describe what happens to Saul in Acts 9, unless we are clear about what we mean. Certainly it is anachronistic to say that Saul converted between religions and religious communities since no one at that time understood Christ-followers as constituting a separate religion.[39] In his own estimation and practice Saul remained Jewish and, by his later testimonies, an even more faithful Jew than before, though based on different criteria. For Saul, hearing and obeying Christ meant not turning from his community, heritage, and rituals but reframing and moving more deeply into them.[40]

Of course, obeying Christ also brought Paul into tension with others in the Jewish community. But consider this: Luke did not portray this tension as resulting from Paul's rejection of or distancing from his Jewish tradition and community. Rather, Jews had every opportunity to, like Paul, embrace Christ and reframe and enter more fully into their own tradition. Indeed, many did so and remained fully Jewish in their identity, even as they reevaluated what this meant in relation to their new allegiance to Christ. In a very real sense it was not and is not the gospel or the nature of the ecclesial community that creates boundaries between communities. The church is called to live in relational shalom with its community, presenting Christ and offering the opportunity for family, friends, and community members to gain new and deepened understanding of their existing identity in light of Christ.

---

[38]Green argues that both readings of 1 Peter, the "sectarian withdrawal from society" and the "optimism toward Babylon," are misguided dichotomies that do not accurately reflect Peter's overall message. Joel B. Green, *1 Peter*, Two Horizons New Testament Commentary (Grand Rapids: Eerdmans, 2007), 1-4.

[39]On this see Brent Nongbri, *Before Religion: A History of a Modern Concept* (New Haven, CT: Yale University Press, 2013). The wider issue that Nongbri addresses, which we will not address here, regards to what degree, if any, people in Paul's time conceived of *religion* in the ways that it is currently understood.

[40]It also meant relativizing this community and its theology, particularly in light of the inclusion of Gentiles into God's church.

Witnessing to Christ and the
Transforming Work of the Spirit

In addition to hearing and obeying the story of Christ, and responding in prayer and praise, the church is also marked by witnessing to Christ and to the ongoing, transformative presence of the Spirit. This marker maintains an important perspective that could be overshadowed or lost in our discussion of previous markers. If hearing, obedience, and worship help form and strengthen the gathering of believers, the marker of witness emphasizes that the church's life together and with God is conducted under the gaze of, and for the benefit of, the world.

In the First Testament God's people were called to be witnesses to the covenant that God had made with them. This covenant, though, was not just for Israel's benefit. The prophets recognize that Israel is living out its covenant on the world stage, in the presence of other nations. In Leviticus 26 God warns Israel of the punishment he will give if they turn away from him. Even if they do, however, he will remember his covenant to them and the way in which he brought them "out of the land of Egypt in the sight of the nations, to be their God" (Lev 26:45). This is a reminder that other nations have observed and continue to observe Israel and her behavior, and thus also God's work among them. As the prophets point out, virtues such as obedience and holiness, including behavior toward and treatment of the marginalized and dispossessed, were meant not only to form and guide God's people but to also mark them as God's possession in the sight of other nations.

If First Testament witness in this sense often operates on a macro level among the nations (though not exclusively), in the New Testament witness is often developed and exemplified at more local and personal levels. The wider scope of witness is not lost (Lk 24:47; Gal 3:8; Rev 15:4) but is now seen through the work of Christ in and through his disciples at local levels. Often this witness is one that is verbally proclaimed. In Luke 24:44-48 Jesus tells his disciples that they would be witnesses to the suffering and resurrection of the Christ and the message of repentance and forgiveness of sins for all nations. The disciples in turn incorporate this into their witness in Acts. Peter's first sermon in Acts 2:14-26, for example, emphasizes Jesus' resurrection triumph over suffering and the need for the listeners to repent and be forgiven.

But the church's witness is not only proclaimed; it is also embodied in space and time. In Acts 3:1-11, shortly after Peter's speech, Peter and John move to the gate of the temple where they encounter a man who was lame from birth. As Willie Jennings notes, the location is instructive: the lame man and disciples encounter each other at the gate of the temple, or "the doorway to worship."[41] As they do so, Peter and John see the man and invite him to look at them as well. In this early, formative moment of disciple witness, and as prelude to their communal worship, the disciples follow the example of Jesus to truly see others. But they also claim a new space in their Jewish community—one that calls people to watch them and for them to be seen. As Jennings says,

> Disciples must call attention to themselves, not as an act of religious hubris, but as the absolute mandate of a witness. As all eyes were fixed on Jesus in the synagogue (Luke 4:20), so in this scene the gaze invites fresh anticipation, unexpected by the lame man but imagined by those of faith: God will move and God will speak.[42]

Peter continues the interaction by contrasting the gifts that are on offer. One choice, which the man expects, consists of silver and gold—the gifts of Caesar. The other comprises the gifts of God—healing and restoration in the name of Jesus. Both "carry power and both lead to worship," but Peter and John witness to the greater claim and authority, God himself.[43] The lame man, after being invited to fix his gaze on Peter and John (Acts 3:4), experiences bodily healing and enters into the space of worship with Peter and John, walking, leaping, and praising God (Acts 3:8). The crowds then join in witness to this work of God as they see and recognize the man, now transformed, touching others and being touched without shame, and inviting wonder and amazement (Acts 3:9-10). This embodied witness is then joined with proclamation as Peter addresses the crowd, calling them to respond and repent so they too can experience "times of refreshing" from the Lord (Acts 3:19-20).

Much more could be said about witness, but this brief discussion highlights several important aspects of witness as an ecclesial marker. First, the

---

[41]Jennings, Acts, 41.
[42]Jennings, Acts, 41.
[43]Jennings, Acts, 42.

church invites the gaze of onlookers through its interactions with the people and structures of its context, but not before it truly sees those to whom it is called to witness. The church is that which allows itself to see and to be seen and touched by others, not sealed off from one another and from the wider community.

Second, as the disciples see and are seen, they in turn witness and make known the gifts Jesus brings to their community. There is no false modesty here, for the church is truly given the role of mediation. We see this in Paul's letters, including in 2 Corinthians 5:11–6:2, where he reminds the church at Corinth about their ministry of reconciliation, the message that God is reconciling people to himself through Christ. The humility of witness is the ongoing recognition that the church is the continual object of reconciliation, even as it bears witness to others about the reconciliation they can experience.

Third, these passages also evoke the way in which the mission of reconciliation and transformation is witness not just to a message, nor to an experience, but also to an emergent reality. To return to Acts 3, the healed cripple dances next to Peter, the restored Jesus-denier. These are part of a larger church of more than three thousand Christ-followers who, though we are not told all their names or stories, have each responded to and joined their personal stories with that of their new Lord, Jesus. In keeping with our argument throughout this book, we suggest that the kingdom Jesus inaugurates and the disciples proclaim is in many ways an emergent kingdom. In this the church witnesses to a reality that emerges out of but also transcends its daily existence, rituals, problems, and joys. As Paul tells the church in Corinth, in Christ there is a new creation in which "everything has become new" (2 Cor 5:17). But that kingdom is also, in some mysterious way, dependent on each person's unique story and the relation between it and other person's stories. So a person healed of his disability joins his story to others that have been touched by Christ, and there emerges a community that embodies a kingdom story and reality that reflects those unique and wonderful particularities. The church is marked by its witness to a new kingdom that transcends our current reality but also reflects and transforms it in profound ways.

CONCLUSION: ECCLESIAL MARKERS, MARKERS OF BEAUTY

During the Civil Rights movement of the 1960s the ideal of the "Beloved Community" emerged. That is, when people are gathered in love around the good news of Christ and the work the Spirit is doing to create spaces of justice, there a beloved community begins to emerge. This is a space that not only welcomes the stranger and foreigner but represents the beauty and peace of a spiritual home. It is a vision of church that explicitly reflects some of the hopes and concerns of those involved in the Civil Rights movement, even though these were markers that are arguably normative for all churches. For, as we have said, the various marks of the church will receive greater or lesser emphasis and be expressed in various ways dependent on the cultural situation, social structures, and numerous other factors. And often, as is typical of emergence, it is not always easy to anticipate what particular characteristics of a group will emerge, let alone in what ways those characteristics will be expressed.

We have argued throughout this book that the particular shape a community of Jesus-followers takes always reflects a reverse hermeneutic, a situated reading of Scripture and the story of Jesus in terms this group can understand and embody. This process prompts us to be attentive to the ways in which God is in the midst of cultural and religious values, practices and identities, seeking to affirm and not replace these. But we must be clear that God's purposes in the kingdom are not satisfied by simply making believers into better Americans or Kenyans or Japanese. Rather, God is always making things new (Rev 21:5). These emergent markers then represent ways that the gospel, the story of Jesus, by the work of the Spirit will create something new in and through the cultural values of any people group. The astounding news of God's love in Christ, the ability to respond in faith and trust, the formation of a community that embodies shalom and witnesses to God's new creation, all these offer ways for us to push back against our cultural situation—both affirming and transcending that culture.

Sadly, as we have implied, the restraining power of culture has often not only shaped the church in ways unique to specific contexts but also prevented them from pushing back against their culture when this has impeded certain markers. Too often churches develop or allow for structures and attitudes that subvert and even deny these markers—too often hypocrisy has trumped humble obedience, violence has replaced peacemaking, and the endorsement of cultural values has muted the witness to God's love. Most Christians are all too aware that our churches rarely, if ever, fully live up to the ideal to which these markers point.

But thanks be to God, there is a new creation that can be glimpsed in these markers and a beauty that emerges as these marks are embraced and embodied. In Revelation 21 John talks about the new Jerusalem, adorned and prepared with the beauty of a bride. It is a vision of summation, a sense of the radiance that will one day characterize God's people and new creation. We will discuss this summation in the next chapter, but here note that the marks of the church are meant to bring beauty and joy to creation now, and in doing so serve as an anticipation of what is to come. They bring joy and beauty now because these practices are the principal means by which God creates something new in and through his people. They also bring beauty because, by design, they display the dazzling diversity and richness of God's people. But they are also indicators of what God plans for his kingdom in its full summation. No church will ever fully or perfectly display the marks given to it by God, but by the power of his Spirit the church points to the ultimate "beloved community" to which it journeys.

8

The Future of the Church

The argument of this book has been that the church is an emergent phenomenon, a community called out by God, joined to Christ, and empowered by the Spirit to embody and witness to God's presence and work in the world. That presence and work we defined in the opening chapter as the kingdom or the reign of God. In that chapter we emphasized that the church exists for the sake of the kingdom, not the other way around. That is, the calling of the church is to proclaim the redemptive reign of God of which it is privileged to be a part. As Karl Rahner put this: "The Church . . . is living always on the proclamation of her own provisional status and of her historically advancing elimination in the coming kingdom of God towards which she is traveling as a pilgrim."[1] Two aspects of this claim call for special attention in this final chapter. We consider first the provisional status of the church and second her elimination in the fulfilled kingdom. How could something as important as the Christian church be considered provisional? And how could it possibly be eliminated?

THE KINGDOM IS COMING

As we noted earlier, the focus of Jesus' preaching was both the arrival and the coming of the kingdom of God. According to Mark, when he came to Galilee, Jesus announced: "The time is fulfilled, and the kingdom of God has come near; repent, and believe the good news" (Mk 1:15). Yet at the same time Jesus indicated that the full realization of this kingdom was a series of events that lay in the future. Jesus tells Peter in Matthew 19 that "at the renewal [lit., the 'regeneration'] of all things, when the Son of Man is seated

---

[1]Karl Rahner, *Concerning Vatican Council II*, vol. 6 of *Theological Investigations*, trans. David Bourke (Baltimore: Helicon Press, 1969), 298.

on the throne of his glory," Peter and the disciples would reign with him (Mt 19:28). So, although Jesus, in his person and work, embodied the powers and reality of the kingdom, the fullness of this lay somewhere in the future. This separation has posed a problem for many of the Jewish faithful—in Jesus' day and up to the present. That Jesus did not bring about the complete renewal of all things meant, in their minds, he could not have been the Messiah. For in Jewish thinking the Messiah and the renewal of all things are inseparably related—something we will consider further below.

Christians, instructed by the New Testament revelation, believe that the revelation of the kingdom has been divided into two parts. One is the initial revelation of God's re-creating work in the teaching, miracles, death, and resurrection of Jesus—what Jesus announced had "come near" in Mark 1:15; the other is the (future) return of the Messiah that Peter referenced in Acts 3:18-21 while preaching in the temple. There he called on people to repent so that God would wipe away their sins and send the Messiah: "that is, Jesus, who must remain in heaven until the time of universal restoration that God announced long ago through his holy prophets" (Acts 3:20-21). While differing about this timetable, Judaism and Christianity both agree that the final purposes of God include the renewal of all things.

It is important that we spend some time reflecting on this because not only is it central to the biblical revelation of God's future purposes, but it is key to understanding the role of the church in these purposes. And recent events have made this issue more salient. Whether because of the last century's history of war and violence, recent dramatic climatic events, or the global movements of peoples in search of a better life, recent theology has paid increasing attention to eschatology—that is, things that happen at the end of history. And this attention has issued in a general consensus that God's purposes relate not merely to the survival of God's special people but to the renewal of all things—literally, the resurrection of creation.[2] If, as

---

[2]Many scholars point to Jürgen Moltmann's *The Theology of Hope: On the Ground and Implications of a Christian Eschatology*, trans. James W. Leitch (New York: Harper & Row, 1967; Minneapolis: Fortress, 1993) as the beginning of this new focus on eschatology, but for evangelicals the key source was George E. Ladd's influential *Jesus and the Kingdom: The Eschatology of Biblical Realism* (New York: Harper & Row, 1964; updated and revised as *The Presence of the Future* [Grand Rapids: Eerdmans, 1974]). Two recent evangelical offerings carry forward his emphasis: N. T. Wright, *Surprised by Hope: Rethinking Heaven, the Resurrection, and the Mission of the Church* (New York: HarperCollins, 2008); and J. Richard Middleton, *A New Heaven and a New Earth: Reclaiming*

many scholars believe, the primary direction of redemptive history in Scripture is toward the final renewal and redemption of the entire created order, the mission of the church, as the body of Christ, must be tied to this future realization of God's purposes. But how exactly are these related, and what does this relationship mean for the present mission of the church?

This is where the provisional character of the church comes into focus. Although the Christian hope is secure, resting as it does on what God has already done in Christ, the exact shape of that future is still unclear. As John says in his letter to the young churches: "Beloved, we are God's children now; *what we will be has not yet been revealed.* What we do know is this: when he is revealed, we will be like him, for we will see him as he is" (1 Jn 3:2, emphasis added). Though we will be like God and see God truly, the shape of this relationship—to each other, to God, and to the renewed creation—has not yet been revealed. Therefore, as Rahner insists, the church lives on the proclamation of its own preliminary status. And since, before Christ returns, the church literally does not know what it will become, there can never be an ecclesial form or structure that is final.

EMERGENT IMAGES OF RENEWAL

The church's uncertainty about its future does not reflect a reticence on the part of Scripture to reference this future. From the first pages of Genesis through to the end of Revelation, Scripture is peppered with references to deliverance, restoration, and new creations. Most such references, however, take the form of metaphors that develop over the course of Scripture. We will focus on three of these in this chapter: garden, temple, and city (Jerusalem), among others we might choose.[3] When one considers the exuberant description of these images, one must conclude that the problem with a full grasp of this future world lies not with God's hesitance to reveal this future but with our human inability to conceive of such realities. When one considers

---

Biblical Eschatology (Grand Rapids: Baker Academic, 2014). A bit earlier the Jewish scholar Jon D. Levenson published his influential *Resurrection and the Restoration of Israel: The Ultimate Victory of the God of Life* (New Haven, CT: Yale University Press, 2006). These sources will be important to our discussion.

[3]By metaphor, as in chapter five, we mean the placing of two (or more) things together for the sake of comparison or their symbolic likeness. Metaphor insists both on the similarity of images and yet also their difference, and its power lies largely in its suggestive character. These images all suggest: "What if the world were like this?"

the explosion of imagery in the book of Revelation, all of which in one way or another reference events in the future, one can hardly say God is holding something back. The problem is our lack of imagination for a future that, according to Paul, is beyond our ability to comprehend. As he explains to the Corinthian believers, "God has revealed to us through the Spirit" (1 Cor 2:10):

> What no eye has seen, nor ear heard,
> nor the human heart conceived,
> what God has prepared for those who love him (1 Cor 2:9)[4]

Let us then spend some time reflecting on these central images and then see how they all extend and apply the earthshaking events associated with Christ's death and resurrection and the pouring out of the Holy Spirit.

Garden. At the very beginning of the First Testament God prepared a place of abundance, beauty, and sustenance as a special home for Adam and Eve, a place called the Garden of Eden (Gen 2:8). And already in this primal environment there is a hint of the future God intended for humans, and an implicit covenant that guaranteed that future. God had prepared this place of plenty with flowing waters, gems and precious stones, and "every tree that is pleasant to the sight and good for food" (Gen 2:9) as a place where Adam and Eve would live in tranquil relationship with "God walking in the garden at the time of the evening breeze" (Gen 3:8). The instructions God gave the man and woman "to till it and keep it" were accompanied by the assurance that they could "freely eat of every tree of the garden," provided they kept away from the tree of life in the center (Gen 2:15-16). That is to say, if they were faithful and cared for this place, it would continue to provide for them, as a kind of embodiment of God's promise to always care for the special objects of his regard—created in his image.

The garden theme plays a continuing—and expanding—role in the development of God's program in Scripture. Though Israel could not reenter the literal Garden of Eden, guarded as it was by cherubim and flaming sword, the metaphor of Eden continued to assert itself throughout the First Testament

---

[4]Paul claims that this is written somewhere, though scholars have been unable to determine where this might be. Isaiah 64:4 has some resemblance and may have been in Paul's mind:
> From ages past no one has heard,
> no ear has perceived,
> no eye has seen any God besides you.

and right up to the end of the New Testament. When God delivers Israel from Egypt he brings them into the "good land" (a phrase that is repeated 300 times in Deuteronomy). And there the description of this land of plenty recalls the provision of Eden. As Moses explains to the people at the mountain:

> The LORD your God is bringing you into a good land, a land with flowing streams, . . . a land of wheat and barley, of vines and fig trees and pomegranates, a land of olive trees and honey, a land where you may eat bread without scarcity, where you will lack nothing. (Deut 8:7-9)

But this promise is bookended with the proviso that Israel is to "keep" the commandments, and not forget the Lord God. As Jon Levenson says of this constant refrain, though, there is always an awareness of death in the First Testament, this reality does not have the last word. Parallel to this awareness is the "ubiquitous promise of life as a reward for the careful and faithful obedience to God and his will"—as God enjoins his people to "choose life."[5]

In Ezekiel God can even bless the Gentile nations with the blessing of Eden. Assyria is called "a cedar of Lebanon," towering above all the trees and nourished by streams (Ezek 3:3-4), so that

> no tree in the garden of God
> was like it in beauty.
> I made it beautiful,
> with its mass of branches,
> the envy of all the trees of Eden
> that were in the garden of God (Ezek 31:8-9).[6]

But pride replaced gratitude, and God brought Assyria down. The same Edenic imagery, however, assures Israel of God's provision:

> he will comfort all her waste places,
> and will make her wilderness like Eden,
> her desert like the garden of the LORD. (Is 51:3)

---

[5]Levenson, *Resurrection and the Restoration of Israel*, 168. Cf. Deuteronomy 30:19-20: "I call heaven and earth to witness against you today that I have set before you life and death, blessings and curses. Choose life so that you and your descendants may live, loving the LORD your God, obeying him."

[6]The King of Tyre was also said to be "in Eden, the garden of God; / every precious stone was your covering" (Ezek 28:13).

As Levenson notes, Eden hovers over the First Testament record as a promise of Israel's eventual resurrection.

In the New Testament the garden theme takes on additional resonance. The garden is where Christ prays the night before his crucifixion (Lk 22:39-46); it is where he is buried in a tomb where "no one had ever been laid" (Jn 19:41); and it is the place where Mary encounters him as a gardener, and he tells her not to touch him "because he had not yet ascended to the Father" (Jn 20:17). When we reach the end of John's visions in Revelation, the garden has been placed in the midst of the city, which is also the cosmic temple. John sees

> the river of the water of life, bright as crystal, flowing from the throne of God and of the Lamb through the middle of the street of the city. On either side of the river is the tree of life with its twelve kinds of fruit, producing its fruit each month; and the leaves of the tree are for the healing of the nations. (Rev 22:1-2)

Now the tree of life produces its fruit for all (for "the nations"); it is no longer forbidden. Thus, Richard Middleton notes, Eden comes to symbolize in Scripture a kind of holy of holies in its relation to the rest of the earth. Like the holy of holies in the temple, it was the place where the priest went to meet God. For it was there in Eden where humans knew their closest fellowship with God and where they experienced their first judgment for their disobedience.[7] The implication is clear that if humans had obeyed God they would have chosen life; the abundance and provision of the garden would have spread to cover the earth. But because of their disobedience Eden symbolizes loss and death, that is, until God takes up the metaphor and breathes new life into it, in Revelation 22, where it stands as a beacon of hope, a place of abundance, safety, and provision. Meanwhile, throughout Christian history the enclosed garden has symbolized a place where—in beauty and safety—humans can meet God in peace and security, whether this is the cloister of monasteries and convents or the fruitful enclosed garden so common in medieval paintings.

The temple. Throughout Scripture the temple becomes an increasingly central metaphor in illuminating God's presence in creation and, eventually, God's purposes for that creation—what the New Testament calls "new creation." Early in the First Testament (see Ex 27–31, 35–40) God gives instructions for

---

[7]Middleton, *New Heaven and a New Earth*, 164.

constructing the tabernacle, or the "tent of meeting" as it is called (see, e.g., Ex
27:21; 35:21). This structure, destined for replacement by the temple in Jerusalem,
was constructed as the place where the priests would enter to make sacrifices
for the sins of the people—the place, that is, where meeting and reconciliation
between God and humans would be realized. Jon Levenson points out that
many interpreters of Scripture (he points to Christians in particular) believe
that the tabernacle and temple are meant to replace Eden, which has now been
closed because of Adam and Eve's sin. But, he argues, this interpretation is
mistaken; the temple itself, he argues, encompassed the symbolism of Eden.[8]
This points up the rich interrelationship that exists among First Testament
biblical images, something that reflects a Hebrew aesthetic wherein various
images are placed together to spark new and broader meanings.[9]

Consider, for example, the association of the tabernacle with the imagery
of paradise. The detailed instructions for building the tabernacle and temple
are filled with references to the splendor of creation—gems and precious
stones, rare wood, and a restored beauty of the people themselves, represented by the priests. In Psalm 92 the psalmist similarly conflates imagery
of temple, Eden, and God's people:

The righteous flourish like the palm tree,
and grow like a cedar in Lebanon.
They are planted in the house of the LORD;
they flourish in the courts of our God.
In old age they still produce fruit;
they are always green and full of sap. (Ps 92:12-14)

Scholars have noted that cedar and hyssop, so important to temple imagery, could have been grown only in the specially protected gardens that
were planted in Jerusalem during the time of the Davidic kings.[10] But this
Edenic imagery is also extended to the human priests and worshipers at the

---

[8]Levenson, *Resurrection and the Restoration of Israel*, 83-92.
[9]On this Hebrew symbolism see Othmar Keel, *The Symbolism of the Biblical World: Ancient Near Eastern Iconography and the Book of Psalms*, trans. Timothy J. Hallett (New York: Seabury, 1978).
[10]Levenson, *Resurrection and the Restoration of Israel*, 85, 86. He refers here to the work of Law-rence Stager. Levenson notes that even the tree of life has not been left behind in Eden. Proverbs 3:18 calls wisdom the tree of life "to those who lay hold of her." Levenson notes: "The torah . . . became the Tree of Life through which God, in the words of the familiar blessing, 'planted eternal life within us'" (83, 84).

temple as Psalm 92 shows. Recall the extensive description of the beauty of the priestly robes in Exodus. Moses is to "make sacred vestments for the glorious adornment of your brother Aaron" (Ex 28:2). Here then is the beauty and perfection of human creation entering (again) the paradise that God has prepared for them, exhibiting all the stately splendor they were created to display, meeting and standing once again in the presence of God. Thus the temple not only carries forward the symbolism of garden and paradise but, with these added layers of meaning, becomes itself an image of the future destiny of the earth and its people.[11] This future orientation of temple imagery, and its conflation with Eden, becomes even clearer in Ezekiel's (sixth century before Christ) vision of the future temple. In Ezekiel 47 the prophet is brought to the entrance of the temple, which faces east. There he sees water flowing from the south end of the temple, on its banks are a great many trees with their leaves for healing, and the water teems with fish and every living creature (Ezek 47:1-12). This central place of provision and abundance becomes a centerpiece for Ezekiel's assignment to divide the land justly among the tribes of Israel (including the aliens and their children who shall be counted as citizens, Ezek 47:22).

Temple references become even more significant in the New Testament narrative. John recalls that Jesus, when asked for a sign (or miracle) while teaching in the temple, promised that if they destroy this temple, "in three days I will raise it up" (Jn 2:19). When the people wonder how the great temple could be rebuilt in such a short time, John explains that "he was speaking of the temple of his body" (Jn 2:21). This, together with the Gospels' description of the rending of the curtain of the holy of holies at Jesus' death (Lk 23:45), indicates that for these apostles Jesus himself has become the place of meeting between God and humans, a place of safety and provision. This symbolism has been picked up by medieval Christian art, in which Mary herself often becomes identified with the enclosed garden, bearing a son who is the reconciling space of abundance and beauty.

Paul will later extend this metaphor of temple to include believers, though in a way different from the association we noted in Psalm 92. In his letter to the Corinthians, Paul notes that Christians have been united with the Lord

---

[11]An excellent description of these multiple references is found in Meredith G. Kline, *Images of the Spirit* (Grand Rapids, Baker, 1980).

in their baptism so that they should not defile their bodies, concluding, "Or do you not know that your body is a temple of the Holy Spirit within you, which you have from God, and that you are not your own?" (1 Cor 6:19). Paul would not have dared such a comparison unless he intended to appropriate the many layers of meaning this word *temple* carried—the place of meeting between God and humans, a restored order and dignity (recalling the First Testament priests who served in the temple), and indeed a future fulfillment.[12]

The future of the temple comes into full view with John's vision on Patmos. In Revelation 21–22, when John sees the holy city coming down from heaven and from God, what arrives can also be described as a temple—or better, what will replace the temple. John says "I saw no temple in the city, for its temple is the Lord God the Almighty and the Lamb" (Rev 21:22). This is the revelation of what has been called the cosmic temple, where in a transformed creation God dwells with humans. As we noted earlier, the imagery of Eden is also highlighted: the tree of life freely available, the river, and trees bearing their fruit. Temple and garden have become one, and indeed one with the city of God, the new Jerusalem.

John announces here the new temple:

> The home of God is among mortals.
> He will dwell with them;
> they will be his peoples,
> and God himself will be with them. (Rev 21:3)

Notice the plural, "his peoples," indicating the diversity of those now welcomed. John had earlier recorded his vision of "a great multitude that no one could count, from every nation, from all tribes and peoples and languages, standing before the throne and before the Lamb" (Rev 7:9). They cried, "Salvation belongs to our God who is seated on the throne, and to the Lamb" (Rev 7:10). In this temple, difference matters. And it must, for relationship can only occur among beings who are differentiated from each other in various ways. In that future temple, what is it that allows people to see one another as different? We see glimpses of this in their worship. Just

---

[12]As this entire Corinthian letter makes clear, we should avoid reading this in terms of the modern autonomous individual—it is the holiness of the body of Christ, not the individual Christian, that Paul has in view here.

as at Pentecost, when all the people heard the word in their own language, these will now praise God in their own way. They will bring their histories— their tastes and treasures—with them for these are essential not only to their identities but also to their eventual praise of God (see Rev 21:24). We see here that difference and diversity are not sources of division and discord, as they have so often been in our present church age. Rather, in some mysterious way, some of the emergent diversity among global churches will continue and form the basis for the ongoing praise and relationships that occur. Thus, the difference that is already on full display in the worldwide communities of God's people is a very real anticipation of that which will be at work within the new temple.

The city—Jerusalem. Individuals in the First Testament were deeply engaged with their social identity; each person defined herself or himself by family and tribe, and the tribes in turn by their connection to the ancestors and God's promises to them.[13] In such a situation it is not surprising that the seat of power, and the location of the temple, could become identified with the people themselves. Such was the case of the founding of Jerusalem in the First Testament in 1000 BCE, when David conquered the city and it became the city of David and the capital of the united Davidic kingdom. Jerusalem, also referred to as Zion, over time became identified with the mountain of the Lord and with the temple that was built there. Here as well, the symbolism of Eden and temple is often fused with that of Jerusalem and the Mountain of the Lord. The river Gihon, identified as one of the four rivers in Genesis 2, flows in Jerusalem into the Kidron Valley, irrigating the gardens planted by the Davidic kings.[14] Like Eden and the temple, Jerusalem becomes not simply the king's dwelling but the special dwelling place of God. In Psalm 133, when the blessing is pronounced on those who dwell together in unity, it is not clear whether this refers to the temple or to Jerusalem or indeed to both. This blessing is

> like the dew of Herman,
> which falls on the mountains of Zion.

---

[13]On this see Levenson, *Resurrection and the Restoration of Israel*, 112, 113, where he cites the work of Robert DeVito on the individual's social identity that found authenticity in dependence on the community.

[14]Levenson, *Resurrection and the Restoration of Israel*, 87.

For there the LORD ordained his blessing,

life forevermore. (Ps 133:3)

This psalm belongs to the famous Songs of Ascents, which were sung by people journeying up to Jerusalem to worship at the temple. As they sang, they blessed the Lord and prayed: "May the LORD, maker of heaven and earth, / bless you from Zion" (Ps 134:3). Levenson sums up the goal of this journey to Jerusalem: "To journey to the temple is to move toward redemption, to leave the parched land of wasting and death for the formation of life and the revival and rejuvenation it dispenses."[15] For, the psalmist writes, "Those who trust in the LORD are like Mount Zion, / which cannot be moved, but abides forever" (Ps 125:1). They pray:

The Lord bless you from Zion.

May you see the prosperity of Jerusalem

all the days of your life. (Ps 128:5)

As with the temple and Eden, Jerusalem—often identified with God's people themselves—becomes a symbol of God's presence and blessing, but more than this, it comes to stand for the place where one can already taste the world that is coming. Isaiah gives a further picture of the Jerusalem that is to come. God says through the prophet:

For I am about to create new heavens

and a new earth;

the former things shall not be remembered

or come to mind.

But be glad and rejoice forever

in what I am creating;

for I am about to create Jerusalem as a joy,

and its people as a delight.

I will rejoice in Jerusalem,

and delight in my people;

no more shall the sound of weeping be heard in it,

or the cry of distress. (Is 65:17-19)

In the New Testament the city of Jerusalem takes on a similar range of resonances. It is still the city of David, the seat of the temple and site of

---

[15]Levenson, *Resurrection and the Restoration of Israel*, 92.

pilgrimage, but in the ministry of Jesus the historical reality overshadows its symbolic character. On his visit to Jerusalem the week of his death, Jesus is welcomed by crowds shouting, "Hosanna to the Son of David!" (Mt 21:1-11), though Jesus is not swayed by the crowds. In Matthew's version, immediately after this he enters the temple and turns over the tables of the moneychangers, saying, "'My house shall be called a house of prayer'; / but you are making it a den of robbers" (Mt 21:13). Afterward, in his famous lament over the city, Jesus cries: "Jerusalem, Jerusalem, the city that kills the prophets and stones those who are sent to it! How often have I desired to gather your children together as a hen gathers her brood under her wings, and you were not willing!" (Mt 23:37). Jerusalem would become "desolate," Jesus predicted, until he would return and be truly welcomed (Mt 23:38-39). Later that week Jesus is crucified as a criminal just outside the city walls and is buried in a garden tomb.

It is well known that the direction of mission in the New Testament is the reverse of that in the First Testament. In the latter, the movement is up to Jerusalem and the temple, where God dwells and God's blessing is to be found. In Acts the instructions to the apostles urge them to move outward from Jerusalem to the ends of the earth. And though the apostles continue regular fellowship in the temple (Acts 2:46; 3:1; 5:12; 5:25), they soon leave the temple and Jerusalem behind as they pursue their missionary journeys.

But if Jerusalem loses some of its centrality, it does not give up its symbolic role. When John glimpses the holy city coming down from heaven and from God in Revelation 21, it is the new Jerusalem that he sees—as a bride adorned for her husband. Indeed, Jerusalem here becomes a stand-in for the church, which is elsewhere in the New Testament called the bride of Christ.[16] As we have noted, the imagery of Eden and the temple is brought together with that of the city of the Lord to indicate that now heaven and earth have become one. "It is God's intent," Richard Middleton notes, "that the divine presence extend from heaven to earth, to unify heaven and earth."[17] This is a foursquare city whose gates are always open and into which the honor and

---

[16]In Ephesians 5:22-33 Paul likens the relationship between the church and Christ to that between a wife and her husband. In 2 Corinthians 11:2-4 Paul expresses his jealousy that though the Corinthians are espoused to one husband (Christ), as the virgin of Christ they have been led astray.

[17]Middleton, *New Heaven and a New Earth*, 168.

glory of the nations will come and be celebrated (Rev 21:24-26), where the trees and water give life and healing, and where God will wipe away every tear. There will be no night in this city, and no more sea,[18] and nothing unclean will enter it, only those whose names are written in the Lamb's book of life (Rev 21:27).

CHRIST AND HIS PEOPLE

We have been referencing Jon Levenson's book on the First Testament and its relationship to resurrection. That important work argues, contrary to what is often thought, that the resurrection of the dead is a "weight bearing beam" in the edifice of Judaism: "Resurrection is one key element in the whole panorama of redemptive and recreative events that characterize the rabbinic vision of the end of history."[19] For the Jewish people, Levenson stresses, God was not a distant deity but one deeply involved with Israel's history, delivering them from slavery, bringing them into the Good Land, restoring the fortunes of Job, and dwelling among them in the tabernacle and temple. Indeed, the temple itself, with its Edenic character, is where God ordained the blessing of eternal life (Ps 133) and where, in Ezekiel's vision (Ezek 47), a future restoration of Israel is envisioned.[20]

Thus, if Levenson is right, resurrection and renewal are already part of the central structure of biblical revelation when Jesus appears in Palestine preaching the kingdom of God. But at the time of Jesus that story was largely told in the future tense—like Simeon, the Jewish people were "looking *forward* to the consolation of Israel" (Lk 2:25, emphasis added). As with Mary and Martha at the tomb of Lazarus (Jn 11:1-44), they believed resurrection and restoration were still in the future. In his teaching and miracles Jesus challenged that assumption and demonstrated the reality that the kingdom had come near in his person and ministry. As Jesus tells Mary and Martha when he stands before Lazarus's tomb: "I am the resurrection and the life. Those who believe in me, even though they die, will live" (Jn 11:25). Further, with his death on the cross and his resurrection on the third day, the kingdom

---

[18]The people of Israel were famously afraid of the sea. They were not seagoing people, a fact that is important to the story of Jonah.

[19]Levenson, *Resurrection and the Restoration of Israel*, 6.

[20]Death is alien to the temple, Levenson notes in *Resurrection and the Restoration of Israel*, 92.

is made manifest and establishes itself in the center of human history. N. T. Wright makes this point strongly in his bestselling book *Surprised by Hope*. He notes, "The resurrection completes the inauguration of God's kingdom."[21] This is to say that with the resurrection of Jesus and the gift of the Holy Spirit given as a result, the renewal of all things has begun; something definitive has been added to human history that will change the way that history will be told. Indeed, Wright notes, with the resurrection of Jesus, the story of Israel itself must be told in a new way.[22] The resurrection is both the sign of victory over all that keeps creation from realizing the purposes God has for it and the emergence of the first fruits of a new creation.

But what does this radical intervention mean for the nature and mission of God's people? Here we need to recall the interconnection of the renewal of all things we have been tracing, including the deliverance and restoration of God's people. On the one hand, this means that restoration of creation involves centrally the realization of God's purposes for the human creation. Central to the First Testament is the promise that the righteous will be rewarded with life. As the Wisdom of Solomon notes:

> The righteous live forever,
> and their reward is with the Lord;
> the Most High takes care of them.
> Therefore they will receive a glorious crown
> and a beautiful diadem from the hand of the Lord. (Wisdom 5:15-16)

During the Second Temple period (when this was written), Jewish people looked forward with assurance to the resurrection of the righteous. As Richard Middleton puts this, they expected the restoration of humans to their rightful status, especially as this was described in Psalm 8—where humans are, "made . . . a little lower than God, / and crowned . . . with glory and honor" (Ps 8:5).[23] So, for Jewish people, it would have been unthinkable that the renewal of all things would not have centrally involved the restoration of the people of God. John Calvin similarly insists that God's preservation of the church is of such a character that it will involve nothing less

---

[21]N. T. Wright, *Surprised by Hope*, 234. See 236-37 for what follows.

[22]Though perhaps the argument of Levenson nuances this claim. Actual resurrections were not unknown in the First Testament, as Elisha's ministry makes clear.

[23]Middleton, *New Heaven and a New Earth*, 144.

than a renewal of all things. In his commentary on the Isaiah 65 passage that we cited above, Calvin comments: "As if God had said he has . . . the power not only to restore his Church, but to restore it in such a manner that it shall appear to gain a new life and to dwell in a new world."[24] Similarly, in his commentary on Isaiah 40:5, Calvin writes: "The deliverance of the Church, from its commencement down to the coming of Christ, might be called a renewal of the world."[25] So the new creation that God will bring about will also be a deliverance, a vindication, and an elevation of God's people.

On other hand, the church is also called—now in this period of history—to embody and live by its praise of God's power and glory, thus anticipating, showing something of the future renewal that God will bring about. The Spirit that "intercedes with sighs too deep for words" in Romans 8:26 at the same time calls on God to bring about the revelation of his glory: "For the creation waits with eager longing for the revealing of the children of God" (Rom 8:19). This revealing is a part of the creation being set free from its "bondage to decay" (Rom 8:21). But with their praises God's people do even more. As Belden Lane notes, in extolling God's glory, in sharing in the groaning of creation and the prayers of the Spirit, "the praise of the faithful helps restore the earth to its original order and wholeness."[26]

Clearly, the future of God's people is central to the renewal of all things; the renewal of creation is, at the same time, the renewal of God's people—those whose names, John says, are written in the Lamb's book of life. But are these to be equated simply with the church? Can we say that the church will exist together with God in the new creation? Not any more than we can say that the temple simply now exists in heaven. Rather, we need to say the temple will *become* the new heaven and new earth; similarly, we can say God's people will *become* a part of the new heaven and new earth. Perhaps then we should modify Rahner's claim that the church looks to its "historically advancing elimination."[27] The church does not disappear; it is transformed. But this is no cause for sadness; rather, it is a reason to celebrate.

---

[24]John Calvin, *Commentary on the Book of Isaiah*, trans. John King (1844–1856), electronic edition, Isaiah 65:17.

[25]Calvin, *Commentary on the Book of Isaiah*, Isaiah 40:5.

[26]Belden C. Lane, *Ravished by Beauty: The Surprising Legacy of Reformed Spirituality* (New York: Oxford University Press, 2011), 67.

[27]Rahner, *Concerning Vatican Council II*, 298.

The kingdoms of this world, including the church, will become the kingdoms of our Lord. The church becomes something else; it merges with the renewal of all things even as it celebrates and partakes in that renewal—the chrysalis becomes a butterfly.

CHURCH AND KINGDOM

Finally, we need to return to the question that puzzles many and that is determinative for present attitudes and practices of church. If the kingdom is the goal, what specifically is the relation between the church in all its multiple forms and this emerging program of renewal? George Ladd addressed this question fifty years ago in his influential book *Jesus and the Kingdom*. In biblical language, he argued, "the kingdom is not identified with its subjects." Ladd wrote, "The Church is the community of the kingdom, but never the kingdom itself."[28] He noted that the first missionaries preached the kingdom, not the church. The kingdom—or the good news of what God has begun in Christ—is the dynamic force in history whereas the church is always some form of human community that witnesses to this reality. This does not belittle the role of the church so much as establish it. The church is an instrument of the kingdom of which it is a custodian.

But what does it mean to be an instrument of the kingdom? And what are the implications of this for the form it ought to take in the world? Here we take our cue from the preaching of Jesus: How did he conceive of what he was bringing about? In his first sermon in Nazareth (recorded in Lk 4), he reads passages from the prophet Isaiah referring to the Jubilee year:

> The Spirit of the Lord is upon me,
>> because he has anointed me
>>> to bring good news to the poor.
> He has sent me to proclaim release to the captives
>> and recovery of sight to the blind,
>>> to let the oppressed go free,
> to proclaim the year of the Lord's favor. (Lk 4:18-19)

Jesus' comment on this passage was simply that "today this scripture has been fulfilled in your hearing" (Lk 4:21). In other words, on that day this

---

[28]Ladd, *Jesus and the Kingdom*, updated as *Presence of the Future*, 262-64.

Jubilee was becoming visible in Christ's ministry. The themes of these verses resonate with the images that we have described in this chapter: provision, healing, release, recovery, deliverance, and, most of all, God's grace (favor) toward his creation. The church then, as the body of Christ and continuing his ministry, should be people on whom the Spirit has come, enabling them to bring about, by their words, their lives, and their actions, visible evidence of God's restorative rule over all creation. As N. T. Wright notes, the church needs constantly to be recalibrated and renewed for this mission, which is a "*mission to* the world, based on Christ's *lordship over* the world."[29] Here is his summary of this mission:

> The revolutionary new world, which began in the resurrection of Jesus—the world where Jesus reigns as Lord, having won the victory over sin and death— has its frontline outposts in those who in baptism have shared his death and resurrection.[30]

Wright goes on to describe the character of this people as self-giving rather than self-seeking—as people who learn about the world by loving and serving it. To make use of emergent language, the kingdom is constituted by particular ways of relating people to God, to the earth, and to each other that embody justice and righteousness, and the metaphors of garden, temple, and city provide imaginative forays into the world that is coming.

Conclusion

The church, and churches, comprise historical communities appearing in multiple forms and speaking many languages. All are important to God, but as we noted earlier, short of the eschaton, none are final. Or perhaps we should rather say, all are on the way to a final incorporation into God's kingdom. In an earlier chapter we referenced Andrew Walls's well-known suggestion that God's people struggle with the tension between the indigenizing and pilgrim principles.[31] But we should not misunderstand the role of these impulses. It is not the case that we can choose one or another as our focus since both are a necessary part of our present situation as God's people.

---

[29]N. T. Wright, *Surprised by Hope*, 235 (emphasis original).
[30]N. T. Wright, *Surprised by Hope*, 249.
[31]Andrew F. Walls, "The Gospel as Prisoner and Liberator of Culture," in *The Missionary Movement in Christian History: Studies in the Transmission of Faith* (Maryknoll, NY: Orbis, 1996).

We necessarily reflect the culture that has shaped us; we cannot choose to free ourselves from culture since we are, after all, pilgrims—indeed even pilgrimage is rooted in culture. As we noted in chapter three, here is where Walls's principle breaks down, for we are never able to rise above or simply travel through a culture. So, while our reading of the gospel may lead us to counter aspects of our culture (Walls's point), cultural escape is not an option that is open to us. And it is not open to us because we do not control the trajectory of our pilgrimage; we have no map or strategy to follow. We do not know what we will become, John says, though we know that we will be like our Lord (1 Jn 3:2). Meanwhile, we are called to make our discipleship indigenous in the particular places we find ourselves.

We argue that in God's program the church both celebrates and transcends these particularities: accumulating layers of significance from its origins in a garden and its foundation in a cross and an empty tomb, finding its life by the Spirit who works to make all things new, and drawing inspiration from a future that confounds all wisdom while fulfilling every hope. The church is not a garden, but this image suggests the peace and provision that the church provides; the church is not a temple, but it is a place where humans and God meet and grow together; the church is not a city, but it does propose a polis that all cities struggle to embody. In providing a space where humans meet God, share the gifts of the Spirit, and progressively and corporately reflect the love that God has for all creation, the church both represents and gestures toward the future renewal of all things.

The church is a journey defined by its goal in the new creation. That new creation we have likened to a garden, a city, a temple, but John in Revelation 19 also calls it the marriage supper of the Lamb: "And the angel said to me, 'Write this: Blessed are those who are invited to the marriage supper of the Lamb'" (Rev 19:9). The bride John sees has made herself ready, clothed in fine linen, which is "the righteous deeds of the saints" (Rev 19:8). And the angels, the twenty-four elders, the people from every tongue and nation celebrate together; they sing "Hallelujah!" (Rev 19:1).

All human beings yearn for a community in which they are welcomed and at home. And many today are seeking technical means to move toward that global human community. Mark Zuckerberg, founder of Facebook, often speaks of his desire to create a global community where all have access and no one is excluded. But sadly he has come to realize that the platform he developed can also be used to recruit Muslim youth for the global jihad, or vulnerable girls from the majority world into human trafficking. So he has recently said that connecting people was only step one. It is time, he says, to move to the next step. Here is how he described this: "The next focus will be developing the social infrastructure for community—for supporting us, for keeping us safe, for informing us, for civic engagement and for inclusion of all."[32] To see a community that is open and caring is what we all want, but Zuckerberg is right: we do not yet have the appropriate social infrastructure. However, what Zuckerberg is describing is the biblical heart of the church: an open and caring community. However, that is something that is only truly embodied in the vocation of God's people. In this sense all human communities aspire to be the church. Of course, we don't always see this in our local parish though—God be praised—sometimes we do. For those who are looking for a city whose builder and maker is God, this future is not merely aspirational; it is eschatological. We do yearn for some final and healthy community that covers the earth. But we are not prepared for that now. First *we* must be renewed; first the *earth* must be renewed. And the fix that we await is not technical (pace Zuckerberg); it is the resurrection of all things. And it is this toward which history leads, and toward which God's people gesture with their lives and witness. When that world comes, we will truly celebrate. Meanwhile we pray with the apostle John: "Amen. Come, Lord Jesus!" (Rev 22:20).

---

[32]Quoted in Farhad Manoo, "Can Facebook Fix Its Own Worst Bug?," *New York Times Magazine*, April 30, 2017, 42, www.nytimes.com/2017/04/25/magazine/can-facebook-fix-its-own-worst-bug.html.

Bibliography

Abbott, Walter M., ed. *The Documents of Vatican II with Notes and Comments by Catholic, Protestant, and Orthodox Authorities.* Translations edited by Joseph Gallagher (New York: Guild Press, 1966).

Acoba, E. [pseud.]. "Towards an Understanding of Inclusivity in Contextualizing into Philippine Context." In *The Gospel in Culture: Contextualization Issues in an Asian Context,* edited by M. P. Maggay, 416-50. Manila: OMF Literature/ISACC, 2013.

Adam, A. K. M. "Saint-Spotting in Scripture: Οἱ Ἅγιοι in the New (and Old) Testament." Paper presented at Saints Without Borders: 47th International Ecumenical Seminar, Strasbourg, France, July 3, 2013.

Adams, Edward. *The Earliest Christian Meeting Places: Almost Exclusively Houses?* New York: Bloomsbury; T&T Clark, 2016.

Allmen, J.-J. von. *Worship: Its Theology and Practice.* New York: Oxford University Press, 1965.

Alvarez, Miguel, ed. *The Reshaping of Mission in Latin America.* Oxford: Regnum, 2015.

Antony, Prem. "The Khrist Bhakta Way: A New Way of Being the Church." In *The Emerging Challenges to Christian Mission Today,* edited by S. M. Michael and Jose Joseph, 231-48. New Delhi: Ishvani Kendra and Christian World Imprints, 2016.

The Apostolic Fathers in English. Translated and edited by Michael W. Holmes. 3rd ed. Grand Rapids: Baker Academic, 2007.

Appasamy, A. J., V. Chakkarai, and P. Chenchiah. *A Christian Theological Approach to Hinduism: Being Studies in the Theology of A. J. Appasamy, V. Chakkarai, and P. Chenchiah.* Madras, India: Christian Literature Society, 1956.

Archer, Margaret S. *Being Human: The Problem of Agency.* New York: Cambridge University Press, 2000.

———. *Realist Social Theory: The Morphogenetic Approach.* New York: Cambridge University Press, 1995.

Ascough, Richard S. "Greco-Roman Philosophic, Religious, and Voluntary Associations." In *Community Formation in the Early Church and in the Church Today,* edited by Richard N. Longenecker, 3-19. Peabody, MA: Hendrickson, 2002.

————. *Paul's Macedonian Associations*. Tübingen: Mohr Siebeck, 2003.

Augustine. "Sermon 341." In *Sermons on Various Subjects, 341-400*. Part 3, vol. 10 of *The Works of Saint Augustine: A Translation for the 21st Century*, translated by Edmund Hill and edited by John E. Rotelle, 19-29. Brooklyn, NY: New City Press, 1995.

Badcock, Gary D. "The Church as 'Sacrament.'" In Husbands and Treier, *Community of the Word*, 188-200.

Balcomb, Anthony. "From Liberation to Democracy: Theologies of Bread and Being in the New South Africa." *Missionalia* 26, no. 1 (1998): 54-73.

Banks, Robert J. *Paul's Idea of Community: The Early House Churches in Their Cultural Setting*. Rev. ed. Peabody, MA: Hendrickson, 1994.

Banton, Michael, ed. *Anthropological Approaches to the Study of Religion*. London: Routledge, 1966.

Baptism, Eucharist and Ministry. Geneva: World Council of Churches, 1982.

Bauman, Chad M. "Hindu-Christian Conflict in India: Globalization, Conversion, and the Coterminal Castes and Tribes." *Journal of Asian Studies* 72, no. 3 (2013): 633-53.

Bauman, Chad M., and Richard Fox Young, eds. *Constructing Indian Christianities: Culture, Conversion and Caste*. New Delhi: Routledge, 2014.

Bazzell, Pascal, and Aldrin Peñamora, eds. *Christologies, Cultures and Religions: Portraits of Christ in the Philippines*. Manila: OMF, 2016.

Bediako, Kwame. "Jesus in African Culture: A Ghanaian Perspective." In *Jesus and the Gospel in Africa: History and Experience*, 20-33. Maryknoll, NY: Orbis, 2004.

Bender, Harold S. "Bible." In *Global Anabaptist Mennonite Encyclopedia Online*. Herald Press, 1953. Last modified January 18, 2019. http://gameo.org/index.php?title=Bible&oldid=144829.

Berger, Peter L., ed. *The Desecularization of the World: Resurgent Religions and World Politics*. Grand Rapids: Eerdmans, 1999.

Bharati, Dayanand. *Living Water and Indian Bowl: An Analysis of Christian Failings in Communicating Christ to Hindus, with Suggestions Toward Improvements*. Delhi: ISPCK, 1997.

Blickle, Peter. *From the Communal Reformation to the Revolution of the Common Man*. Translated by Beat Kumin. Boston: Brill, 1998.

Blue, Bradley. "Acts and the House Church." In *The Book of Acts in Its Graeco-Roman Setting*, edited by David W. J. Gill and Conrad Gempf, 119-221. Grand Rapids: Eerdmans, 1994.

Bonhoeffer, Dietrich. *Sanctorum Communio: A Theological Study of the Sociology of the Church*. German edited by Joachim von Soosten. English edition translated by Reinhard Krauss and Nancy Lukens and edited by Clifford J. Green. Minneapolis: Fortress, 1998.

Bosch, David J. *Transforming Mission: Paradigm Shifts in Theology of Mission*. Maryknoll, NY: Orbis, 1991.

Bouyer, Louis. *The Church of God: Body of Christ and Temple of the Spirit*. Translated by Charles Quinn. Chicago: Franciscan Herald, 1982.

Bradshaw, Paul F., and Maxwell E. Johnson. *The Eucharistic Liturgies: Their Evolution and Interpretation*. Collegeville, MN: Liturgical Press, 2012.

Brady, Thomas A., Jr. *Communities, Politics, and Reformation in Early Modern Europe*. Boston: Brill, 1998.

Brueggemann, Walter. *Old Testament Theology: An Introduction*. Nashville: Abingdon Press, 2008.

Caldarola, Carlo. *Christianity the Japanese Way*. Leiden: Brill, 1979.

Calvin, John. *Commentary on the Book of Isaiah*. Translated by John King. Electronic Ed. 1944–1956.

———. *Institutes of the Christian Religion*. Edited by John T. McNeill. Translated by Ford Lewis Battles. 2 vols. Philadelphia: Westminster, 1960.

"The Cape Town Commitment: A Confession of Faith and a Call to Action." *Kairos* 5, no. 1 (2011): 165-224.

Cardoza-Orlandi, Carlos F. "An Invitation to Theological Dialogue." In *What Young Asian Theologians Are Thinking*, edited by Leow Theng Huat, 128-35. Singapore: Trinity Theological College, 2014.

Carter, Craig A. "Beyond Theocracy and Individualism." In Husbands and Treier, *Community of the Word*, 173-87.

Chan, Simon. *Grassroots Asian Theology: Thinking the Faith from the Ground Up*. Downers Grove, IL: InterVarsity Press, 2014.

Charry, Ellen T. "Sacramental Ecclesiology." In Husbands and Treier, *Community of the Word*, 201-17.

Clasen, Claus-Peter. *Anabaptism: A Social History, 1525–1618*. Ithaca, NY: Cornell University Press, 1972.

Clifford, James. "Introduction: Partial Truths." In James Clifford and George E. Marcus, eds., *Writing Culture: The Poetics and Politics of Ethnography*. Berkeley: University of California Press, 1986.

Committee on Cooperation in Latin America. *Christian Work in Latin America*. New York: Missionary Education Committee, 1917.

Congregation for the Doctrine of the Faith. "Declaration 'Dominus Iesus': On the Unicity and Salvific Universality of Jesus Christ and the Church." June 16, 2000. www.vatican.va/roman_curia/congregations/cfaith/documents/rc_con_cfaith_doc_20000806_dominus-iesus_en.html.

Cyprian. *The Letters of St. Cyprian of Carthage.* Translated and annotated by G. W. Clarke. 4 vols. New York: Newman Press, 1984–1989.

Dalrymple, William. *The Last Mughal: The Fall of a Dynasty, Delhi, 1857.* New York: Penguin, 2006.

Dilley, Andrea Palpant. "The World the Missionaries Made." *Christianity Today,* January 8, 2014. www.christianitytoday.com/ct/2014/january-february/world-missionaries-made.html.

Donati, Pierpaolo, and Margaret S. Archer. *The Relational Subject.* Cambridge: Cambridge University Press, 2015.

Douglas, J. D. *Let the Earth Hear His Voice: International Congress on World Evangelization, Lausanne, Switzerland.* Minneapolis: World Wide Publications, 1975.

Doyle, Dennis M. "Henri de Lubac and the Roots of Communion Ecclesiology." *Theological Studies* 60 (1999): 209-27.

Driedger, Michael. "Anabaptists and the Early Modern State: A Long-Term View." In Roth and Stayer, *Companion to Anabaptism and Spiritualism,* 507-44.

Duerksen, Darren Todd. *Ecclesial Identities in a Multi-Faith Context: Jesus Truth-Gatherings* (Yeshu Satsangs) *Among Hindus and Sikhs in Northwest India.* American Society of Missiology Monograph 22. Eugene, OR: Pickwick, 2015.

Dulles, Avery. "Nature, Mission, and Structure of the Church." In *Vatican II: Renewal Within Tradition,* edited by Matthew L. Lamb and Matthew Levering, 25-36. New York: Oxford University Press, 2008.

Durkheim, Émile. *Suicide: A Study in Sociology.* Edited by George Simpson. Translated by John A. Spaulding and George Simpson. New York: The Free Press, 1951. First published in French in 1897.

Dyrness, William A. *Insider Jesus: Theological Reflections on New Christian Movements.* Downers Grove, IL: InterVarsity Press, 2016.

———. *A Primer on Christian Worship.* Grand Rapids: Eerdmans, 2009.

———. "Spaces for an Evangelical Ecclesiology." In Husbands and Treier, *Community of the Word,* 251-72.

Elder-Vass, Dave. *The Causal Power of Social Structures: Emergence, Structure and Agency.* New York: Cambridge University Press, 2010.

Endō, Shūsaku. *Silence: A Novel.* Translated by William Johnston. New York: Picador, 2016. First published in Japanese under the title *Chinmoku* by Monumenta Nipponica, 1969.

Escobar, Samuel. "Evangelical Missiology: Peering into the Future at the Turn of the Century." In *Global Missiology for the 21st Century: The Iguassu Dialogue,* edited by William D. Taylor, 101-22. Grand Rapids: Baker Academic, 2000.

Faith and Order Secretariat. *Baptism, Eucharist and Ministry.* Paper no. 111. Geneva: World Council of Churches, 1982.

Farquhar, J. N. *The Crown of Hinduism.* 1913; reprint, New York: Oxford University Press, 1919.

Finger, Thomas N. *A Contemporary Anabaptist Theology: Biblical, Historical, Constructive.* Downers Grove, IL: InterVarsity Press, 2004.

Flueckiger, Joyce Burkhalter. *Everyday Hinduism.* Oxford: Wiley Blackwell, 2015.

Francis-Dehqani, Gulnar. "Adventures in Christian-Muslim Encounters since 1910." In Kerr and Ross, *Edinburgh 2010,* 125-38.

Fujimura, Makoto. *Silence and Beauty: Hidden Faith Born of Suffering.* Downers Grove, IL: InterVarsity Press, 2016.

Gaba, Christian R. *Scriptures of an African People: Ritual Utterances of the Anlo.* New York: NOK, 1973.

Gadamer, Hans-Georg. *Truth and Method.* Translated by Richard Heinemann and Bruce Krajewski. New York: Seabury, 1975.

Garrison, David. *A Wind in the House of Islam: How God Is Drawing Muslims Around the World to Faith in Christ.* Monument, CO: WIGTake Resources, 2014.

Geertz, Clifford. "Religion as a Cultural System." In Banton, *Anthropological Approaches to the Study of Religion,* 1-46.

Gehring, Roger W. *House Church and Mission: The Importance of Household Structures in Early Christianity.* Peabody MA: Hendrickson, 2004.

Gell-Mann, Murray. *The Quark and the Jaguar: Adventures in the Simple and the Complex.* London: Abacus, 1995.

Gitau, Wanjiru M. *Megachurch Christianity Reconsidered: Millennials and Social Change in African Perspective.* Downers Grove, IL: InterVarsity Press, 2018.

Goel, Sita Ram. *Catholic Ashrams: Sannyasins or Swindlers?* 2nd ed. New Delhi: Voice of India, 1994.

Goertz, Hans-Jürgen. "Karlstadt, Müntzer and the Reformation of the Commoners, 1521–1525." In Roth and Stayer, *Companion to Anabaptism and Spiritualism,* 1-44.

Goizueta, Roberto S. *Caminemos con Jesús: Toward a Hispanic/Latino Theology of Accompaniment.* Maryknoll, NY: Orbis, 1995.

———. "Liberalism." In *Global Dictionary of Theology*, edited by William A. Dyrness and Veli-Matti Kärkkäinan. Downers Grove, IL: InterVarsity Press, 2008.

Goldingay, John. *Old Testament Theology: Israel's Gospel*. Downers Grove, IL: InterVarsity Press, 2003.

Grant, Robert M. *Augustus to Constantine: The Rise and Triumph of Christianity in the Roman World*. New York: Harper & Row, 1990.

Gravend-Tirole, Xavier. "From Christian Ashrams to Dalit Theology—or Beyond?: An Examination of the Indigenisation/Inculturation Trend Within the Indian Catholic Church." In Bauman and Young, *Constructing Indian Christianities*, 110-37.

Green Joel B. *1 Peter*. Two Horizons New Testament Commentary. Grand Rapids: Eerdmans, 2007.

———. *Conversion in Luke-Acts: Divine Action, Human Cognition, and the People of God*. Grand Rapids: Baker Academic, 2015.

———. "Conversion in Luke-Acts: The Potential of a Cognitive Approach." Paper presented to the Consultation on the Use of Cognitive Linguistics in Biblical Interpretation, Society of Biblical Literature, Washington, DC, November 2006.

Gritsch, Eric W., and Robert W. Jenson. *Lutheranism: The Theological Movement and Its Confessional Writings*. Philadelphia: Fortress, 1976.

Haight, Roger. *Christian Community in History*. Vol. 2, *Comparative Ecclesiology*. New York: Continuum, 2005.

Hanciles, Jehu J. *Beyond Christendom: Globalization, African Migration and the Transformation of the West*. Maryknoll, NY: Orbis, 2008.

Harding, Christopher. *Religious Transformation in South Asia: The Meanings of Conversion in Colonial Punjab*. New York: Oxford University Press, 2008.

Hatch, Nathan O. *The Democratization of American Christianity*. New Haven, CT: Yale University Press, 1989.

Hiebert, Paul G. "French Structuralism and Modern Missiology." Paper presented at the Christian Perspectives on Anthropological Theory Conference, Biola University, La Mirada, CA, April 6-8, 2000.

Hocking, William Ernest. *Living Religions and a World Faith*. New York: Macmillan, 1940.

Hsia, R. Po-Chia. "The Myth of the Commune: Recent Historiography on City and Reformation in Germany." *Central European History* 20, no. 3 (1987): 203-15.

Humphreys, Paul. *Emergence: A Philosophical Account*. New York: Oxford University Press, 2016.

Husbands, Mark, and Daniel J. Treier, eds. *The Community of the Word: Toward an Evangelical Ecclesiology*. Downers Grove, IL: IVP Academic, 2005.

Iannaccone, Laurence R. "Rational Choice: Framework for the Scientific Study of Religion." In *Rational Choice Theory and Religion: Summary and Assessment,* edited by Lawrence A. Young, 25-44. New York: Routledge, 1997.

Isomae, Jun'ichi. "The Conceptual Formation of the Category 'Religion' in Modern Japan: Religion, State, Shintō." *Journal of Religion in Japan* 1, no. 3 (2012): 226-45.

Jennings, Willie James. *Acts.* Louisville, KY: Westminster John Knox, 2017.

———. *The Christian Imagination: Theology and the Origins of Race.* New Haven, CT: Yale University Press, 2010.

Jorgensen, Jonas Adelin. *Jesus Imandars and Christ Bhaktas: Two Case Studies of Interreligious Hermeneutics and Identity in Global Christianity.* New York: Peter Lang, 2008.

Joshi, A. P., M. D. Srinivas, and J. K. Bajaj. *Religious Demography of India: A Summary.* Chennai: Centre for Policy Studies, 2003.

Kabir. *One Hundred Poems of Kabir.* Translated by Rabindranath Tagore and assisted by Evelyn Underhill. New York: Macmillan, 1915.

Kaplan, Benjamin J. *Divided by Faith: Religious Conflict and the Practice of Toleration in Early Modern Europe.* Cambridge, MA: Belknap Press, 2007.

Kärkkäinen, Veli-Matti. *An Introduction to Ecclesiology: Ecumenical, Historical & Global Perspectives.* Downers Grove, IL: InterVarsity Press, 2002.

———. *An Introduction to the Theology of Religions: Biblical, Historical and Contemporary Perspectives.* Downers Grove, IL: InterVarsity Press, 2003.

Kauffman, Stuart A. *At Home in the Universe: The Search for Laws of Self-Organization and Complexity.* London: Oxford University Press, 1995.

Keel, Othmar. *The Symbolism of the Biblical World: Ancient Near Eastern Iconography and the Book of Psalms.* Translated by Timothy J. Hallett. New York: Seabury, 1978.

Kelly, J. N. D. *Early Christian Creeds.* 3rd ed. London: Longman, 1972.

———. *Early Christian Doctrines.* Rev. ed. New York: Harper, 1978.

Kerr, David A., and Kenneth R. Ross, eds. *Edinburgh 2010: Mission Then and Now.* Oxford: Regnum, 2009.

Kim, Jaegwon. "Making Sense of Emergence." *Philosophical Studies* 95 (1999): 3-36.

Kim, Sung-Sup. "Evangelicalism and Empire: Evangelicals in Korea and Japan Under Japanese Imperialism." Paper presented to Evangelical Studies Section of the American Academy of Religion, San Antonio, TX, November 19, 2016.

Kim, Yung Suk. *Christ's Body in Corinth: The Politics of a Metaphor*. Minneapolis: Fortress, 2008.

King, Richard. *Orientalism and Religion: Postcolonial Theory, India and "The Mystic East."* New York: Routledge, 1999.

Kline, Meredith G. *Images of the Spirit*. Grand Rapids: Baker, 1980.

Kloppenborg, John S. "Associations, Christ Groups, and Their Place in the Polis." *Zeitschrift für die neutestamentliche Wissenschaft* 108, no. 1 (2017): 1-56.

Kolg, Robert, and Timothy J. Wengert, eds. *The Book of Concord: The Confessions of the Evangelical Lutheran Church*. Translations by Charles P. Arand. Minneapolis: Fortress, 2000.

Kool, Anne-Marie. "Changing Images in the Formation for Mission: Commission Five in Light of Current Challenges; A Western Perspective." In Kerr and Ross, *Edinburgh 2010*, 158-79.

Kosse, Kuzuli. "Unity of Believers." In *Africa Bible Commentary: A One-Volume Commentary Written by 70 African Scholars*, edited by Tokunboh Adeyemo, 1314. Grand Rapids: Zondervan, 2010.

Kraemer, Hendrick. *The Communication of the Christian Faith*. Philadelphia: Westminster, 1956.

Kraft, Charles H. "The Church in Culture: A Dynamic Equivalence Model." In John R. W. Stott and Robert Coote, eds., *Down to Earth: Studies in Christianity and Culture*. Grand Rapids: Eerdmans, 1980.

Kraft, Charles H. "Dynamics of Contextualization." In Charles H. Kraft, ed., *Appropriate Christianity*. Pasadena, CA: William Carey Library, 2005.

———. *Christianity in Culture: A Study in Dynamic Biblical Theologizing in Crosscultural Perspective*. Maryknoll, NY: Orbis, 1979.

Kreider, Alan. *The Patient Ferment of the Early Church: The Improbable Rise of Christianity in the Roman Empire*. Grand Rapids: Baker Academic, 2016.

Kreitzer, Larry Joseph. *Gospel Images in Fiction and Film: On Reversing the Hermeneutical Flow*. Sheffield: Sheffield Academic Press, 2002.

Kuttiyanikkal, Ciril J. *Khrist Bhakta Movement: A Model for an Indian Church?: Inculturation in the Area of Community Building*. Berlin: Lit Verlag, 2014.

Ladd, George Eldon. *Jesus and the Kingdom: The Eschatology of Biblical Realism*. New York: Harper & Row, 1964. Reissued as *The Presence of the Future* (Grand Rapids: Eerdmans, 1974).

Lane, Belden C. *Ravished by Beauty: The Surprising Legacy of Reformed Spirituality*. New York: Oxford University Press, 2011.

Last, Richard. *The Pauline Church and the Corinthian Ekklēsia: Greco-Roman Associations in Comparative Context*. New York: Cambridge University Press, 2016.

Laube, Adolf. "Radicalism as a Research Problem in the History of Early Reformation." In *Radical Tendencies in the Reformation: Divergent Perspectives*, edited by Hans J. Hillerbrand, 9-24. Kirksville, MO: Sixteenth Century Journal Publishers, 1988.

Levenson, Jon D. *Resurrection and the Restoration of Israel: The Ultimate Victory of the God of Life.* New Haven, CT: Yale University Press, 2006.

Lichtenstein, Benyamin B. *Generative Emergence: A New Discipline of Organizational, Entrepreneurial, and Social Innovation.* New York: Oxford University Press, 2014.

Lingenfelter, Sherwood. *Agents of Transformation: A Guide for Effective Cross-Cultural Ministry.* Grand Rapids: Baker Academic, 1996.

Loisy, Alfred Firmin. *The Gospel and the Church.* Translated by Christopher Home. 1902; Philadelphia: Fortress, 1976.

Lowery, Stephanie A. *Identity and Ecclesiology: Their Relationship Among Select African Theologians.* Eugene, OR: Pickwick, 2017.

Lynch, Joseph. H. *The Medieval Church: A Brief History.* London: Longman, 1992.

Maggay, Melba Padilla, Rey Corpuz, and Miriam Adeney. *Raja Sulaiman Was No Carabao: Understanding the Muslim Question.* Diliman, Quezon City: Institute for Studies in Asian Church and Culture, 2001.

Mallouhi, Mazhar. "Comments on the Insider Movement." In Talman and Travis, *Understanding Insider Movements*, 109-15. Pasadena, CA: William Carey Library, 2015.

Manoo, Farhad. "Can Facebook Fix Its Own Worst Bug?" *New York Times Magazine*, April 25, 2017, 40-43. www.nytimes.com/2017/04/25/magazine/can-facebook-fix-its-own-worst-bug.html.

Marsden, George M. *The Evangelical Mind and the New School Presbyterian Experience: A Case Study of Thought and Theology in Nineteenth-Century America.* New Haven, CT: Yale University Press, 1970.

Mascall, E. L. *Words and Images: A Study in the Possibility of Religious Discourse.* London: Longmans, Green, 1957.

Masuzawa, Tomoko. *The Invention of World Religions: Or, How European Universalism Was Preserved in the Language of Pluralism.* Chicago: University of Chicago Press, 2005.

Mbiti, John S. *New Testament Eschatology in an African Background: A Study of the Encounter Between New Testament Theology and African Traditional Concepts.* Oxford: Oxford University Press, 1971.

McDermott, Gerald R., and Harold A. Netland. *A Trinitarian Theology of Religions: An Evangelical Proposal.* New York: Oxford University Press, 2014.

McGowan, Andrew B. *Ancient Christian Worship: Early Church Practices in Social, Historical, and Theological Perspective.* Grand Rapids: Baker Academic, 2014.

Middleton, J. Richard. *A New Heaven and a New Earth: Reclaiming Biblical Eschatology.* Grand Rapids: Baker Academic, 2014.

Miles, Margaret R. *Image as Insight: Visual Understanding in Western Christianity and Secular Culture.* Boston: Beacon Press, 1985.

Miller, Colin D. *The Practice of the Body of Christ: Human Agency in Pauline Theology After MacIntyre.* Cambridge: James Clarke & Co., 2014.

Miller, Nicholas P. *The Religious Roots of the First Amendment: Dissenting Protestantism and the Separation of Church and State.* New York: Oxford University Press, 2012.

Minear, Paul S. *Images of the Church in the New Testament.* Philadelphia: Westminster, 1960.

Moltmann, Jürgen. *The Church in the Power of the Spirit: A Contribution to Messianic Ecclesiology.* Translated by Margaret Kohl. New York: Harper & Row, 1977.

————. *The Theology of Hope: On the Ground and Implications of a Christian Eschatology.* Translated by James W. Leitch. New York: Harper & Row, 1967; Minneapolis: Fortress, 1993.

Mullins, Mark. R. "Christianity as a Transnational Social Movement: Kagawa Toyohiko and the Friends of Jesus." *Japanese Religions* 32, nos. 1 & 2 (2007): 69-87.

Myers, Bryant L. *Walking with the Poor: Principles and Practices of Transformational Development.* Revised and updated ed. Maryknoll, NY: Orbis, 2011.

Neill, Stephen. *A History of Christian Missions.* Edited by Owen Chadwick. 2nd ed. New York: Penguin, 1986.

————. *A History of Christianity in India: 1707–1858.* New York: Cambridge University Press, 1985.

Netland, Harold. *Encountering Religious Pluralism: The Challenge to Christian Faith & Mission.* Downers Grove, IL: InterVarsity Press, 2001.

Nicholls, Bruce J., ed. *The Unique Christ in Our Pluralist World.* (Grand Rapids: Baker Books, 1994).

Noll, Mark. *The New Shape of World Christianity: How American Experience Reflects Global Faith.* Downers Grove, IL: InterVarsity Press, 2009.

Nongbri, Brent. *Before Religion: A History of a Modern Concept.* New Haven, CT: Yale University Press, 2013.

Oak, Sung-Deuk. "Major Protestant Revivals in Korea: 1903–1935." *Studies in World Christianity* 18, no. 3 (2012): 269-90.

Oberoi, Harjot. *The Construction of Religious Boundaries: Culture, Identity and Diversity in the Sikh Tradition.* Delhi: Oxford University Press, 1994.

Oddie, Geoffrey A. *Imagined Hinduism: British Protestant Missionary Constructions of Hinduism, 1793–1900.* Thousand Oaks, CA: Sage, 2006.

Odoyuye, Mercy Amba. *Hearing and Doing: Theological Reflections on Christianity in Africa.* Maryknoll, NY: Orbis, 1986.

Okorocha, Cyril. "The Meaning of Salvation: An African Perspective." In *Emerging Voices in Global Christian Theology,* edited by William A. Dyrness, 59-92. Grand Rapids: Zondervan, 1994.

Ortner, Sherry B. "Theory in Anthropology since the Sixties." *Comparative Studies in Society and History* 26, no. 1 (1984): 126-66.

Packull, Werner O. *Hutterite Beginnings: Communitarian Experiments During the Reformation.* Baltimore: John Hopkins University Press, 1995.

Paredes, Tito. "Integrity of Mission in the Light of the Gospel: Bearing the Witness of the Spirit. Perspectives from Latin America." *Mission Studies* 24, no. 2 (2007): 233-45.

Park, Heon-Wook. "Die Vorstellung vom Leib Christi bei Paulus." PhD diss., Tübingen, 1988.

Parker, Cristián. *Popular Religion and Modernization in Latin America: A Different Logic.* Maryknoll, NY: Orbis, 1996.

Partonadi, Sutarman Soediman. *Sadrach's Community and Its Contextual Roots: A Nineteenth-Century Javanese Expression of Christianity.* Amsterdam: Rodopi, 1990.

Paul VI (pope). *Gaudium et Spes.* December 7, 1965. Papal Archive. The Holy See. http://www.vatican.va/archive/hist_councils/ii_vatican_council/documents/vat-ii_cons_19651207_gaudium-et-spes_en.html.

Payne, Richard E. *A State of Mixture: Christian, Zoroastrians, and Iranian Political Culture in Late Antiquity.* Berkeley: University of California Press, 2015.

Peñamora, Aldrin M. "The Christ of the Eucharist and Moro-Christian Relations." In Bazzell and Peñamora, *Christologies, Cultures and Religions,* 169-83.

Peterson, Cheryl M. "Who Is the Church?" *Dialog: A Journal of Theology* 51, no. 1 (2012): 24-30.

Pickett, J. W. *Christian Mass Movements in India: A Study with Recommendations.* New York: Abingdon, 1933.

Pinnock, Clark H. *A Wideness in God's Mercy: The Finality of Jesus Christ in a World of Religions*. Grand Rapids: Zondervan, 1992.

Porpora, Douglas V. *Reconstructing Sociology: The Critical Realist Approach*. Cambridge: Cambridge University Press, 2015.

Powell, Brian. "Manobo Blood Sacrifice and Christ's Death." In Bazzell and Peñamora, *Christologies, Cultures and Religions*, 87-93.

Rahner, Karl. *Concerning Vatican Council II*. Vol. 6 of *Theological Investigations*. Translated by David Bourke. Baltimore: Helicon Press, 1969.

———. *Ecclesiology, Questions in the Church, the Church in the World*. Vol. 14 of *Theological Investigations*. Translated by David Bourke. London: Darton, Longman & Todd, 1976.

Ramachandra, Vinoth. "A World of Religions and a Gospel of Transformation." In Kerr and Ross, *Edinburgh 2010*, 139-53.

Richard, H. L. "New Paradigms for Religion, Multiple Religious Belonging, and Insider Movements." *Missiology* 43, no. 3 (2015): 297-308.

———. "Religious Syncretism as a Syncretistic Concept: The Inadequacy of the 'World Religions' Paradigm in Cross-Cultural Encounter." *International Journal of Frontier Missiology* 31, no. 4 (2014): 209-15.

Romanowski, William, and Jennifer L. Vander Heide, "Easier Said Than Done: On Reversing the Hermeneutical Flow in Theology and Film Dialogue." *Journal of Communication and Religion* 30, no. 1 (2007): 40-64.

Roth, John D., and James M. Stayer, eds. *A Companion to Anabaptism and Spiritualism, 1521–1700*. Boston: Brill, 2007.

Rots, Aike P. "Shinto's Modern Transformations: From Imperial Cult to Nature Worship." In *Routledge Handbook of Religions in Asia*, edited by Bryan S. Turner and Oscar Salemink, 125-43. New York: Routledge, 2015.

Rouwhorst, Gerard. "The Roots of the Early Christian Eucharist: Jewish Blessings or Hellenistic Symposia?" In *Jewish and Christian Liturgy and Worship: New Insights into Its History and Interaction*, edited by Albert Gerhards and Clemens Leonhard, 295-308. Boston: Brill, 2007.

San Chirico, Kerry P. C. "Between Christian and Hindu: *Krist Bhaktas,* Catholics and the Negotiation of Devotion in the Banaras Region." In Bauman and Young, *Constructing Indian Christianities*, 23-44.

Sanders, James. "First Testament and Second." *Biblical Theology Bulletin* 17, no. 2 (1987): 47-49.

Sanders, John. *No Other Name: An Investigation into the Destiny of the Unevangelized*. Grand Rapids: Eerdmans, 1992.

Sawyer, R. Keith. *Social Emergence: Societies as Complex Systems*. New York: Cambridge University Press, 2005.

Schineller, Peter. "Inculturation: A Difficult and Delicate Task." *International Bulletin of Missionary Research* 20, no. 3 (1996): 109-12.

Schreiter, Robert J. *Constructing Local Theologies*. Maryknoll, NY: Orbis, 1985.

Scribner, Bob. "Communities and the Nature of Power." In *Germany: A New Social and Economic History*. Vol. 1, *1450–1630*, edited by Bob Scribner, 291-326. New York: Arnold, 1996.

Searle, John R. *The Rediscovery of the Mind*. Cambridge, MA: MIT Press, 1992.

Sebastian, Mrinalini. "Vamps and Villains or Citizen-Subjects?: Converting a Third-Person Self-Conception of the Indian Christians into a First-Person Narrative." *Studies in World Christianity* 16, no. 2 (2010): 109-25.

Shaw, R. Daniel. "Beyond Contextualization: Toward a Twenty-First-Century Model for Enabling Mission." *International Bulletin of Missionary Research* 34, no. 4 (2010): 208-15.

Singh, Giani Ditt. *The Khalsa Akhbar*, May 25, 1894. Quoted in Nikky-Guninder Kaur Singh, *The Feminine Principle in the Sikh Vision of the Transcendent* (New York: Cambridge University Press, 1993), 153.

Smith, Christian. *Religion: What It Is, How It Works, and Why It Matters*. Princeton, NJ: Princeton University Press, 2017.

———. *To Flourish or Destruct: A Personalist Theory of Human Goods, Motivations, Failure, and Evil*. Chicago: University of Chicago Press, 2015.

Smith, Dennis E. *From Symposium to Eucharist: The Banquet in the Early Christian World*. Minneapolis: Fortress, 2003.

Smith, James K. A. *Desiring the Kingdom: Worship, Worldview, and Cultural Formation*. Grand Rapids: Baker Academic, 2009.

———. *The Fall of Interpretation: Philosophical Foundations for a Creational Hermeneutic*. Downers Grove, IL: InterVarsity Press, 2000.

———. *Imagining the Kingdom: How Worship Works*. Grand Rapids: Baker Academic, 2013.

Smith, Jonathan Z. *Imagining Religion: From Babylon to Jonestown*. Chicago: University of Chicago Press, 1982.

Smith, Wilfred Cantwell. *The Meaning and End of Religion*. New York: Macmillan, 1963.

Snyder, C. Arnold. *Anabaptist History and Theology: An Introduction*. Kitchener, Ont.: Pandora, 1995.

———. *The Life and Thought of Michael Sattler*. Scottdale, PA: Herald Press, 1984.

———. "Swiss Anabaptism: The Beginnings." In Roth and Stayer, *Companion to Anabaptism and Spiritualism*, 45-81.

Stanley, Brian. *The World Missionary Conference, Edinburgh 1910*. Grand Rapids: Eerdmans, 2009.

Stark, Rodney, and Roger Finke. *Acts of Faith: Explaining the Human Side of Religion*. Berkeley: University of California Press, 2000.

Stayer, James M. *The German Peasants' War and Anabaptist Community of Goods*. Montreal: McGill-Queen's University Press, 1991.

Stoll, Laurie C. "Church Growth and Decline: A Test of the Market-Based Approach." *Review of Religious Research* 49, no. 3 (2008): 251-68.

Stott, John R. W., and Robert Coote, eds. *Down to Earth: Studies in Christianity and Culture*. Grand Rapids: Eerdmans, 1980.

Study Team on Worship and Culture. "Nairobi Statement on Worship and Culture: Contemporary Challenges and Opportunities." *Lutheran World Federation*. Calvin Institute of Christian Worship, January 1996. https://worship.calvin.edu/resources/resource-library/nairobi-statement-on-worship-and-culture-full-text.

Sugimoto, Yoshio. *An Introduction to Japanese Society*. 2nd ed. Port Melbourne, Australia: Cambridge University Press, 2003.

Synod of Bishops. "Special Synod of Bishops for Africa, Message of the Synod." English text released May 6, 1994. www.ewtn.com/new_evangelization/africa/synod/message.htm.

Talman, Harley, and John Jay Travis, eds. *Understanding Insider Movements: Disciples of Jesus Within Diverse Religious Communities*. Pasadena, CA: William Carey Library, 2015.

Tanner, Kathryn. *Theories of Culture: A New Agenda for Theology*. Minneapolis: Fortress, 1997.

Thiselton, Anthony C. *The Hermeneutics of Doctrine*. Grand Rapids: Eerdmans, 2007.

Tocqueville, Alexis de. *Democracy in America*. 1863; Cambridge: Sever & Francis, 1963.

Travis, John Jay. "Insider Movements Among Muslims: A Focus on Asia." In Talman and Travis, *Understanding Insider Movements*, 133-42. Pasadena, CA: William Carey Library, 2015.

———. *Personal Correspondence*. Darren Duerksen, July 11, 2017.

Turner, Max. "The 'Spirit of Prophecy' as the Power of Israel's Restoration and Witness." In *Witness to the Gospel: The Theology of Acts*, edited by I. Howard Marshall and David Peterson, 327-48. Grand Rapids: Eerdmans, 1998.

Twiss, Richard. *Rescuing the Gospel from the Cowboys: A Native American Expression of the Jesus Way.* Downers Grove, IL: InterVarsity Press, 2015.

Verhey, Allen. "'Able to Instruct One Another': The Church as a Community of Moral Discourse." In Husbands and Treier, *Community of the Word*, 146-70.

Volf, Miroslav. *After Our Likeness: The Church as the Image of the Trinity.* Grand Rapids: Eerdmans, 1998.

Walia, Noormallu. "Open the Eyes of Your Heart." Sikh Punjabi Music Video (English subtitles). India/Pakistan: Create International, 2010. www.indig-itube.tv/video/sikh-punjabi-music-video-engsub.

Walls, Andrew F. "The Evangelical Revival, the Missionary Movement, and Africa." In *The Missionary Movement in Christian History: Studies in the Transmission of Faith*, 79-101. Maryknoll, NY: Orbis, 1996.

———. "The Gospel as Prisoner and Liberator of Culture." In *The Missionary Movement in Christian History: Studies in the Transmission of Faith*, 3-15. Maryknoll, NY: Orbis, 1996.

Wandel, Lee Palmer. *The Reformation: Towards a New History.* New York: Cambridge University Press, 2011.

Weaver, J. Denny. *Becoming Anabaptist: The Origin and Significance of Sixteenth-Century Anabaptism.* Scottdale, PA: Herald Press, 2005.

Weaver-Zercher, David L. *Martyrs Mirror: A Social History.* Baltimore: Johns Hopkins University Press, 2016.

Webster, John C. B. *A Social History of Christianity: North-west India Since 1800.* New Delhi: Oxford, 2007.

Wendel, François. *Calvin: The Origins and Development of His Religious Thought.* Translated by Philip Mairet. London: Collins, 1963.

White, L. Michael. *The Social Origins of Christian Architecture.* Vol. 1, *Building God's House in the Roman World;* Vol. 2, *Text and Monuments for the Christian Domus Ecclesiae in Its Environment.* Valley Forge, PA: Trinity Press International, 1997.

Williams, Rowan. *The Edge of Words: God and the Habits of Language.* London: Bloomsbury, 2104.

Wilson, Peter H. *The Heart of Europe: A History of the Holy Roman Empire.* Cambridge, MA: Harvard University Press, 2016.

Witherington, Ben III. *The Acts of the Apostles: A Socio-Rhetorical Commentary.* Grand Rapids: Eerdmans, 1998.

Wolterstorff, Nicholas. *Justice: Rights and Wrongs.* Princeton, NJ: Princeton University Press, 2008.

———. *Until Justice and Peace Embrace.* Grand Rapids: Eerdmans, 1983.

Woodberry, Robert. "The Missionary Roots of Liberal Democracy." *American Political Science Review* 106, no. 2 (2012): 244-74.

Wright, Christopher. "Confronting Our Idols." Conference on Integrity. Cape Town: Lausanne Movement, 2010. Video. www.lausanne.org/content/confronting-idols.

Wright, N. T. *Surprised by Hope: Rethinking Heaven, the Resurrection, and the Mission of the Church.* New York: HarperCollins, 2008.

Wrogemann, Henning. *Intercultural Theology.* Vol. 1, *Intercultural Hermeneutics.* Downers Grove, IL: InterVarsity Press, 2016.

Yoder, John Howard. *The Royal Priesthood: Essays Ecclesiastical and Ecumenical.* Edited by Michael G. Cartwright. Grand Rapids: Eerdmans, 1994.

Young, Richard Fox. *Resistant Hinduism: Sanskrit Sources on Anti-Christian Apologetics in Early Nineteenth-Century India.* Publications of the De Nobili Research Library 8. Leiden: Brill, 1981.

Name and Subject Index

Scripture Index

MISSIOLOGICAL ENGAGEMENTS

Series Editors: Scott W. Sunquist,
Amos Yong, and John R. Franke

Missiological Engagements: Church, Theology, and Culture in Global Contexts charts interdisciplinary and innovative trajectories in the history, theology, and practice of Christian mission at the beginning of the third millennium.

Among its guiding questions are the following: What are the major opportunities and challenges for Christian mission in the twenty-first century? How does the missionary impulse of the gospel reframe theology and hermeneutics within a global and intercultural context? What kind of missiological thinking ought to be retrieved and reappropriated for a dynamic global Christianity? What innovations in the theology and practice of mission are needed for a renewed and revitalized Christian witness in a postmodern, postcolonial, postsecular, and post-Christian world?

Books in the series, both monographs and edited collections, will feature contributions by leading thinkers representing evangelical, Protestant, Roman Catholic, and Orthodox traditions, who work within or across the range of biblical, historical, theological, and social-scientific disciplines. Authors and editors will include the full spectrum from younger and emerging researchers to established and renowned scholars, from the Euro-American West and the Majority World, whose missiological scholarship will bridge church, academy, and society.

Missiological Engagements reflects cutting-edge trends, research, and innovations in the field that will be of relevance to theorists and practitioners in churches, academic domains, mission organizations, and NGOs, among other arenas.